HIPPIE

HIPPIE

BARRY MILES

STERLING PUBLISHING CO., INC.
NEW YORK

Text by Barry Miles
Designed by Grant Scott
Edited by Mal Peachey
Assisted by Dea Brovig

Produced by Essential Works
168a Camden Street
London NW1 8PT

Library of Congress Cataloging-in-Publication Data Available

3   5   7   9   10   8   6   4   2

Published 2004 by Sterling Publishing Co., Inc.
387 Park Avenue South, New York, NY 10016
First published in Great Britain in 2003 by Cassell Illustrated
a division of Octopus Publishing Group Limited
2–4 Heron Quays, London E14 4JP
Copyright © 2003 Essential Works Limited
Distributed in Canada by Sterling Publishing
c/o Canadian Manda Group, One Atlantic Avenue, Suite 105
Toronto, Ontario, Canada M6K 3E7

1-4027-1442-4

The author and publishers have made every reasonable effort to contact all copyright holders. Any errors that may have occurred are inadvertent and anyone who for any reason has not been contacted is invited to write to the publishers so that a full acknowledgment may be made in subsequent editions of this work.

To all the old freaks and hippies everywhere

CONTENTS

INTRODUCTION BY MILES

Call them freaks, the underground, the counter-culture, flower children or hippies—they are all loose labels for the youth culture of the 60s that transformed life in the West as we knew it, introducing a spirit of freedom, of hope, of happiness, of change and of revolution.

Its beginnings were small, growing from the Beat Generation of the 50s. Many of the Beats remained central to the movement throughout the 60s: poets Gary Snyder, Michael McClure, Lawrence Ferlinghetti and Allen Ginsberg were all regarded as statesmen and gurus of the movement in the USA, as was William Burroughs in his self-imposed exile in London. Like the Beats, hippies rejected the stultifying boredom of American 50s' consumer society, offering an alternative to the then prevalent idea of living in identical suburbs, sleeping in twin beds, driving virtually identical cars, watching mind-numbing sitcoms on television or staring through picture windows at the neighbors' identical picture window. What became known as "straight society" went to church, satisfied that they were the moral guardians of the world in their fight against godless communism.

But that doesn't explain a similar movement in Europe, particularly Britain, where hardly anyone could afford a car and there seemed no space to build tacky suburban housing. In Britain the counterculture came about as a reaction to post-war austerity. The invention of the teenager came late to Britain and it was only in the 60s that young people had any money of their own to spend. They looked around and saw that everything was controlled by old people—those hypocrites intent on maintaining the status quo as if World War II had never happened. The changes in Britain came through the organized opposition to nuclear weapons in CND, the growth of home-produced rock 'n' roll—most of which originated in the art schools—and, of course, from the use of drugs, which set young people apart from their parents' generation and the authorities.

The campaign against nuclear weapons was never a big issue in the USA, but opposition to the Vietnam War certainly was. It is a mistake to see the anti-war movement, or "the movement" as many people called it, simply as a youth movement, however. It took much of its energy and enthusiasm from young people, but the majority of people involved were adults over 30 who believed in American representative democracy and the individual right to make themselves heard and affect government policy. The CIA, the FBI and various other institutions tried their utmost to discredit them, often by using illegal methods, including denying people their constitutional right of assembly. They claimed that the movement was financed and organized by foreign powers, that it was just made up of a bunch of bomb-throwing kids.

"Johnny Pot wears gold sandals and a black derby hat."

Chapter heading in Playpower by Richard Neville

Throughout the late 60s, until the last American helicopter escaped from the roof of the US embassy in Saigon in 1975, the anti-war movement was a continual presence. The protests took scores of different forms, including letters to congressmen and presidents from concerned citizens and church groups, to collecting signatures on petitions and names for advertisements in the press. There were many marches and demonstrations, vigils in public places and at government installations; there was tax refusal and public draft card burnings, as well as widespread desertion from the army or self-imposed exile in friendly Canada, which refused to extradite draft-resisters. There was nonviolent civil disobedience, which usually resulted in tear gas and mass arrests and inevitably in brutality and violence on the part of the police; there were rallies and strikes, sit-ins and occupations. As the murder and destruction in Vietnam grew in pace, so did the actions at home—"bringing the war home" was one of the slogans—and a small faction turned to bombing, to burning draft board offices and destroying military records. There were even a few suicides.

Some hippies were involved, particularly after the police riot in Chicago in 1968 when so many people got injured, but on the whole the movement activists looked on hippies with disdain. They couldn't see how these people could spend their time taking drugs, making music, meditating and contemplating the void when people were being murdered by their own government in a nondeclared war.

Why then, are hippies important? Because it was only by stepping outside society that people were able to look at it objectively—to see what was wrong with it, to see how they'd like to change it.

The ecology movement had its beginnings in the 60s counterculture. The writings of Beat Generation poets Gary Snyder and Michael McClure, both based in or near San Francisco, appeared in the underground press and their books became very popular. Scientists such as Gregory Bateson also helped change people's consciousness, largely by being cited and quoted by movement activists like Allen Ginsberg. It was Bateson who first sounded the warning about global warming at the Dialectics of Liberation Congress in London in 1967. The work of R. Buckminster Fuller was very popular in the 60s, in particular his book Operating Manual for Spaceship Earth, which helped spread an awareness of how frail the ecosystem of the planet actually is. The move towards vegetarianism also heralded a move towards organic food and by the end of the decade the natural food movement

ABOVE: The Beatles' "All You Need Is Love" is broadcast live worldwide. RIGHT: Hippie style in New York, 1968.

"The more I revolt, the more I make love."

was well established. Bucky himself also invented the geodesic dome, used as a model by many commune builders.

The counterculture questioned sexual morality and proposed many different models: extended sexual families, sex orgies, sex-therapy groups, acceptance of homosexuality and, most of all, a positive, joyful celebration of sexuality, as opposed to the uptight morality of the previous generation. In mid-60s America, television situation-comedy shows could only depict a married couple in twin beds, and unmarried couples were not allowed to be shown in bed at all. Most sitcom sets didn't have a bedroom. This was why

the Beats were so shocking to people in the late 50s, with their sex orgies and their acceptance of homosexuality. Ginsberg wrote, "America, I'm putting my queer shoulder to the wheel." He wasn't ashamed of it, even though it was illegal.

It was from this questioning of sex roles that the women's movement began. Hippies were notorious in their treatment of women, who were regarded as "chicks" or "old ladies" and expected to do all the chores as if they were suburban housewives, but without any of the security that straight women had. Naturally they also looked after the children. In political circles it was even worse, as the men did all the talking while the women did the paperwork. But the introduction of the contraceptive pill gave women freedom of choice in sexual partners for the first

time. The "loose" sexual morality in counter-cultural circles gave rise to a questioning of all sexual roles, including whether it was right for women to do the housework, the cooking and washing while her stoned partner grooved on the latest sounds wearing his headphones. Out of all this the women's movement was born.

On 7 September 1968 the women's movement announced its existence to the world by disrupting the Miss America Pageant broadcast live on nationwide television from Atlantic City. With the protest seemingly confined to the picket signs outside the hall the organizers were not expecting further trouble, but one of the contestants had been converted to the cause and she managed to shuffle the cue-cards of presenter Bert Parks, causing his perfect plastic smile to

LEFT: Women's Liberation activists interrupt the Miss World Beauty Contest. ABOVE: A psychedelic Bentley on London's Kings Road.

falter. Then twenty brave sisters began chanting "Freedom For Women" and hung a huge banner proclaiming "Women's Liberation" from the balcony rail. Millions of viewers saw the action and the show was stopped for ten minutes. One woman was arrested for "emitting a noxious odor"—in fact it was Toni Hair Conditioner, made by the sponsor of the show, that was sprayed near the mayor's box.

In October 1968 Robin Morgan, one of the organizers, wrote, "Some male reactionaries in the Left still think Women's Liberation 'frivolous' in the face of 'larger, more important' revolutionary problems … What is frivolous, for that

reflect alternative life-styles to this whole sick culture, only to hear a male SDS leader ask for 'chicks to volunteer for cooking duty'?"

Also out of the counterculture came the gay rights movement, sparked by the Stonewall bar riots in New York in 1969, when gays on Christopher Street had finally had enough of having their heads broken by police clubs any time the cops wanted to move them along and suddenly fought back. It wasn't a big riot—a few police car windows were smashed and stones thrown—but the newspapers the next day proclaimed Gay Power, and nothing was ever the same again.

with World War II military hygiene. The fact that it made them look like criminals was irrelevant. In America there was greater conformity than in Europe, but anyone stepping too far away from the norm was in trouble. In Britain, the male put on a cheap suit the day he left school and shirts and ties were essential. People are sometimes surprised to see early photographs of the Beatles and Stones in their neat suits and thin ties. By the end of the 60s, jeans and t-shirts or worn work-shirts and ex-army jackets were the new uniform in the States, but the hippie revolution meant you could wear virtually anything you wanted, from a robe to a cape. And the hair, of

"A new generation is finally getting an education, though the college may have to be destroyed in the process."

Mayday magazine

matter, about a woman who isn't rich enough to fly to Puerto Rico for an abortion and so must lie on some kitchen table watching cockroaches on the ceiling articulate the graph of her pain? What is frivolous about the young black woman, proud and beautiful and militant, whose spirit cracks when she hears Stokely Carmichael say that 'the only position for women in SNCC (Student Nonviolent Co-ordinating Committee) is prone?' … What is frivolous about the migrant-worker mother who must be yet one step lower than her oppressed husband, must let him beat her up a bit, impregnate her just after she's dropped her seventh child, and maybe disappear for a year now and then so that he, at least, can feel a little of his 'manhood'? And what is frivolous about the women in Fayerweather Hall at Columbia last spring, new-minted revolutionaries ready to be beaten and busted as well as anybody (and they were), ready to form a commune that would

The 60s counterculture really was about sex and drugs and rock 'n' roll; most other aspects of change during the 60s were forged by other members of society as well. But though President Kennedy's sex life was closer to that of Mick Jagger than to that of Billy Graham, the media preferred to cover up anything which threatened the American Dream. The hippies did it out in the open: "Sex and Drugs and Fucking In the Streets" was the rallying cry of Detroit's MC5, and even Paul McCartney suggested, "Why don't we do it in the road?"

The hippies attracted opprobrium because they were visible. Their clothes, for instance, outraged the conservative members of the population—which in America was just about everyone and in Britain tended to be men on building sites. Before the 60s men's hair and sideburns were cut short in Britain, while in America the norm was a crew cut, in keeping

course, was long. In fact, by the end of the 60s it was often accompanied by a moustache and beard as well.

For women, the early 60s was a time of skirts and dresses; trouser-suits did not come in until the late 60s and caused a sensation when they did. Hair was permed and sprayed and thick lipstick and make-up made even teenage girls look like they were in their mid-30s. The hippies and the influence of hippie fashion did away with the rollers and long natural hair took over; pony-tails were now only for the boys and both sexes wore hairbands. This new androgynous look made the straights particularly upset. Clearly they felt strangely threatened to find that the difference between boys and girls might be something more than the length of their hair.

PREVIOUS PAGE: An Acid Test examinee passes with flying colors, San Francisco, 1966. RIGHT: A Be-In, San Francisco, 1967.

"If the Beatles meant a lot in Britain, they meant very much more in America. They changed things."

Nik Cohn

Girls looked for old-fashioned, second-hand dresses in thrift stores, favoring worn, soft fabrics like lace and velvet and often opting for long granny dresses. If they felt like dressing up, then anything went—handmade clothes, often tie-dyed in earth colors or psychedelic rainbows, hand-strung beads and, if the climate was temperate as in California, bare feet. Maybe even flowers in their hair. The dictatorial control over fashion once exerted by the fashion houses was broken—to the relief of all women, not just those in the counterculture. No longer were women told how high the hem of their skirt was to be that year. After the hippie movement it could be anywhere you wanted it to be.

Then there was the music. The 60s transformed pop music into rock music, from entertainment to art. The greatest difference between the two was that rock groups, generally speaking, returned to the blues or rhythm and blues for their inspiration. The Rolling Stones' early work includes cover versions of many R&B classics, and the Beatles live act in Liverpool and

in Hamburg also included many R&B numbers. It took the British Invasion, led by the Beatles, to reawaken the North American musicians' interest in their own black originals. And it worked. Before they became the Grateful Dead, that band was known as the Warlocks and specialized in extended blues jams. Other seminal 60s bands made no excuses and simply called themselves the Butterfield Blues Band, or the Blues Project. Canned Heat was nothing but a blues band, and Janis Joplin a blues singer. Add to this the intense awareness of the sound that LSD or marijuana brings and you have so-called psychedelic music. The great catalyst of change was the Beatles, in particular Sgt. Pepper, but tracks like "Tomorrow Never Knows" had paved the way. This was no longer pop, it was some new form of art. Most art forms go through this process, of course. Cinema began as pure entertainment, as did opera and photography, but as artists saw the potential of the new medium a separate strain of development began, so that now photography can be found in galleries as well as in news

papers. Art cinemas show avant-garde offerings while the latest Hollywood blockbuster exhibits round the corner.

With some groups and musicians, this development was more obvious than others. Dylan began locked into the folk tradition of Woody Guthrie, but outraged his traditionalist fans even before he went electric by incorporating some outrageous lyrics into his work. It took the Byrds to realize that he was really singing rock 'n' roll and they virtually made a career of setting his music to a psychedelicized backing. The hypnotic jangling of Roger McGuinn's 12-string Rickenbacker on "Mr. Tambourine Man" was music from the future when it appeared in 1965.

The Byrds played the Strip in Los Angeles, and the rest of LA listened. It was in Los Angeles that most of the new music developed. The Mothers of Invention were clearly like nothing that came before; both musically and lyrically they were a complete breakthrough. The Doors, similarly, combined almost pretentiously serious lyrics with ambitious musical arrangements, to

take pop music to a new level. The San Francisco groups were much more blues based and the Grateful Dead's playing, though informed by acid, was still an extended blues jam. Similarly the Jefferson Airplane were very pop-oriented and it was really their lyrics that set them apart from other chart bands. Jimi Hendrix combined R&B and pop to forge a new art form. His improvisation and distortion of "The Star Spangled Banner" at Woodstock did for rock what extended improvisation did for be-bop, setting it apart from traditional jazz. It was significant that he had to go to Britain to do it, away from the grind of the R&B circuit.

In London, where there was no R&B circuit, Hendrix could combine his experience of working with the Isley Brothers and Little Richard with the weird new sounds of the psychedelic London bands to create the Jimi Hendrix Experience. With no rock 'n' roll tradition to form them, a band like the Who saw nothing strange in attempting a rock opera—a new seriousness of intent in rock music

previously unheard of. And the post-Syd Barrett Pink Floyd, using their background as architectural students, moved into areas previously unknown in rock, building extended musical constructions. In New York, despite some lingering Beach Boys chords, the Velvet Underground entered entirely new, unquestionably adult territory, drawing a firm line between their work and songs aimed at 12-year-olds.

The Velvets had in their ranks John Cale, a classically trained musician and avant-garde performer, as did the Grateful Dead with Phil Lesh and, from 1967, the Mothers of Invention with Ian Underwood. Zappa himself had been composing classical music since the age of fifteen. All of which provided evidence of the huge difference between the commercial offerings from the Brill Building and Denmark Street and the psychedelic musings of "White Rabbit" or "Arnold Layne."

LEFT: The Sgt. Pepper's Lonely Hearts Club Band sleeve by Peter Blake, 1967. ABOVE: Tim Hardin backstage at Woodstock, 1969.

The 60s brought us rock festivals, which, even in the mud and cold of an English summer, are enjoyable community experiences, beloved by thousands. It brought us marketed culture: ias opposed to folk music that belonged to all, rock culture did not belong to the hippies. Despite Columbia Records' series of ads proclaiming "The Man Can't Bust Our Music," it turned out that Columbia Records was "The Man." They owned the copyrights and they wanted money every time a cassette was made of one of their records (or, later, every time a song was downloaded from the Internet). Many rock bands found themselves in a quandary: they had always claimed to be part of the community, part of street culture, but as soon as the first big record company advance came along the vast majority of them sold out. Very few bands allow fans to even tape their concerts, let alone condone bootlegs. But in the early days, there was a short period when it seemed that rock 'n' roll really was the people's music and was going to change the world.

"A hand on your cock is more moral— and more fun—than a finger on the trigger."

Lawrence Lipton

The stated aim of many hippies was to build a counterculture—their own version of whatever was needed from straight society. The straight press ran Al Capp and Andy Cap, the underground press ran the Furry Freak Brothers and Mr. Natural. The straight press ran articles on Hollywood stars and their wardrobes; the underground press ran reviews of rock bands and happenings. The straight press gave out the government line on crime and the Vietnam War; the underground papers reported on dope busts, the price of drugs and the anti-war movement. The straight press ran features on middle-class consumer life, while the underground press ran long pieces on LSD, flying saucers, the workless society, communes and group sex. By 1969 there were over 500 underground papers worldwide, serving various communities and constituencies, plus a further thousand in American high schools—though these were usually strong on the anti-war rhetoric and wisely kept quiet about drugs.

Some communes did become self-sufficient, or else made things or provided services that other people in the hip community wanted.

Communes brought food into the cities for sale at green markets, potters and craftspeople made clothes, carved wooden objects, cups and plates and bowls. Hippie high streets sprang up. Among them were St Mark's Place in New York, Sunset Strip in Los Angeles, Telegraph Avenue in Berkeley, Mifflin Street in Madison, Haight-Ashbury in San Francisco, Wells Street in Chicago and The Grove in London, where there were boutiques, vegetarian stores and restaurants, bookstores, record stores, poster and head shops. By 1971 there were so many communes that just for Berkeley there was a daily commune newsletter, delivered by hand to more than 50 communes and posted on a special board in the hallway.

The notice boards in the communes and hippie shops were filled with posters and leaflets for yoga classes, meditation classes and talks by gurus. One very durable aspect of the 60s counterculture that is still with us today and growing each year was the personal growth movement—new age therapy. The yoga classes and gestalt therapy of the 60s developed into a mass movement of self-examination and self-

therapy among the middle classes. Modern dance, jogging, health foods, vegetarianism, veganism, tai chi, meditation groups, acupuncture, massage, sex-therapy clinics, Esalen Institute therapies, bioenergetics, Reichian therapy, Orgonomy, Rolfing, Silva Mind Control, Arica, Erhard Seminars Training (est), More House and most forms of preventative medicine, all came from or were popularized in the 60s.

Let's not forget the Maharishi's Transcendental Meditation, Krishna Consciousness, the Naropa Institute (the Tibetan Buddhist followers of Chogyam Trungpa), Scientology, the Process, various Zen Buddhist sects including the tantric fire-eating members of Kailas Shugendo (Yamabushi) and the quiet bread-makers of Tasahara. There were scores of Hindu swamis, mostly in competition with each other and denouncing the others as frauds. There were also western witches, wiccas and wizards, the followers of the OTO, the Golden Dawn Society, the Great Beast Crowley, the followers of lay lines

RIGHT: A hippie cafe on London's Kings Road, 1968.

20

and the flying-saucer watchers. No other period can have produced such a quantity of such imaginative speculation and belief in so short a time.

In America, the 60s heralded the entry of both blacks and women into politics and the higher levels of business; these are both battles not yet won, but this decade saw the first steps. The struggle of blacks was much harder and more bloody. The 60s was not only the time of Martin Luther King, who became a targeted man as soon as he began to oppose the war in Vietnam, but also the time of the Black Panthers, who saw the police mowing down their brothers and decided to arm themselves and fight back. The statistics are terrible to read: in 1967, while the hippies were having the summer of love, there were 83 people killed in riots, including 23 in Newark and 43 in Detroit, as well as thousands injured. That July Detroit was in flames, there were snipers on the roofs and 4,700 US Army paratroopers, supported by 8,000 National Guardsmen, were called in to occupy the burning ghetto. No wonder the Panthers got themselves guns—particularly after the murder of Martin

Luther King, which to them simply showed that peaceful protest was not going to change the racist establishment one iota. The growth and virtual slaughter of the Black Panthers by police, who were shooting to kill, is outside the scope of this book, but it represented a parallel development to the counterculture that the middle-class hippies were striving for.

There was a political strain to the underground, particularly in the late 60s, which followed in the footsteps of the old left and which combined, to quote David Widgery, "Bolshevism at its most libertarian and Marxism at its most warmhearted and witty." Jerry Rubin had this, so did Ed Sanders, Wavy Gravy and other movement "leaders," though it was often distorted by massive ego trips. By and large the underground could be said to be Left, but it tended more towards anarchism than toward any organized Marxist or Socialist party. The true impact of the hippie movement of the 60s, however, can be measured in political terms both in the US and the UK. The establishment is no longer sacrosanct and a much greater degree of accounta-

bility and transparency is required by society at large these days, both of public institutions and among politicians. In Britain the hippie movement delivered a massive blow to the entrenched class system, though this is also a battle not completely won, as a look at the letterhead of any large bank or corporation will show. In America, both women and blacks have entered all levels of society, from business to the military, and are integrated to a degree that would have shocked many people 30 years ago. But most of these gains were not the result of the counterculture as such. They were more the work of the general population who, thanks to the counterculture, began questioning and examining the society they lived in and finding it wanting.

ABOVE and RIGHT: Album sleeves grew more innovative, and were ultimately exhibited as art in their own right. OVER: Easy Rider, 1969.

Hippies didn't just pop up overnight, but 1965 was the first year in which a discernible youth movement began to emerge. Most of the key "psychedelic" rock bands formed this year. On the new developing Haight-Ashbury there were the Grateful Dead, Big Brother and the Holding Company, the Charlatans and the

65 66 67 68 69 70 71

Jefferson Airplane. On the Strip there were Love, the Byrds and the Doors. In New York the Fugs were just getting known and the Velvet Underground were getting together. This is the year that the use of LSD became widespread thanks to massive media coverage. Tim Leary went on the lecture circuit and his Millbrook mansion hosted hundreds of controlled LSD sessions. On the West Coast, thanks to underground chemist Augustus Owsley Stanley III and Ken Kesey and the Pranksters, thousands of people took uncontrolled trips at the Trips Festivals and in the new psychedelic dancehalls. The drug was still legal, but the authorities were beginning to grow restless and talk of how to control it. Over in London the Beatles took their first LSD trip and smoked a lot of marijuana. Michael Hollingshead opened his World Psychedelic Centre and the Beat Generation poets Allen Ginsberg, Lawrence Ferlinghetti and Gregory Corso read at the Royal Albert Hall. This reading acted as a catalyst for underground activity in London, as people suddenly realized just how many like-minded people there were around. This was also the year that London began to blossom into colour with the opening of the Granny Takes a Trip and Hung On You clothes shops.

SAN FRANCISCO

"If you're going ...
be sure to wear some
flowers in your hair."

John Philips

THE SCENE

The San Francisco scene began not in the City of Brotherly Love, but in a renovated ghost town called Virginia City, a three-hours away, just over the state line in Nevada. Once the center of the Comstock Lode silver rush, it was now the home of an offbeat community of artists and drug takers. Folk music enthusiast Mark Unobsky bought the old Comstock House and decided to open a folk club together with Chan Laughlin, a one-time folk club owner, and Don Works, who had moved to Virginia City in order to take peyote with the Washoe and Paiute Indians.

More than twenty carpenters, masons and electricians, together with their girlfriends and wives, were hired from the Haight and the three-story brick building was restored to its former Victorian grandeur, complete with a shaded wooden sidewalk and bat-wing doors. They painted it red and called it the Red Dog Saloon, a common name for bars in the old west of the 1860s. Antique fittings were purchased and a newly formed, inexperienced group called the Charlatans were hired to play there, chosen for their looks as opposed to their folk music playing ability—they were, in fact, a rock 'n' roll band.

PREVIOUS PAGE: LOVE was everywhere.
RIGHT: The Red Dog Saloon in Virginia City.

"A man should have the right to be as big as he feels it's in him to be."

Ken Babbs

Their leader, George Hunter, was impeccably dressed in Edwardian clothes that fitted perfectly into the old west image of the Red Dog. Hunter had formed the band more as an artistic statement than as a musical group; he wanted to counter the London-style mini-skirts and mod clothes that everyone was wearing by returning to something he saw as authentically American. They had not previously played in public when they auditioned at the Red Dog and their performance was not enhanced by the fact they had all been given LSD.

The Charlatans wore cowboy boots, waistcoats and straw boaters or cowboy hats and all of them were armed to the teeth. The Red Dog saloon opened for business on June 29, 1965. Soon everyone around the bar was wearing nineteenth century clothes, cowboy hats and chaps, string ties and long dresses. The waitresses dressed as Miss Kitty with fishnet stockings and bodices and carried ceramic doorknobs in case the action got a little too rowdy. The bar was closed on Mondays, when the staff had an LSD party. The Charlatans got so into the western tradition that they all bought Winchester rifles that they leaned against their amplifiers on stage.

Mothers, run by KYA disc jockey "Big Daddy" Tom Donahue, opened in San Francisco on July 4, 1965. He spent a lot of money on it, with wooden sculpture on the walls, murals in the bathrooms and an expensive light show, but the fact that Donahue served drinks meant that it was illegal to let young people in and the place was empty. Then on August 4, the Lovin' Spoonful, whose "Do You Believe In Magic?" was climbing the charts, opened a four-week gig. Suddenly Mothers was packed with older rock fans, all wearing Edwardian-style clothing and dancing to the music.

They came from Haight-Ashbury, the area with wealthy Pacific Heights to the south and the black Fillmore neighborhood to the east that they were gradually colonizing for themselves. It was only a couple of blocks south of the Panhandle, the long thin park that led to Golden Gate Park itself, and the University of San Francisco was just two blocks further north. It had always been a cheap student area.

In San Francisco hippies were seen as a new, younger, inexperienced version of the older hipsters—hence the name, which some people claim was given them by the older, hipper North Beach residents. Hippies loved the English Invasion groups, but also related to a certain extent to the folk boom of the early 60s. They wore the "swinging London" style mini-skirts and Beatles haircuts, but also raided the thrift stores for Victorian and Edwardian clothing.

San Francisco had the advantage of having an abundance of actual Victorian houses—unlike New York or Los Angeles—particularly in the Haight-Ashbury area, where you could rent an apartment in a Victorian quite cheaply. Some people, like the Charlatans, went overboard and dressed like Edwardians and decorated their houses that way.

One of the most important of the houses was a condemned mansion which had a sweeping rosewood and oak staircase and magnificent parquet floors, located at 1090 Page. There was a ballroom in the basement with rooms off on either side and a bandstand with moonstone glass windows around it. It was managed by Rod Albin—a harpsichord player who was taking psychology at San Francisco State—and was owned by his uncle. His brother, Peter Albin, started Big Brother and the Holding Company there. Though Janis Joplin never lived there, she was often to be found hanging out or rehearsing.

RIGHT: The Charlatans, the first house band at the Red Dog Saloon in Virginia City, perform in western gear.

"Look at you, look at me Walkin' ten feet tall are we Smilin' silly smiles all day How'd we ever get that way?"

Mario Rocuzzo & Joe Heims, from a poem printed on the back of Sonny & Cher's Look At Us LP, 1965

LSD

On February 21, 1965 state narcotics agents raided the home of Augustus Owsley Stanley III in Berkeley, California and busted him for operating a Methedrine laboratory. Berkeley was awash with speed and Owsley was responsible for much of it, but although his lab equipment was there, they found no drugs. Not only did he get off, but he successfully sued the State to get his confiscated equipment back.

After two months in Los Angeles he returned to Berkeley with a new batch of pills. This time they contained very powerful doses of LSD. By May, Owsley's Beat Research Group had enough ergotomine to make a million and a half doses. It was still legal then, but those who used it kept it more or less a secret, knowing that as soon as the word got out the authorities would clamp down on it.

Psilocybin had been popularized on the East Coast by Allen Ginsberg and Timothy Leary, who had conducted a series of controlled sessions in 1960 with artists and writers such as Thelonious Monk, Jack Kerouac and Robert Lowell. The idea was that when the expected drive to make it illegal came, there would be a number of informed, articulate people available to speak in its favor.

Ginsberg had first taken LSD at the Mental Research labs at Palo Alto in 1959 as part of a series of experiments they were conducting and was a vocal advocate of its benefits. He was not the only connection with the Beat Generation. Lawrence Ferlinghetti's City Lights bookshop on Columbus Avenue remained a gathering place for writers and poets and there was also the very active presence of Neal Cassady, who had been Jack Kerouac's great hero—celebrated as Dean Moriarty in On The Road—and who now drove Ken Kesey's psychedelic bus.

In 1962 Ken Kesey had scored a great success with his brilliant novel One Flew Over The Cuckoo's Nest, which he had written while working as a psychiatric aide with mental patients at Veteran's Memorial Hospital in Menlo Park.

In 1964 Kesey received the last part of a large advance for a second novel, Sometimes A Great Notion (published later that year), and used some of the money to buy a 1939 International Harvester school bus. Once Kesey had bought a bus they set to work to transform it into THE bus. A hole was cut in the roof and a platform built so that people could ride on top. Huge outdoor speakers were installed on the roof along with microphones so that people inside could hear what was happening outside. At one point there was also a drum kit, guitar and bass to entertain people in the towns they passed through. Everything spoken inside or outside the bus could be recorded, submitted to tape delay and played back through speakers or headphones. There were a number of cameras and tape recorders onboard to record the whole thing.

Then the bus was painted: a terrible, sloppy, amateur psychedelic paint job that certainly drew attention to it. Roy Seburn painted the destination sign on the front to read "Furthur" with two 'u's (later corrected), and Kesey and his Pranksters left to discover America and subject it to their own Acid Test on June 14, 1964.

Fourteen people set out on the bus to cross America. Some of them wanted to see friends in the east, but most of them were hard-core Pranksters who regarded the entire thing as a work of art. They included Ken Babbs and his brother John, Sandy Lehmann-Haupt, Mike Hagen, George Walker, Mike Bevirt, Kesey's brother Chuck and his cousin Dale Kesey. Kathy Casano was there because she wanted to be in the film that Mike Hagen was shooting, provisionally titled The Merry Pranksters Search For The Cool Place. The film was sometimes given as the whole reason for the trip, but the Prankster's spirit was one of rejoicing in amateurism, which made the completing of the movie impossible.

Books devoted to describing the journey have included Tom Wolfe's The Electric Kool-Aid Acid Test, Paul Perry's On The Bus and Kesey's own The Further Inquiry, published in 1990.

"You're either on the bus, or off the bus."

Ken Kesey

LEFT: Dr. Timothy Leary (left) laughs with Neal Cassady onboard the Merry Pranksters" bus, Further. In 1964, Cassady had driven the bus across America with various Pranksters onboard, including head Prankster, author Ken Kesey, to visit Millbrook, the home of Leary's East Coast LSD-soaked community. The visit was unexpected.
OVER (LEFT): Kesey meets the Hell's Angels at a party he hosted to get to know them. OVER (RIGHT): The Further bus in San Francisco.

> ## "If society wants me to be an outlaw, then I'll be an outlaw and a damned good one. That's something people need. People at all times need outlaws."
>
> ### Ken Kesey

THE TRIP

The principal bus driver was Neal Cassady, who had his own microphone suspended in front of him so that he could keep up a continuous amphetamine-inspired monologue as he drove, smoked joints, made faces, crashed his way through the gears and hallucinated that the gas pedal had turned to spaghetti or that he was being attacked by phantom cockroaches.

No one else could have driven a bus that was periodically lacking in brakes, clutch and reverse gear and still have arrived at their destination. Kesey sat on the roof in his role as Captain Flag, wrapped in the Stars and Stripes and reading Captain America comics, while Soul and R&B blasted from the roof-mounted speakers as the bus travelled south.

Their route took them through Wikieup, Arizona, where they had their first group acid experience, through Phoenix to Houston, Texas, where they lost Kathy Casano (aka Stark Naked), up through New Orleans to New York City.

THE DRUGS

A trip up to Millbrook to drop in unexpectedly on the East Coast acid guru, Timothy Leary, proved far from successful.

Leary's approach to the LSD experience was about as far from that of the Pranksters as could be imagined. He thought it should be taken in a peaceful setting to produce a personal, contemplative, spiritual experience. The intention being to cause a "brain-change", or, to use one of Leary's slogans, "You have to be out of your mind to use your head." Kesey and Babbs, in particular, saw it as more of a sport, a test of endurance for the very hip. They thought LSD should be taken in an atmosphere where anything could happen and went out of their way to organize tricks and scary, edgy situations for themselves to encounter while on a trip, just to see what would happen. It was this that got Babbs and his buddies their name: the Merry Pranksters.

Timothy Leary was not at Millbrook when they arrived: the bus roared up the long drive, around the lake, American flags flying all over it, rock 'n' roll blaring from the speakers.

As they drew near to the giant 63-room Victorian gothic stone mansion, the Pranksters began lobbing green smoke bombs, expecting the members of the League for Spiritual Discovery to run out and welcome them with open arms as fellow travellers. But nothing hap-pened. Eventually Dr. Richard Alpert (he was not yet Ram Dass), accompanied by Peggy Hitchcock and Susan Metzner came wandering out to see what all the fuss was about.

Really the names said it all. The League for Spiritual Discovery meets the Pranksters; two more different approaches could not be imagined. Leary, Kesey and Babbs did meet, quietly in Leary's room. "We looked each other in the eye and promised to stay in touch as allies," wrote Leary in Flashbacks.

Later, Leary said, "I'm not sure what their real intention of coming to Millbrook was anyway, except to just say 'hi.' It is in the nature of the tribe that they don't meld. The genius of the tribal system is that each one has its own totem and its own gods. When you get into merging tribes you get into feudalism. The very nature of the stuff is that you're not supposed to be organized and you respect the other person's style." Leary said that he learned a lot from their visit—to be less formal and to have more of a sense of humour.

Neal Cassady returned to the Coast ahead of the others, where he met young Carolyn Adams, an energetic, loud eighteen-year-old from upstate New York who drove a big black motorcycle. Cassady immediately gave her a new name, Mountain Girl, and persuaded her to go with him to La Honda.

By the end of August 1964 the Pranksters were all back at home base and each day there seemed to be more of them. Mountain Girl fitted right in and she and Kesey became very close.

Together they had a daughter, Sunshine. Mountain Girl later married Jerry Garcia from the Grateful Dead.

"What are they on?" asked Dr. Leary. "Looks like speed to me," replied Dick Alpert. Leary groaned.

Ken Kesey & his Pranksters visit Millbrook, 1964

LEFT: Ken Babbs rides shotgun as Neal Cassady drives the Further bus, wearing headphones and dark glasses.

"Never trust a Prankster."

Ken Babbs

THE DEAD & AIRPLANE

On their first tour of America the Rolling Stones missed San Francisco, but on May 21, 1965 they played the Civic Auditorium in San Jose. All the local musicians and hipsters were there. People arrived in fancy dress, men in lipstick, women in long granny dresses. People in the audience even lit up joints for the first time in public.

There was a real feeling of community and afterwards people gathered in the basement music room of 1090 Page. Janis Joplin was there, jamming with some members of the Charlatans, the Albin brothers, who managed the building, were also there, as were David Freiberg and Gary Duncan, who maybe got the idea of starting Quicksilver Messenger Service that very night.

Jerry Garcia, who was playing around the San Mateo area, told Phil Lesh, "Come on down next week; we've got a gig at a pizza joint called Magoo's." The Grateful Dead did not yet exist. The line-ups had been together in various formations since the early 60s, coming together and breaking apart like amoebae. Ron McKernan, also known as "Pig-Pen", and Bill Kreutzmann had a band called the Zodiacs, with Pig-Pen on keyboards and Bill on drums. Jerry Garcia and his songwriting partner Robert Hunter had a folk-blues band called the Wildwood Boys. Then Garcia, Kreutzmann and Pig-Pen formed Mother McCree's Uptown Jug Champions, which, as their name implies, was more of a good-time jug band than a serious rock 'n' roll outfit.

Then, after the Stones concert, a band came together called the Warlocks, with a line-up that was to become the Grateful Dead: Jerry Garcia on guitar, Pig-Pen on Vox organ and blues harp, Bill Kreutzmann on drums, Bob Weir on rhythm guitar and Phil Lesh on bass.

They played their first club gig at the Fireside Club on El Camino Real in San Mateo in June 1965, where they had ID problems with the club because Bob Weir was only seventeen—and looked fifteen. The Warlocks was mostly Pig-Pen's idea; though he grew up in Palo Alto, he could sing like an old-time southern blues man and, at first, he was the assumed leader of the group.

In the beginning they played mostly R&B numbers—Pig-Pen's father was the only white DJ on a black R&B station and Pig-Pen himself worked in a record store, so he really knew the stuff. Then, leadership drifted naturally to Jerry Garcia, possibly because Pig-Pen was a drinking man and refused to have anything to do with drugs. The Pranksters naturally spiked him—LSD rubbed on the top of a sealed beer can—but he hated it. Drunk though he was, he was often the only one in the right key.

On 13 August singer Marty Balin and Matthew Katz, who had earned a fortune making a machine that put plastic lids on coffee cans, took over the Honeybucket on Fillmore Street, a small bar that used to be a hang-out for plain clothes police, stool pigeons and afternoon hookers. Now it became the Matrix—from underworld to underground. It was intended as a venue for Balin's group, the Jefferson Airplane, who were to be the house band, with Katz acting as their manager.

Their unusual name was thought up by Steve Talbot, a friend of Jorma Kaukonen's in Berkeley, after an evening of inventing spoof names for blues musicians offered up "Blind Thomas Jefferson Airplane."

Balin furnished and decorated the club with a wall of Egyptian hieroglyphs, used as the background for many photographic portraits from the

ABOVE: Millbrook, East Coast home of Leary and his League for Spiritual Discovery.

period. The biggest problem that ultimately remained unresolved came from the neighbors. The club was in a residential area and its wooden walls were not designed for amplified music. It was on the ground floor without even the natural soundproofing qualities that basement clubs have. You walked into the main room straight off the street.

Balin—real name Martyn Jerel Buchwald—was a painter and a sculptor; he had danced in West Side Story and played with a variety of groups, including the Town Criers. He settled on rock 'n' roll after seeing the Beatles performing on Ed Sullivan and exclaiming, like so many other American musicians, "That's where it's at!" He watched A Hard Day's Night nine times.

In March 1965 he was in Los Angeles working as a folk singer, when the Byrds had a hit with "Mr. Tambourine Man": "That record sent me beetling back to San Francisco to start my own folk rock group." He tried out a large number of players until one day in June 1965 he ran into Paul Kantner and they jelled. After a spell as a folk group Balin bought an electric guitar and they became a rock band.

Balin then met Skip Spence, a guitarist, auditioning for the Quicksilver Messenger Service. He had never played drums in his life but Balin persuaded him to try it and, if he could play in a week, he could join the band. A week later, Balin called and told him, "Come down tonight, we have a job." Balin, Kantner and Spence hired Signe Anderson as vocalist; she had been around the San Francisco folk scene for some time and had hung out with Ken Kesey. A bluegrass player, Bob Harvey, was hired on bass, which left only a lead guitarist. Jorma Kaukonen stood in while an electric guitarist was sought.

At first Kaukonen copied Roger McGuinn and bought a 12-string Rickenbacker, but soon had to change it for a Gibson, which gave him his distinctive sound: "I really had to learn to play guitar all over again."

Balin's roommate worked as a copy boy at the San Francisco Chronicle and used his influence to get their jazz columnist, Ralph J Gleason, a pipe-smoking, patches on the elbows, tweed-jacketed hipster, to write them up. Gleason had caused a great deal of controversy in local jazz circles by suggesting that some of the British

Invasion rock bands might actually be worth seeing. He even wrote positively about folk-rock—anathema to the jazz diehards.

Bob Harvey left in November and was replaced by Kaukonen's friend Jack Casady, whom they flew in from Washington, DC, excited by the promise of fame and fortune. He got both and soon became the archetypal San Francisco hippie, with his wide smile, long hair and head-band. The band immediately went into the studio to record their first album, Jefferson Airplane Takes Off.

"San Francisco can be the American Liverpool. Dancing is the thing, they've got to give people a place to dance. That's what's wrong with those Cow Palace shows. The kids can't dance there! There'll be no trouble when they can dance."

Luria Castell

RIGHT: The Rolling Stones toured America in 1965 and attracted the coolest, proto-hippie crowds to their gigs on the West Coast.

"Rock 'n' roll is the new form of communication for our generation."

Paul Kantner

THE FAMILY DOG

In October 1965 three posters went up in San Francisco: one on the notice board in Enrico's Coffee House on Broadway near the City Lights Bookshop, one in the Committee's box office and the final one on the wall of the Matrix on Fillmore Street. They were designed and hand silk-screened by Marty Balin and read: "The Family Dog Presents / A Rock 'n' Roll Dance and Concert / The Jefferson Airplane, The Marbles, / The Great Society / and in High Gear / Those Charlatans Announce Their Arrival / Oct. 16 / 9 to 2 / Longshoreman's Hall".

It was the first dance organized by a new outfit, called The Family Dog. They consisted of Luria Castell, who had once been a political activist and who looked like the archetypal hippie-chick, with wire-rimmed glasses, long granny dresses and very long straight hair; Ellen Harmon, who had apparently lived in a tree in Mexico for at least six months, possibly a year

("It's good for you, you do a lot of thinking"); Alton Kelly, an ex-commercial artist who later became a leading psychedelic poster artist; and Jack Towle, a dealer who was reputed to have established $10 as the ceiling price for an ounce of grass in San Francisco.

All four had lived at the Red Dog Saloon in Virginia City that summer and were hoping to continue the same community spirit in San Francisco. They borrowed money from their parents and soon booked some dates at the Longshoreman's Hall.

They called their first dance "A Tribute To Dr. Strange". No one had given a dance a name before. They approached Russ Syracuse, a DJ whose "All Night Flight" on KYA was the hippest show on the radio, to act as MC for the evening—another clever idea because people had never seen him in person.

RIGHT: The Jefferson Airplane debut LP, 1965.

"The march should be led by grandmothers carrying flowers, young women with babies in arms and girls dressed in pretty costumes."

Allen Ginsberg on the Vietnam Day Committee Anti-War march, 16 October 1965

The Longshoreman's Hall, down on the waterfront, had often been the venue for jazz concerts. It was the first large venue that the Jefferson Airplane ever played and it established them as central to the burgeoning new scene. As Donovan later sang after attending Jefferson Airplane rehearsals with Paul McCartney, "Fly Jefferson Airplane—gets you there on time!"

The Family Dog booked the Longshoremen's Hall for three weeks in a row. The second dance was called "A Tribute to Sparkle Plenty", this time featuring the Lovin' Spoonful and The Charlatans. The third was "A Tribute to Ming the Merciless" and featured the Charlatans and the Mothers of Invention.

The same night as the "Tribute to Ming the Merciless" show, on November 6, there was an appeal party for the San Francisco Mime Troupe (see page 52). The Family Dog helped them to organize it and many people took in both events. After the first three dances, the original members of the Family Dog decided to leave town for various reasons, leaving Chet Helms—who had assisted on the first three and had money invested in a fourth—to take over the organization.

There was a lot of underground activity in San Francisco and the Bay Area in the summer of 1965—individual actions and events which together gave rise to the extraordinary phenomenon of Haight-Ashbury.

On August 13, 1965 Max Scherr started The Berkeley Barb, a strongly anti-war, pro-student protest weekly that was started, in part, as a response to the university's ban on radical political activities on campus. Aimed at the student and hippie community in the Bay Area, the Barb gave the people their voice and a place to announce underground activities when other newspapers were too expensive to advertise in or simply would not touch the subject matter.

A NEW MUSIC

A lot of new bands and theatre groups came together that summer. In August the Great Society was formed, consisting of Grace Slick on vocals, her husband, filmmaker Jerry Slick, on drums, his brother Darby Slick on lead guitar, David Minor on rhythm guitar and Peter Vandegilder on bass. They auditioned at Tom Donahue's club, Mothers, and after a one-nighter at the Coffee Gallery they got a two-week steady gig there. Donahue released a single, "Someone to Love/Free Advice", as the first record on his North Beach label and live tapes from the Matrix were later released by Columbia after Grace Slick joined the Jefferson Airplane and became famous.

Guitarists Jim Murray and John Cipollina began putting together a group which was to have Dino Valente as its singer. They got in Gary Duncan on guitar, David Freiberg on bass and vocals and Greg Elmore on drums and named themselves the Quicksilver Messenger Service. Unfortunately Dino was serving a jail sentence for possession and by the time he got out, there was no place for him in the line-up that had originally been put together at his request. Soon they were a fixture in the San Francisco underground scene and one of the most popular psychedelic bands in the Bay Area. Dino did eventually join then, as did Nicky Hopkins, the British keyboard player who worked a lot with the Stones.

On August 30 the Charlatans played in San Francisco for the first time. One of the Committee, a Beat generation-era North Beach satirical theatre group, had made a movie of himself and wanted a band as part of the evening's entertainment. One of the creators of the extravaganza was Stewart Brand, later publisher of the Whole Earth Catalog, who described it as "a peyote meeting without the peyote." On September 13 the Committee began a series of regular Monday events, a mixed-media happening called America Needs Indians, with three movie projectors, four American Indian dancers and two separate soundtracks playing.

Another Haight-Ashbury-based theatre group was The Open Theatre on Pine Street, which specialized in mixed-media effects, light projections and, for a while, projections onto nude bodies.

RIGHT: A Vietnam Day Committee member protests against US involvement in Vietnam on a march, 16 October 1965.
OVER: Hell's Angels attack anti-war protesters.

ANGELS & HIPPIES

Each Saturday there was a big party at La Honda that Kesey and the Pranksters would spend all week preparing for. The woods were wired for sound, with speakers suspended in the trees and microphones hidden in the bushes, and everything was controlled by a complex sound mixing and recording system. There were sculptures in the garden, a stage in a little amphitheater behind the house, complicated lighting systems: everything was designed to amaze and confuse. The Pranksters ran around with their faces painted wearing American flags or goggles. Everything was spiked with acid. The police would park outside, but they couldn't enter the property without a warrant. As soon as anyone left the property, they would be pulled over and their car would be searched. Even rental cars were ticketed for some minor infraction.

Neal Cassady would stand in the bushes near the road, stark naked, haranguing the police with his mile-a-minute motormouth. LSD was still legal, but the police had a good idea of what else they might find if they could only get in. The raid came on April 24, 1965, when eighteen cops searched the place for pot. They found Kesey trying to flush it down the toilet. He and fourteen Pranksters were arrested on charges of marijuana possession and Kesey was additionally charged with resisting arrest and operating a premises where marijuana was furnished.

After fifteen court appearances the charges against the other Pranksters were dropped and Kesey was given a suspended sentence on the condition that he would no longer associate with the other Pranksters. It was towards the end of the summer that Kesey met the Hell's Angels. He was introduced by Gonzo journalist Hunter S. Thompson, who was living on the Haight and writing a book about them. Against Thompson's advice, Kesey invited them down to La Honda for a party in early December and hung a fifteen-foot banner outside the property saying, "The Merry Pranksters Welcome the Hell's Angels."

The woods were filled with the roar of Harley Davidsons as forty or so Hell's Angels descended on the Kesey spread. The Pranksters had food and beer ready and, after a few joints, the Angels were persuaded to try LSD. Soon they were tripping wildly.

The party lasted for two and a half days and continued on and off for months, until Kesey, wife Faye, their kids and Mountain Girl all moved to "The Spread," Babbs' 400-acre place in Soquel, outside Santa Cruz. The septic tank at la Honda had backed up and there were too many Hell's Angels around even for the Pranksters' liking.

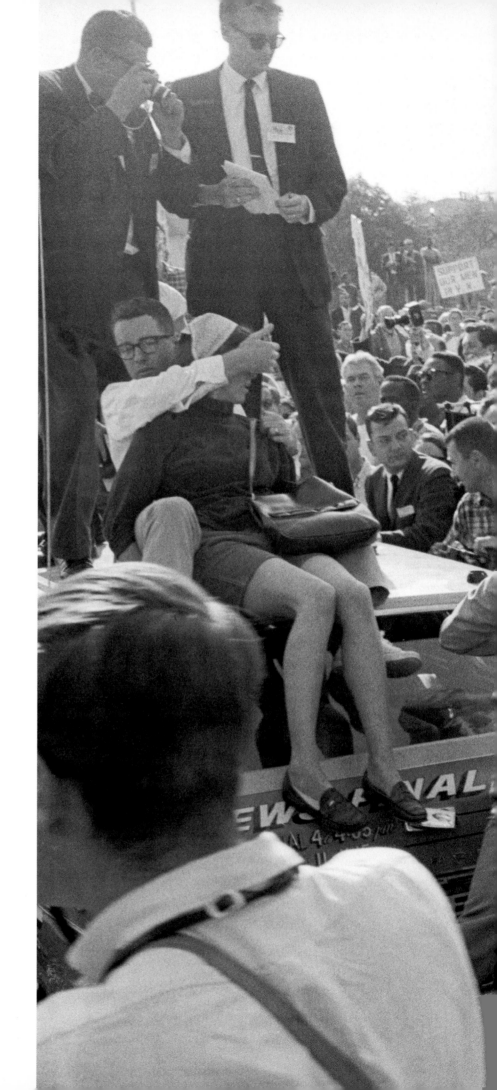

There were anti-war demonstrations in all the major cities across America and, as more and more troops were sent to Vietnam, the trickle of anti-war protesters crossing the border to Canada to avoid the draft became a stream. Country Joe wrote songs for the people who protested or ran.

STOP THE WAR

On October 16 a massive anti-war march was organized by the Vietnam Day Committee to go from the Berkeley campus, through the black district of Oakland to the Oakland Army Terminal. However, at the Oakland city line, they were stopped by the Oakland police, equipped with full riot gear, gas masks, and guns. The marchers sat down in the street and there were some speeches from the sound truck. At this point, seven Hell's Angels rushed out from behind the police lines and one named Tiny tore down the "Peace In Vietnam" banner that had led the march. Then, as police stood by and watched, he cut the wires to the sound truck so that no more speeches could be made.

This was the day the Family Dog put on their first dance, "A Tribute To Dr. Strange," and many of the political radicals who had participated in the Berkeley Vietnam Day rally earlier that day attended, including some Hell's Angels. They all joined in a snake-dance, weaving circles and figure eights through the hall. The marchers were determined to exercise their constitutional rights and planned another demonstration and march for November.

The Hell's Angels announced their intention to beat up anyone who marched, so Ken Kesey organized a meeting between the two sides, to be held at Ralph "Sonny" Barger's house in Oakland. Barger was the president of the Oakland chapter of the Hell's Angels, the most powerful of the outlaw gangs operating on the coast. Ginsberg, Neal Cassady, Ken Kesey, some of his Merry Pranksters in costume and one or two people from the Vietnam Day Committee arrived and were met by about twenty Angels, also in costume. All but Ginsberg dropped acid and they began talking. The Angels held a classic anti-Communist position and the discussion became heated. Ginsberg unpacked his harmonium and began to chant the Prajnaparamita Sutra, the "Highest Perfect Wisdom." After a few minutes, Tiny, the Angel who had torn up the "Peace In Vietnam" banner, joined in, singing "Om, om, zoom, zoom, zoom, om!" Gradually the other Hell's Angels joined in, followed by Neal and Kesey, until in the end the whole room was chanting. "I was absolutely astounded," said Ginsberg, "I knew it was history being made. It was the first time in a tense tight, situation that I

relied totally on pure mantric vocalization, 'breath-chant' to alleviate my own paranoia and anxiety." By the time the meeting broke up the tensions had dissipated.

Barger insisted that they had been inaccurately reported and said they had already made American flags for their own, peaceful, pro-American counterdemonstration. Several days later the Angels issued their Newspaper Edict, printed in the San Francisco Examiner, saying that it would demean them to attack the filthy Communist marchers and that they had sent a telegram to President Johnson offering to fight the Communists in South Vietnam as "gorilla [sic] soldiers." The Angels had found a way to save face and the march was safe from attack.

Joe McDonald, a protest singer who was also the editor of Rag Baby, a folk music magazine from Berkeley, decided to put out a "talking issue" of the magazine to coincide with the organized protests against the Vietnam war. He got together with another guitarist, Berry Melton,

RIGHT: Bob Dylan went from being an acoustic protest singer-songwriter to an electrified spokesman for a generation in 1965.

and they formed a folk duo. A little later he added three more musicians—Bruce Barthol on bass, John Gunning on drums and Paul Armstrong on tambourine—to become Country Joe and the Fish. Rehearsals and regular gigs at the Jabberwock in Berkeley perfected their sound.

One of the most successful of the protest bands, they managed to marry rock 'n' roll with genuine political protest—something that sounded phony in Barry McGuire, strained in Phil Ochs and was hard to take in the Fugs. Country Joe whooped it up with the "I Feel Like I'm Fixin To Die Rag" and had the audience singing along on the famous "Fish" cheer: "Gimmee an F! Gimmee a U! Gimmee a C …!"

BILL GRAHAM

The San Francisco Mime Troupe was founded by Ronny Davis in an old church on Capp Street in the Mission. In many ways they were the intellectual end of the scene. They performed what came to be known as agitprop: radical political plays in the tradition of Artaud's Theatre of Cruelty, but rendered in the form of the commedia dell'arte. They updated the old texts to reflect present day events such as the Vietnam War or the Civil Rights movement. There were a lot of people involved with the Mime Troupe, including a young businessman called Bill Graham.

Bill Graham was a German Jew who escaped from Berlin at the age of eight in 1938. He was the office manager of Allis-Chalmers, a heavy equipment manufacturer of trucks, conveyor belts and hydraulic equipment. He earned a high salary, wore a three-piece suit and had an interest in the theatre. In 1965 he was introduced to the people in the San Francisco Mime Troupe, who asked him to transliterate Giordano Bruno's seventeenth-

century play Il Candelaio—the Candle Bearer—into a three-act play suitable for a park performance. This was his entry test. He certainly produced a controversial script.

In August, the San Francisco Recreation and Parks Commission revoked the Mime Troupe's permit to perform in the park, on the grounds that Il Candelaio was "not in good taste" or "suitable" for "their" parks. Believing that the parks belonged to the people and that they had a right to perform on the principle of free speech, they defied the law and, naturally, got busted. After a farcical four-day trial, Ronny Davis was found guilty of performing in the parks without a permit. He was due to be sentenced on December 6 and, in the meantime, a benefit was organized to pay for an appeal. By now the Mime Troupe had moved to a loft at 924 Howard Street between 5th and 6th Streets, part of which they shared with the local branch of SDS—Students for a Democratic Society, one of the main anti-war organizations.

The loft was large, big enough for a party. The Jefferson Airplane agreed to perform, as did folk singer Sandy Bull. The Fugs, who were visiting from New York, said they'd play, as did the John Handy Quintet jazz group. Lawrence Ferlinghetti said he'd read and the Family Dog offered their experience in staging concerts.

At that time Bill Graham, who wrote the poster, didn't know what was happening on the scene and listed them as one of the acts. The party was on November 6. It was a success beyond anyone's wildest dreams. The line went down the block. In fact it was such a success that they had another on December 10, this time at the Fillmore Auditorium. Significantly, the third San Francisco Mime Troupe Dance Concert, on January 14, 1966—again at the Fillmore—was headed "Bill Graham presents."

"The band was playing but I couldn't hear the music . . . people were dancing . . . someone came up to me and I shut my eyes and with a machine he projected images on the back of my eyelids…I sought out a person I trusted and he laughed and told me that the Kool-Aid had been spiked and I was just beginning my first LSD experience."

from the jacket of Tom Wolfe's The Electric Kool-Aid Acid Test

ACID TESTS

The first Acid Test was held on November 27, 1965, at Ken Babbs" place near Santa Cruz, a chicken ranch known as "The Spread." Jerry Garcia and Phil Lesh from the Warlocks had been hanging out and talking about the possibilities of a multimedia show. "Why don't we do one?" said Babbs. Allen Ginsberg chanted Hindu and Buddhist mantras, Neal Cassady rapped into an open microphone, Owsley supplied the LSD—clear Sandoz in red wrinkled capsules—and the Warlocks, shortly to become the Grateful Dead, played. It lasted until dawn and everyone had a good time except Kenneth Anger, who left in a huff when someone suggested sacrificing a chicken.

On December 4 the second Acid Test was held at a house near San Jose State University. The Rolling Stones played the Auditorium in San Jose that evening and the Pranksters passed out crayon-lettered handbills at the concert with the street address and the line: "Can YOU Pass the Acid Test?" Three to four hundred people descended on the venue and the Warlocks played until the cops arrived and proceeded to send everybody home.

There was a third Acid Test in Mountain View, between Palo Alto and San Jose. About 200 people showed up and the Warlocks were in full R&B mode. The police naturally came too, but Jerry Garcia met them in the parking lot and talked to them. LSD was still legal and whatever he said clearly satisfied them. As they walked away, Jerry made a gesture of touching his hat and said, "The trips, captain." Denise Kaufmann, who had witnessed the transaction, liked the way he said it and reported it to Kesey. Thus Jerry Garcia got the name "Captain Trips."

The fourth Acid Test was held at the wooden lodge in the State Park at Muir Beach, ten miles up the highway north of San Francisco. Some 300 people watched bits of the bus movie and danced to the Warlocks. There were no police because they went instead to Stinson Beach, further north, where the event was originally planned to happen. Kesey, however, did not have a good time and at dawn he announced to the Pranksters that the Acid Tests were over. "No more," he declared. They were getting too big and there were too many bad vibes. No one listened though, and they carried right on planning the next one.

Malcolm X was shot and killed on February 21, 1965 and three men were convicted of his murder. It was a year of profound racial unrest. Dr. Martin Luther King led a march from Selma, Alabama to the state capital in Montgomery, which took in over 25,000 marchers, and was held from March 21 to 25, with the protection of federal troops. A white civil rights worker, Mrs. Viola Liuzzo, was killed driving some of the black marchers back to Selma on March 25 .
The previous year, at the age of 35, Martin Luther King, Jr had become the youngest man to have received the Nobel Peace Prize. When notified of his selection, he announced that he would turn over the prize money of $54,123 to the furtherance of the civil rights movement. On August 6, 1965 a voting rights bill was signed by President L. B. Johnson, allowing African-Americans the right to vote.

RIGHT: Dr. Martin Luther King on the Selma march.
OVER: Troops confront Dr. King's marchers at Montgomery, Alabama.

HOLLYWOOD

"We stepped on the dance floor and from then on it was music and dance for months and months! All right!"

Karl Franzoni, an original Freak

FREAKS

The first hippies in Hollywood, perhaps the first hippies anywhere, were Vito, his wife Zsou, Captain Fuck and their group of about thirty-five dancers. Calling themselves Freaks, they lived a semi-communal life and engaged in sex orgies and free-form dancing whenever they could. Vitautus Alphonsus Paulekas was born in 1910, the son of a Lithuanian sausage-maker who settled in Massachusetts. He spent a year and a half in a reformatory as a teenager followed by six months as a marathon dancer during the Depression, which was where he perfected his dancing techniques. He was already in his 50s in 1962 when he began dancing every two weeks with a Top-40 covers band, Jim Doval & The Gauchos, at a club on the Strip across from Ben Frank's. His hair was brushed forward in a Beatle cut and, though he had a very youthful body, his age was betrayed by his lined face and graying moustache. Vito was something of a guru, described by Richard Goldstein as "not the most articulate of wizards, but he comes on booming like thunder. His theories make meagre sense but they are expounded with a galactic joy."

Vito made a living of sorts by giving clay modeling lessons to Beverly Hills matrons who found the atmosphere in his studio exciting; the walls were painted like a Mayan tomb and one wall was covered with a collage of newspaper headlines. Vito had the first crash pad in LA, an open house to countless runaways where everyone was welcome for a night, particularly young women. The studio was in the basement of 303 North Laurel Street and could be reached through his wife Zsou's dress shop on the ground floor. Zsou was an ex-cheerleader who got together with Vito when she was only sixteen. Vito had a little curtained alcove in the back of Zsou's shop with a mattress in it, in case he was ever able to waylay one of her customers. His hand would often emerge and run up the leg of a surprised girl. Vito's best buddy was Karl Franzoni—known as "Captain Fuck"—who joined the troupe in 1963.

Karl Orestes Franzoni had a bald pate surrounded by tight greasy curls, a goatee and an unusually long, pointed tongue which he used to shoot out like a Gila monster. He wore red tights that exaggerated the size of his sex organs, garish tops and a cape with an "F" emblazoned on it which stood, not for "Franzoni," but for "Captain Fuck." Like Vito, he was a sexual predator, forcing his attention upon the teenage girls who hung around the dance troupe at concerts.

Zsou was a forerunner of the thriftstore look; her shop was filled with tatty lace and velvet from the 20s and 30s, frocks and scarves and sequined bags. Karl Franzoni said, "She became, in the 60s, the seller of elegant things for freaks to wear. They all bought their clothes from her and when we went out dancing you would see these bright colored people. Women all wore see-through, no panties, no bras—and that was it ..."

RIGHT: A napkin from the Whisky A Go Go on Sunset Strip in Los Angeles.

"The Beatles came out and changed the whole game for me. I saw a definite niche where the two of them blended together. If you took Lennon and Dylan and mixed them together ... that was something that hadn't been done before."

Jim McGuinn

THE BYRDS etc

In March 1965 Vito and his freaks met up with the Byrds and found the perfect band to dance to. The members of the Byrds had been playing for some years in various combos, mostly folk or folk rock outfits—Jim McGuinn was in the Chad Mitchell Trio, Gene Clark was in the New Christie Minstrels and David Crosby was one of Les Baxter's Balladeers. All of them had been inspired to become musicians by the Beatles, whose impact on American music is incalculable. McGuinn liked them so much that he used to do "Beatles imitations" in the coffee shops of Greenwich Village and even bravely sang their songs solo, first at the Troubadour in Los Angeles, then in the West Coast headquarters of "authentic"—in other words, purely acoustic—folk music. It was after seeing A Hard Day's Night in 1964 that McGuinn, Crosby and Clark had first got together to form a band and had cut some acoustic demos at World Pacific Studios with producer-manager Jim Dickson. He brought in bass player Chris Hillman and David Crosby knew drummer Michael Clarke from Big Sur. The line-up was complete.

At first they called themselves the Jet Set, after McGuinn's love of planes; then they changed their name to the Beefeaters for a single, "Please Let Me Love You," cut for Elektra. It went nowhere, but that November Dickson managed to sign them with Columbia and set about creating excitement about the group. He saw that Ciro's was reopening as a rock venue and managed to get the Byrds (as they now called themselves, with crafty Beatles-like mis-spelling) booked as the first attraction.

RIGHT: The Byrds, the first Los Angeles hippie act to make it big with a mixture of Dylan, Beatles and 12-string pyrotechnical guitar play.

"We started the whole hippie thing: Vito, Karl, Zsou, Beatle Bob, Bryan and me. Bryan put a ribbon in his hair and people would come to Ben Frank's after we played."

Arthur Lee

The Byrds were the first group to make a successful synthesis of LA country rock, acoustic Bob Dylan and the spikier English invasion group sound.

By applying this sound directly to the songs of Bob Dylan they had a winning formula. On January 20, 1965 they recorded their first single: Dylan's "Mr. Tambourine Man." McGuinn's ringing, bell-like 12-string Rickenbacker guitar featured heavily on it and the song went straight to No. 1. Ciro's was once more packed with Hollywood stars and celebrities. The Byrds were a huge hit; even Lenny Bruce's mother went to see them. With their Beatles haircuts, McGuinn in his small rectangular granny glasses and David Crosby in his green cape, they were something entirely new to the Hollywood crowd. Just as the Byrds were taking off, another new group appeared on the scene in Los Angeles: Arthur Lee and Love.

Love was the house band at Bido Lito's, which was located on Cosmo Alley between Hollywood Boulevard and Selma, and they built up a strong local following. Their music was a gritty mixture of the English sound—the Rolling Stones in particular—mixed with LA folk rock—the Byrds—but it had a dark and slightly sinister edge to it. Rock critic Lillian Roxon described Love as "One of the first integrated groups. Arthur Lee produced one of the most amusing paradoxes in rock—a Negro, he came on like Mick Jagger, a white singer who built his whole style around accurate imitations of Negroes."

In the spring of 1965 the three Manzarek brothers, Ray, Rick and Jim, were playing in a Santa Monica bar band called Rick and the Ravens. Ray was studying film at UCLA and living in Venice, the oceanfront beatnik section of LA just south of Santa Monica. In July, he ran into fellow UCLA film student Jim Morrison on the beach and Morrison played him some of his songs, the first one being "Moonlight Drive." Ray Manzarek noted, "I said, 'That's it!' I'd never heard lyrics to a rock song like that before. We talked a while before we decided to get a group together and make a million dollars." In September they recorded six Morrison originals at World Pacific with Ray's brothers and drummer John Densmore, who Ray had met at the Maharishi's

Third Street Meditation Center. Ray's brothers didn't like Jim's songs, but the Maharishi turned up another group member, Robbie Krieger, and the line-up was complete. Taking their name from Aldous Huxley's Doors of Perception, the Doors began rehearsing. Their first club date was at London Fog, a few doors down from the Whisky, between Hamburger Hamlet and the Galaxy on the Strip. Supported by student friends from the UCLA film school, they soon developed a following, but club owners found their music too strange. They played four audition sets at Bido Lito's only to be turned down, but each week they improved their act and it was only a matter of time before they were discovered.

Also playing on the Strip were the Mothers of Invention and, though Zappa's music was never as danceable as the Byrds and required a lot more concentration, Vito and company began to show up at Mothers' gigs to dance. They became so much part of the Mothers' act that they got dubbed as "the Mothers Auxiliary" and Karl Franzoni, in particular, was included in a lot of group photographs.

LEFT: Love, headed by Arthur Lee (on stairs) were a true product of the hippie scene.
OVER: Two teenage girls run screaming from a police charge in Watts.

WATTS RIOTS

On August 11, 1965, in the middle of the summer heat wave, a minor incident in the black South Central neighborhood of Watts flared into full scale rioting. It was an area with poor housing, overcrowding, high unemployment and a high crime rate. When police flagged down 21-year-old Marquette Frye, who they suspected of being drunk, a crowd gathered and began to taunt the policeman who called for backup. The second policeman responded to something said by the crowd by striking them with his baton. It was the spark that led to five days of rioting, during which more than thirty-four people died, almost all of them black. At least 1,000 people were injured and an estimated $200 million in property was destroyed by looting and burning, including the whole Watts business district, which was raised to the ground. Meanwhile, in LA's comfortable suburbs, people watched the riot live on television each night, brought to them by television reporter teams in helicopters—the first such use of this technology.

It took 16,000 National Guardsmen, city police and county deputies to quell the riots, in which an estimated 35,000 African-Americans took part. The protesters focussed their rage largely against the overpriced white shop-keeper's stores, as well as the all-white Los Angeles Police Department protecting them. Black businesses, churches, libraries and private homes were virtually untouched. Though the authorities tried to claim that outside left-wing agitators were at work, studies showed that the overwhelming majority of rioters were born there. The outcome of the riot was predictable: rather than improve conditions, the population reacted by replacing the liberal governor Pat Brown with the right wing law and order candidate, Ronald Reagan.

THE NEW BEATS

EAST COAST HIPPIE

In New York, what became the hippie scene was in many ways simply a continuation of the Beat Generation activities of earlier in the decade and the late 50s. Andy Warhol had been painting since the 50s and his "factory" was at its peak in 1964. Warhol differed from his contemporaries—Lichtenstein, Rauschenburg, Johns and company—in that he surrounded himself with an entourage of young people who spent much of their time hanging out and taking drugs. The entourage included the Velvet Underground. Though they had a lot in common with a band like the Mothers of Invention—they both employed dancers, Tom Wilson produced both bands, they were on the same label and played to much the same crowd—the Velvets would never have thought of themselves as hippies. At least, not in the San Francisco sense of the term.

The Fugs were a natural product of the downtown poetry scene that had begun five years before, in 1959, and involved many of the old Beats such as Allen Ginsberg, who was one of the few figures to make an easy transition from the Beats to the Hippies. His great friend Jack Kerouac could not make the jump. Ginsberg was also responsible for introducing Timothy Leary to the counterculture, by his active participation in lining up volunteers for Leary's psilocybin program at Harvard back in 1961. Leary was the oldest of all the hippie

gurus. Born in 1920, he was already in his mid-40s when he took the stage at the Human Be-In. How he came to be there is a long story.

DR. TIMOTHY LEARY

By 1960 the well-respected, brilliant psychologist Dr. Timothy Leary of Harvard University had become convinced that to alleviate psychic suffering, something more than behavioral analysis was needed. He began to examine existing research into hallucinogenics. He spent that summer in Cuernavaca, where he learned about the pre-Hispanic Mexican civilizations and their use of magic mushrooms to induce visions. In August, sitting next to his swimming pool, he went on his first magic mushroom trip: "You are never the same after you have had that one flash glimpse down the cellular time tunnel," he wrote. "You are never the same after you have had the veil drawn …"

By early 1961 Leary had obtained funding for a Harvard approved project: "A Study of Clinical Reactions to Psilocybin Administered in Supportive Environments." He handed out 3,500 doses to over 400 people, ranging from jazz musicians and writers to prison inmates and Harvard grad students. A huge 90% said they would like to repeat the experience, 83% said they had "learned something or had insight" and a massive 62% said that it had changed their life

for the better. Leary was more than ever convinced that he had found the answer to society's ills. Realizing that the likelihood of such a powerful drug remaining legal was remote, he took steps to influence the public debate by targeting "opinion makers" so that it would at least remain available to researchers and scientists. He gave the drugs to poets like Robert Lowell, Charles Olson, Allen Ginsberg; he gave it to the jazz musicians Maynard Ferguson, Charles Mingus, and Thelonius Monk; he also gave it to publishers and educators and tried hard to get some to President Kennedy.

It was all very academic and above board. The trouble came because Tim and everyone in his household were taking the stuff constantly. In December 1961 Leary switched to the even more potent LSD, introduced to him by Michael Hollingshead. The more acid he took, the more he saw God, and by early 1962 his sessions often included ministers and theological students. One time they took LSD in goblets and read aloud from the New Testament. This, however, was balanced by Hindu "sex rituals" (or tantric sex) held in the attic in a room filled with erotic tapestries.

Inevitably other administrators began to complain because Tim had gathered a clan of about 40 Harvard students around him who, like him, believed that it was "… time to free the brain from the mind," or rather, it was time to kill the mind and cultivate a mindless vision. This, the other

"Let's welcome the gentlemen who may well be responsible for a great deal of the New York scene … The Fugs!"

Introduction to The Fugs Live at Fillmore East, June 1968

RIGHT: The Fugs from New York operated out of a bookshop (they're seated in front of it), published magazines and satirized everything.

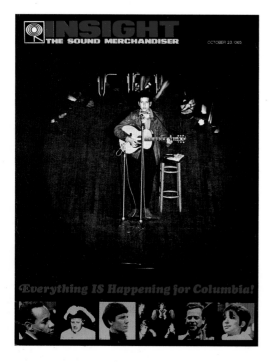

ABOVE: CBS Records flyer, 1965.
RIGHT: Dr. Timothy Leary, wrote The Politics of Ecstasy and The Psychedelic Experience among many pro-psychedelic titles.

academics argued, was not why parents sent their children to Harvard. The Harvard Crimson ran the headline "Campus Drug Cult" and in April 1962 Leary was banned from providing psychedelics without a certified physician being present. Leary kept his head down until the three-month summer break, then with about 35 friends and associates he decamped to Mexico, where he took over an entire hotel in Zihuatanejo for an intense summer season. With him was Richard Alpert, an assistant professor at Harvard, ten years Leary's junior and one of his main disciples. Also along for the trip was Peggy Hitchcock, one of the heirs to the Mellon millions (her grandfather had started Gulf Oil). Tim's in-group saw themselves as visionaries who were together founding a new universal society based on psychedelics and a synthesis of Eastern religions.

Back in Harvard, Alpert and Leary saw that there was no way they could get official approval to continue their work. They founded an off-campus organization called the International Federation for Internal Freedom—known as IF-IF—with a headquarters within sight of Harvard. The university reacted with outrage and a number of anti-psychedelic articles appeared in the Harvard Crimson warning students away from the drugs. Early in 1963 IF-IF organized public summer sessions at the hotel in Zihuatanejo and of the more than 5,000 applica-

tions, 500 were accepted (the hotel held 50 people). Rates were cheap, at $200 a month plus $6 per guided LSD session. In late April Leary flew down to Mexico to make the final preparations and on May 6 the Harvard Board of Trustees fired him for "absenting himself from Cambridge without permission." Leary actually had verbal permission to travel, which meant that this was the first time a faculty member had been fired that century for such a minor infringement of the rules. Twenty days later Alpert was fired for giving psychedelics to an undergraduate, contravening the agreement he had signed the previous November. (The undergraduate was his boyfriend, whose father was on the Harvard Board.)

There was more trouble ahead. The season had barely started in Mexico when IF-IF foolishly invited the press and television to visit. The newsmen were greeted by a hysterical, naked, middle-aged woman with a crude rendering of the crucified Christ painted on her body. She was in the middle of a bad trip and jumped out of a doorway. In Catholic Mexico this was heavy stuff. Leary and his companions were rounded up, put into trucks and shipped back to the States in a sealed plane.

Leary had inadvertently become a martyr to the psychedelic movement. He attempted to set up a center in Antigua and was thrown out; they then went to Dominica, where they rented an entire hotel called the Bucket of Blood, but it was not long before they were expelled from there, too. An 11th-hour reprieve came from Peggy Hitchcock's brother Billy. He and another brother, Tommy, had bought a 64-room Victorian mansion set in three square miles of woodland in Millbrook, New York, about 80 miles north of New York City. Billy and Tommy found the dark wooden paneling and Gothic ambiance of the "big house" oppressive so they turned it over to Leary.

They operated it through the Castalia Foundation, named after the Castalian Brotherhood in Herman Hesse's Magister Ludi (The Glass Bead Game) which was required reading that summer. One of the hundreds of visitors to Millbrook was the model Nena von Schlegrugge, who swept Leary off his feet. They married on December 12, 1964 and in January flew to India on a combination honeymoon and religious pilgrimage. Nena was bored and by the time they returned in May the marriage was over. Everything had changed while Leary was gone. By the spring of 1965 there were already an estimated four million acid users and, to the press and the authorities, it was all Timothy Leary's fault. He played to this by going on lecture tours and generally presenting himself as the leader of the psychedelic movement.

TIMOTHY LEARY
THE POLITICS OF ECSTASY

"I could look back and see my body on the bed. I relived my life, and re-experienced many events I had forgotten. More than that, I went back in time in an evolutionary sense to where I was aware of being a one-celled organism. All of these things were way beyond my mind ... The discovery that the human brain possesses an infinity of potentialities and can operate at unexpected space-time dimensions left me feeling exhilarated, awed, and quite convinced that I had awakened from a long ontological sleep. A profound transcendent experience should leave in its wake a changed man and a changed life."

Timothy Leary on his first Trip

PALADIN

Like A Rolling Stone/Tombstone Blues/It Takes A Lot To Laugh, It Takes A Train To Cry/From A Buick 6/Ballad of A Thin Man/Queen Jane Approximately/Highway 61 Revisited/Just Like Tom Thumb's Blues/Desolation Row

Track listing for Bob Dylan's Highway 61 Revisited, 1965

It was therefore very foolish and arrogant for Leary to drive across the border at Laredo to Mexico on December 23, 1965 in a car filled with marijuana. It was a joke that they were smuggling pot into Mexico, and the stuff was not even well hidden. They drove across the International Bridge, expecting to get tourist cards at the other end and go straight on, but there waiting for them was Jorge Garcia, a secret policeman, and one of the people who deported Leary from Mexico the last time. "Sorry Timoteo," he said, "but you are persona non grata in Mexico." They had to go back. Tim asked his son, Jackie, to flush all the pot down a nearby public toilet, but he did not do a very good job. There was grass all over the floor of the car and when Tim's daughter Susan saw a silver snuff box filled with pot, she hid it in her panties. At United States Immigration they were very thoroughly searched and all the pot was found. They were charged with importing marijuana from Mexico, even though they had never reached it.

Despite Leary's novel defense—he claimed that as a practicing Hindu he had the constitutional right to smoke his "sacrament" under the First Amendment—the Laredo jury didn't buy it. He was given the staggering sentence of 30 years in jail and a $36,000 fine, the maximum under federal law. He was free on bail, pending an appeal, but now the authorities had him where they wanted him. He would have to devote years of his life to fighting the charge in order to stay out of jail.

PROTEST

As the American involvement in Vietnam escalated, students across the country reacted with demonstrations, marches and teach-ins. In February President Lyndon B. Johnson authorized Operation "Rolling Thunder," a program of sustained bombing raids in which over 100 American fighter-bombers attacked targets in North Vietnam. Scheduled to last eight weeks, Rolling Thunder lasted for three years.

On March 8, 1965 the first US combat troops arrived in Vietnam when 3,500 Marines landed at China Beach to defend the American air base at Da Nang. They joined 23,000 American military "advisors" already in Vietnam. By December 1965 nearly 200,000 American troops were stationed there.

On March 9, 1965 President Johnson authorized the use of napalm made by Dow Chemicals, a petroleum-based anti-personnel bomb that showered hundreds of explosive pellets upon impact, burning any unfortunate person in its path to death.

That March, the New York University Committee to End the War in Vietnam (CEWV) organized one of the earliest American anti-war teach-ins on the NYU campus. This was followed on April 17 by a demonstration in Washington by 15,000 students opposed to the war.

Student demonstrations continued in various forms all through the year. One of the biggest demonstrations in New York City was to be on the NYU campus on October 14, but the protest was pushed off campus by the administration so as not to disturb classes. Students and teachers, led by the War Resistor's League and the Committee to End the War in Vietnam, marched along West 3rd Street and West Broadway. This was followed two weeks later by a civil rights teach-in covering the Vietnam War and the Watts riots.

BOB DYLAN HIGHWAY 61 REVISITED

The "I Feel Like I'm Fixin' To Die Rag" by Country Joe became the song to sing as you landed in 'Nam.

RIGHT: Soldiers land in Vietnam in 1965 expecting a quick tour. They died while Americans protested their presence in Vietnam. By the end of the 60s many soldiers took to protesting their presence there, too.

POETRY

"The Beatles thing had just gone beyond comprehension. We were smoking marijuana for breakfast. We were well into marijuana and nobody could communicate with us, because we were just all glazed eyes, giggling all the time. In our own world."

John Lennon

EUROPE

The beginning of the hippie scene in Britain was quite different from that in the US. Whereas the Americans were having a reaction to one of the richest consumer societies on earth, in Britain, the 60s were the first time that young people had any money in their pocket. The underground scene came from the meeting of a number of different strands in youth culture: the mods, the rockers, the dollybirds of Swinging London, the Campaign for Nuclear Disarmament activists, the radical left students and the latest generation of art school graduates, most of whom were rock musicians. At that time, all this activity was largely unknown to the general population because the media had little interest in it. Unlike the USA, there was very little rock music on either radio or television.

Then came the Beatles, followed rapidly by the Stones and the whole explosion of beat groups that transformed rock 'n' roll, if not overnight, then in a year or so. Between the rock groups, Biba's clothes shop, Mary Quant, the widespread introduction of the pill, full employment, pop art, satirical TV shows such as That Was The Week That Was, the growing availability of marijuana, LSD, books by the Beat Generation, American be-bop, Surrealism, French New Wave

films, association with the West Indian community of West London and myriad other factors, an underground culture emerged. This consisted mostly of young people who had a radically new set of values, hopes and ambitions than society had intended them to have. CND, though more of a moral stance than a political position, pitted its members against the establishment by definition, and illegal drugs set their users apart for fear of arrest.

Drugs first became available to this group of people at Oxford in 1963, when an undergraduate who had gone to Morocco for the summer brought back 40 kilos of hash in shopping bags. He sold it for £4 an ounce, or ten shillings for what was known as a matchbox deal. This scenario seems to have been repeated at Cambridge, London and other universities.

THE START

It is generally agreed that in Britain the underground scene began in the summer of 1965, when 7,000 people attended a poetry reading at the Royal Albert Hall given by American Beat poets Lawrence Ferlinghetti, Gregory Corso and Allen Ginsberg. As the audience arrived, they were handed flowers by girls wearing long granny dresses with faces painted in psychedelic patterns. The huge circular Victorian building had tiers of boxes arrayed around the central oval space where the boxing ring was sometimes set up and where the poets were to read. There seemed to be a party going on in each of the boxes: people had brought wine and pot and were sociably visiting each other, sharing what they had.

In the central oval there were tables with wine and fruit and incense wafted about in great clouds. "Anti-psychiatrist" R. D. Laing brought along some of his patients, who danced and blew bubbles to music heard only in their heads. "Professor" Bruce Lacy, star of the Beatles' Hard Day's Night movie, brought several of his raggedy robots, but they didn't make it up the ramp from the green room. A happening by Jeff Nuttall and John Latham went badly wrong when Latham painted himself in green paint and passed out because his skin couldn't breath. Albert Hall attendants discovered them in Sir John Barbarolli's bath, naked, with Nuttall attempting to scrub the paint off. They naturally thought the worst.

The reading itself was uneven. Instead of reading one of his crowd pleasers like "Bomb," "Marriage" or "Hair," which would have suited such a large audience, Gregory Corso chose an

unknown new poem that he read sitting down. Lawrence Ferlinghetti, a master of public performance, got the audience going with "To Fuck is To Love Again," causing one of the attendants to complain to a reporter, "He's just yelling swear words and they love it." Allen Ginsberg, the star of the show and the one responsible for its genesis, was drunk and irritable and read poorly. But it didn't matter because the audience was the most important thing. For the first time they realized there were lots of other people like themselves, a new constituency of youth, unrecognized, uncatered to. The 60s generation.

During his stay in London Ginsberg acted as a catalyst for underground activity. He named Long Hair magazine and gave it a long section from his Cambodian journals to publish. He travelled to Liverpool and proclaimed, "Liverpool is at the present time the center of the consciousness of the human universe"—a quote which Liverpudlians used for decades afterwards. He gave interviews and poetry readings and introduced poets to publishers and boys to girls. On his second day in London he met all four Beatles in Dylan's suite at the Savoy Hotel. The Beatles had been given a warm reception by Dylan when they stayed in New York, but now that he was on their home territory Dylan was withdrawn, quiet, nervous. The Beatles en masse could be terrifying and Allen was summoned to try and break the ice. He found the four Beatles, complete with their ladies and road managers, sitting in silence. There was nowhere for Allen to sit so he perched on the arm of Dylan's chair. "Why don't you sit a little closer?" mocked Lennon, so Allen tumbled forward into John's lap. Looking up into Lennon's face, Ginsberg asked, "Have you ever read William Blake?"

"Never heard of him," snapped Lennon.

"Oh John, stop lying!" said Cynthia, and everyone laughed. The ice was broken.

Allen was 39 during his summer in London and a party was held for him, to which the Beatles were invited. John and Cynthia and George and Patti arrived late, to find the poet stark naked—except for his underpants, which were on his head—and a "Do Not Disturb" hotel room sign hanging around his cock. They stayed for a drink, but were clearly concerned in case someone photographed them with him. As they turned to go, Lennon was asked why they were leaving so soon.

PREVIOUS PAGE: Preparations for a party in London, 1965.
FAR LEFT (TOP): A ticket to the first hippie happening in London in 1965—Poets of The World, Poets of Our Time.
FAR LEFT (BOTTOM): Alan Price, Bob Dylan and Bobby Neuwirth tune in backstage during Dylan's Don't Look Back Tour.
LEFT: Poet Michael Horovitz points to the stars and tells his tale.

"There are ways of getting high without drugs— with yoga, meditation and all those things."

"You don't do that in front of the birds," Lennon hissed. It was to be several years before he, along with Yoko Ono, presented themselves naked on an album sleeve. Lennon always denied that Ginsberg had initially inspired him to do it.

The Albert Hall reading had come about after a meeting at the Better Books bookshop on Charing Cross Road. Ginsberg had recently arrived in London from Czechoslovakia, Poland and Moscow and was using it as his headquarters while staying with Barry Miles, the shop's manager (generally known as "Miles"). Better Books regularly held poetry readings and a standing room only, unadvertised reading by Allen Ginsberg led to the idea for a Beat poetry reading in a large venue.

When Better Books was sold and its experimental extracurricular activities were threatened, Miles got together with art critic John Dunbar to plan a new bookshop/art gallery. Dunbar was married to Marianne Faithfull, and his best friend was Peter Asher of the pop duo Peter and Gordon. Together Miles, Asher and Dunbar formed a company called MAD Ltd, to start an experimental art gallery and bookshop that would continue the work of Better Books and show avant-garde art. It was to be called Indica. Both Peter and his sister, the actress Jane Asher, still lived at home in a large house on Wimpole Street. Jane's boyfriend, Beatle Paul McCartney, also lived there in a small maid's room in the attic.

ICA BULLETIN

No 150   August September 1965   One Shilling

Through Peter, Paul soon became involved in planning the new Indica bookshop and gallery.

THE BEATLES ON POT

The Beatles at that time were avid pot smokers, having been turned on by Bob Dylan in New York the year before. These were the years of their greatest fame and they were already almost legendary figures, but they were rarely seen in person. However, one or more of them did attend underground events. George and John went to Allen Ginsberg's 39th birthday party, while Paul McCartney could often be found at John Dunbar or Miles' flats, hanging out. And of course there were the so-called in-clubs, where the rich and famous could congregate without fear of harassment: Dolly's on Jermyn Street, Chi-Chi's under the Economist Building, the Ad Lib just off

LEFT: The ICA Bulletin reporting on the Albert Hall reading.
RIGHT: Left to right, Barry Miles, Allen Ginsberg, Ian Sommerville at Ginsberg's 39th birthday party.

Leicester Square and the Scotch of Saint James. But up until 1965 there was no public use of drugs, even in the in-clubs. John Dunbar remembers going to the Ad Lib one night with Paul McCartney and meeting up with John Lennon: "I remember John being very shocked when I lit some hash in a little hash pipe I had—'What are you doing man?' He was very paranoid." In fact they were perfectly safe in these exclusive environs, and by the end of the year the distinctive smell of pot could sometimes be detected at the Scotch, which catered almost entirely to the music business. The club managers didn't like it, since it discouraged the punters from drinking overpriced Scotch and cokes.

Early in the year the Beatles made their second film, Help. Paul McCartney said, "By this time we were beginning to smoke a bit of pot and we were getting a little bit more laissez faire about the whole thing. We would occasionally get stoned on the way to the film set, which was pretty fatal. My main memory is of being in hysterics, because for all of us, one of the great things about early pot was the sheer hysteria, the laughs. Things could appear very, very funny, hilariously so. And nobody quite knew why we were laughing, and of course this made it even funnier. It was like kids giggling at the dinner table, it really was."

As 1965 progressed, George began taking sitar lessons—something which influenced the "psychedelic" sound of many UK and US groups,

"A hippie is supposed to be someone who becomes aware—you're hip if you know what's going on. But if you're really hip, you don't get involved with LSD and things like that. You see the potential that it has and the good that can come from it, but you also see that you don't really need it."

George Harrison

including the Stones. Paul began a series of experiments with loop tapes, culminating in the extraordinary solo on "Tomorrow Never Knows," where the backwards high speed guitar loops around like a flock of seagulls.

By this year the Rolling Stones were moving in the same direction. That summer they released an album called Out Of Our Heads and Brian made his first trip to Tangier. Other groups were also switching from booze to pot—or using both—such as members of the Moody Blues, the Animals and the Hollies. Donovan released his Fairy Tale album with the track "Sunny Goodge Street," which describes the "violent hash smoker." Donovan was familiar with Finch's The One Tun pub on Goodge Street, which had been a hang-out first for the beatniks and was now for proto-Hippies and was one of the few places in London you could go to and score pot or hash. The other was a few doors away, the Duke of York on Cleveland Place, directly across from Finch's. In 1965 it was unusual to see young men with long hair, but outside both these pubs, groups of them gathered wearing thick great-coats, long hair and beards and very often a white scarf. Many of them slept in the caves at Hastings during the winter months and only came to London when it was warm enough to sleep in the rough.

RIGHT: The Beatles try on a marching band outfit in Help!

"LSD isn't a real answer. It doesn't give you anything. It enables you to see a lot of possibilities that you may never have noticed before, but it isn't the answer. You don't just take LSD and that's it forever, you're OK."

George Harrison

THE BEATLES ON LSD

A limited amount of LSD had been available in London through certain sources for years. John Lennon and George Harrison first experienced it courtesy of a cosmetic dentist, whose girlfriend was the supervisor of bunnies at the Playboy Club. She received it from the Playboy Club manager, Victor Lownes, who was glad to turn on the Beatles. The two Beatles, Cynthia Lennon and Patti Boyd had dinner at the dentist's flat and only afterwards did he reveal that he had spiked the coffee. He warned them that it was too dangerous for them to leave the flat and drive around London on a trip. Lennon, paranoid as ever, immediately interpreted this to mean that the dentist was expecting to have a sex orgy with them all and insisted on leaving at once. As they pulled away in George's Aston Martin DB6, the dentist gave chase. Even then George was a fan of formula one racing and soon outpaced the dentist by driving down alleys and one-way streets, but he eventually caught up with them at the Pickwick Club. Here the hallucinations kicked in and they left once more, heading for the familiar Ad Lib Club, the dentist still in hot pursuit. To John the red bulb on the ceiling of the elevator appeared to burst into flames and the dentist turned into a pig. After what seemed an eternity the four of them drove home to George's house in Esher, with George maintaining a steady ten miles an hour while Patti kept wanting to smash shop windows. Long after the others had fallen asleep, John sat at the controls of the submarine that George's bungalow had somehow turned into and floated effortlessly over the eighteen-foot wall at the end of the garden.

John and George took acid again in Los Angeles when the Beatles spent five days there in August. While they were tripping, Peter Fonda told Lennon that he knew what it was like to be dead. Lennon did not like being brought down like this and had him removed, but he used Fonda's line later in "She Said."

LEFT: The International Times launched in October 1966.
RIGHT: The Beatles get spaced out on the ski slope in Help!
OVER: A home visit from Dr. Steve Abrams.

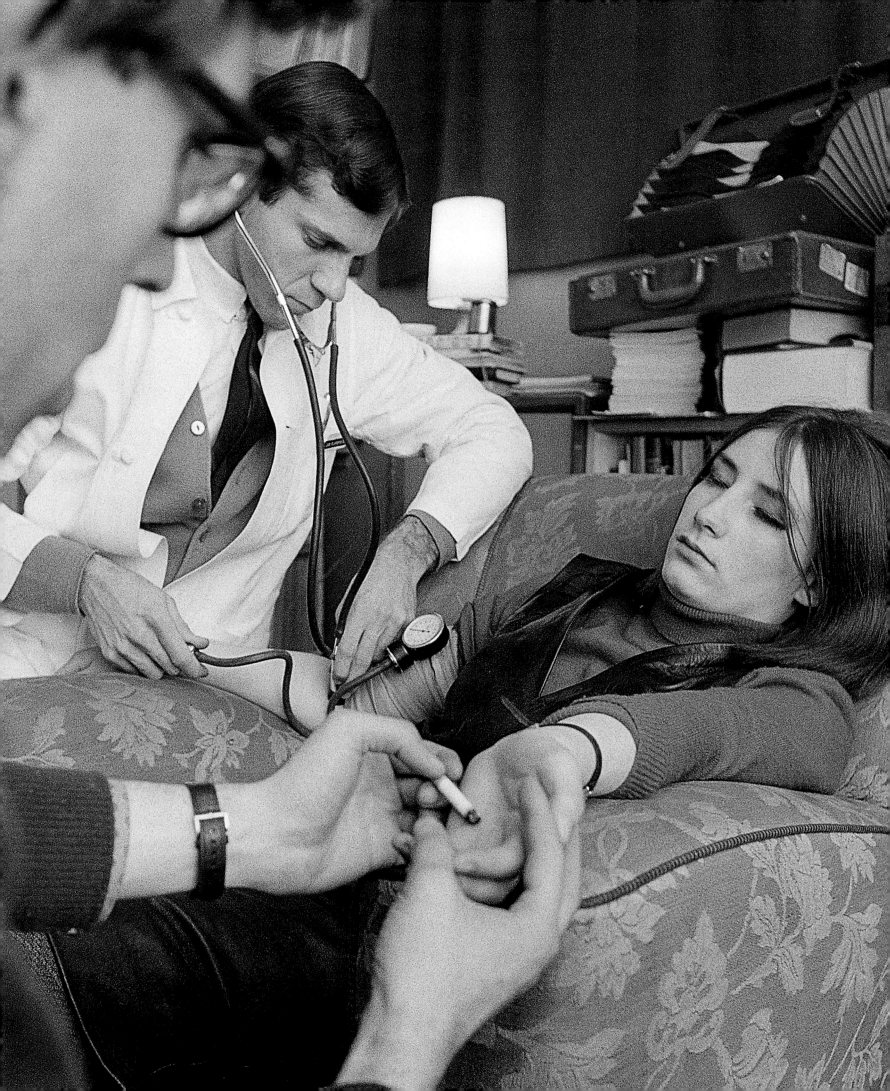

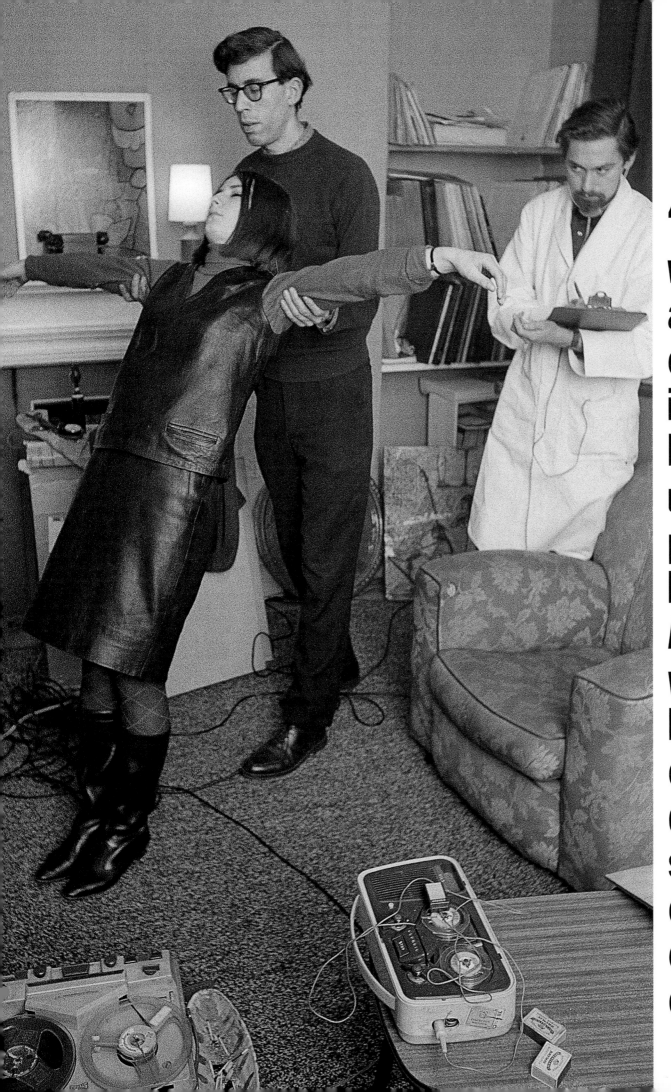

"We don't want to tell anyone else to have it (LSD) because it's up to the person himself. Although it was like a key that opened the door and showed a lot of things on the other side."

George Harrison

LEFT: The poets line up before the event. Left to right, Barbara Rubin (with camera), Harry Fainlight, Adrian Mitchell. Alexander Trocchi, Anselm Hollo, Marcus Field, Michael Horovitz, John Esam, Ernst Jandl, Dan Richter.

HAPPENING
AT SAN REMO

A daring novel of today's Young
Underground—its sexual and mental
excesses—its search for sensation
and conflict ■ BRUCE CASSIDAY

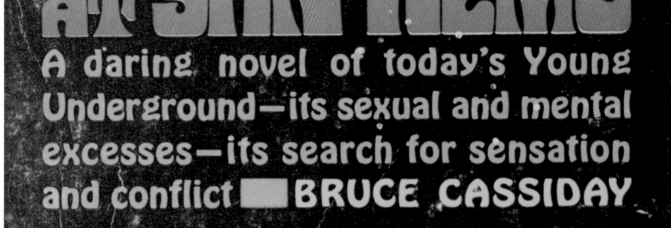

Fashion began to copy the patterns of psychedelic light shows, incorporating flowers and bright colors into fabrics. The mini-dress had appeared in London in 1964 in monochrome. Now mini-dresses came in rainbows and were sold everywhere.

LEFT: An early American exploitation pulp novel cashing in on the burgeoning hippie scene.

OVER: The front window of London's premier hippie clothes store, Granny Takes A Trip, changed constantly. This picture shows a US car, painted bright yellow, emerging from the window.

FASHION

One of the first things that new arrivals in London would do was to exchange boring American jeans and sweaters for some silk and satin from the new hippie shops on the Kings Road. At the far end from Sloane Square were Hung On You, owned by Michael Rainey, and Granny Takes A Trip, owned by John Pearce and Nigel Weymouth. Michael English painted the windows for both of them. Hung On You's window was completely covered by its name in stylized lettering so it was impossible to see in. Initially there was a dollybird theme on the inside wall, but this was replaced by an enormous enlargement of a photograph of Chairman Mao swimming the Yangtse. This was because Michael was convinced that Chinese fashions were going to catch on and that drab, olive Mao jackets would soon be all the rage. At this level there were no clothes to be seen. You had to climb down a precarious stairway through a hole in the floor to the basement, where a few choice items hung on rails and a pile of frilly shirts were available.

At Granny Takes A Trip, the fashion windows were even more extreme and were changed regularly. One time a large American Indian stared out stoically at the World's End Pub over the road; another time it was a stylized dollybird looking rather like Twiggy. The most spectacular was the front half of an American car protruding from the window as if the back half was still embedded inside. Granny's was the place for really frilly shirts—you could buy them with frills that buttoned on over the regular shirt buttons. Both stores sold crushed velvet pants, long lapel satin and silk shirts and soft chiffon and silk scarves.

A glance at album sleeves from the period shows that most of the groups, from the Beatles and Stones on down, patronized both stores. There were others too: Dandy Fashions, which was located across the street from Hung On You and part-owned by Tara Browne, "the man who blew his mind out in a car," as well as a number of boutiques for women—Quorum, Biba, Mary Quant, Foale and Tuffin. But none of these were aimed quite so much at the underground rock 'n' roll market.

The summer of 1966 was the real "Summer of Love"—a phrase now copyrighted by Bill Graham Enterprises. When the year opened there were just a handful of underground papers: the New York East Village Other had just started, the LA Free Press was eighteen months old, the Berkeley Barb less than half a

65 66 66 67 68 69 70 71

year old. By the end of the year there were more than a dozen papers published in cities all across the country—there was even one in London. These included the San Francisco Oracle, with its ground-breaking psychedelic graphics and rainbow printed pages. In New York, 1966 saw the rise of the Fugs, Andy Warhol's Exploding Plastic Inevitable with the Velvet Underground, and Bob Dylan retiring from public view after a motorcycle accident. It also saw the beginning of the Hare Krishna movement and the beginning of St. Mark's Place as the underground high street. In San Francisco the opening of the Psychedelic Shop at Haight and Ashbury gave birth to an era. This was the year the Merry Pranksters, Wavy Gravy and Neal Cassady held more Acid Tests, the year that saw the first Chet Helms Family Dog dances at the Avalon Ballroom and the development of Bill Graham's Fillmore Auditorium. Both dance halls used a new way of advertising, with psychedelic posters so bizarre that only a stoned person could decipher the squiggly, blobby lettering and the insider drug references. It was the year that the notorious underground chemist, Owsley Stanley III, became a millionaire and his main product, LSD, became illegal.

LOVE & HAIGHT

THE SCENE

1966 opened with a portent of things to come when, on January 3, a small store at Haight and Ashbury opened its doors as the Psychedelic Shop and immediately became the place to hang out. Prior to that there had only been the laundromat. It was opened by two brothers, Ron and Jay Thelin, who had grown up in the neighborhood; their father managed the Woolworths across the street. It was a full-service store: they stocked books on drugs and oriental philosophy, rolling papers, roach clips, bells and beads, flutes, posters and a full range of hippie paraphernalia. It was also a major ticket outlet for the dances at the Fillmore and Avalon, and opened just in time to sell tickets to an Acid Test held at the Fillmore Auditorium on January 8.

Two days before the event, one of the Pranksters approached Charles Sullivan, the owner of the Fillmore, asking to rent the hall that Saturday. "You'll never be able to advertise enough to fill it," he told them, but they insisted and he took their $65 booking fee. 2,400 people showed up. As usual Kesey and the Pranksters were established at one end of the space, with their instruments and microphones, light show and gadgets, while the Grateful Dead were set up at the other. In the middle was a baby's bath full of LSD-spiked punch. It was almost the usual Test scene. The big difference was that it had to end at 2am. When the police tried to unplug lights or mikes, the audience applauded; when Mountain Girl followed in their footsteps and plugged them back in again, the audience applauded. When the police picked up a microphone to make an announcement, their words disappeared into a swirl of feedback and echo. Kesey's lawyers eventually calmed the irate police, and the audience dispersed peacefully.

The Trips Festival was organized by Stewart Brand, one of the organizers of the Acid Tests, a biologist who had studied peyote Indian cults and who later was to publish the Whole Earth Catalog. He intended it to be a three-night affair and invited Kesey and the Pranksters to do something on the second night. At 2am, on the night of January 19, two nights before the event, Kesey and Mountain Girl were caught red-handed with a bag of pot on a roof in North Beach. He struggled with the police and threw it over the edge, but they found it on the ground below. His second conviction, it carried a mandatory three-year sentence in the San Mateo County Jail.

Many of his friends thought that he was trying to get busted, that he wanted to become a fugitive for the adventure. Certainly there was a lot of machismo and bravado in his attitude toward it.

The Trips Festival was held at the Longshoremen's Hall on the San Francisco waterfront and Kesey's arrest certainly helped publicize the event. When the hall closed at 2am, there was still a line of people outside waiting to get in. The event grossed $12,500 in three days. Bill Graham, who had been impressed at the financial success of the Mime Troupe benefits he had organized, now moved into promotion full time; the Fillmore Auditorium opened under his name within two weeks. Kesey showed up at the Trips Festival wearing a silver mylar space suit with a helmet. In among all the strange costumes he was not easily recognizable, even though he had a live microphone. He sat hidden on a balcony with Mountain Girl and a few friends and made his presence known with random comments and interjections over the PA system. He met with reporters afterwards and announced that he was running for Governor of California.

After the Trips Festival a warrant was issued and, hoping to get it withdrawn, Kesey staged an elaborate scenario to suggest that he had killed himself. He wrote a suicide note and got his cousin Dale, who looked a lot like him, to drive his old panel truck up the coast to Mendicino and to park it at the edge of some cliffs with the note left on the dashboard: "So I Ken Kesey, being of (ahem) sound mind and body, do hereby leave the whole scene to Faye, corporation, cash, the works. And Babbs to run it." Ron Bevirt rented a red Mustang and drove Kesey to Los Angeles, where he and Ron Boise continued to Mexico in a truck. Kesey was either being theatrical or extremely naive, because anyone, police included, could enquire as to his whereabouts on Haight Street and be told that he was living in Mexico.

With the original partners in Mexico, the Family Dog was now in the hands of Chet Helms, who was also managing Big Brother and the

LEFT: Chet Helms, top dog at the Family Dog.
ABOVE: Bill Graham found his true vocation as a rock promoter running the Fillmore East and The Fillmore West.

Holding Company. A Texan civil rights activist, Helms had arrived in San Francisco in 1962 hoping to make a living as a poet. Soon he was more involved with music than poetry, promoting gigs at a coffee house off Haight. In 1963, on a visit home, Chet Helms met Janis Joplin in Austin and was so impressed by her singing that he convinced her to hitch-hike with him to San Francisco where he was sure she would make it as a singer. All through 1963 and 1964 she ran with the rock and folk music crowd that gathered at, or lived in, 1090 Page.

At the Family Dog Helms brought in two new partners, Rock Scully and Danny Rifkin, who were also attempting to manage the Grateful Dead. However, the Family Dog survived. Chet's first dance was called "Tribal Stomp"; it was held at the Fillmore Auditorium on February 19 and featured a new Family Dog logo—the face of a wizened old American Indian.

There was money in rock dances and many other promoters moved in to hold their own. Competition was fierce, but it really came down to Bill Graham and Chet Helms. Helms had the street credibility, he ran the Family Dog like a

commune, he let hundreds of people in free, he took drugs and was an integral part of the street community, but sometimes the bands didn't get paid or the money wasn't all there or it was late. Graham did not turn on, he had no interest in drugs or their effects. His interest was in making money and putting on a good show. He was a hard-nosed businessman, he was honest and he always paid his bands, but his manner was rude and abrupt and he screamed and swore at his staff and the acts. A lot of people didn't like him, but he delivered the goods.

Graham established a good relationship with the man who owned the Fillmore and was even able to use his dance license until the police began to put pressure on him. It took a lot of good politicking to get a license, but Graham finally achieved it in June by agreeing to not hold dances on religious holidays celebrated at the synagogue next door. At first he allowed the Family Dog to play alternate weekends, and they had what Helms thought was a partnership. But then they had the inevitable falling out over money. Chet had booked the Butterfield Blues Band from Chicago and was putting them up on

"As he walked around in his ethereal manner savoring the tone of his dances, he would sometimes greet newcomers by saying, 'Welcome to our church'."

Charles Perry on Chet Helms

his floor. Their manager, Albert Grossman, was demanding a stiff $2,500 fee, but Chet just knew they'd make it back and more. The concert was a great success, artistically and financially, and as Chet and Graham discussed the band afterwards they agreed that they should get them back again soon. Graham got up very early the next morning and phoned Albert Grossman at 6am to book the group for a weekend three weeks away—one of his own weekends.

With nowhere to hold dances, Chet scoured San Francisco for a new venue and found it eight blocks away: the Avalon Ballroom. Like the Fillmore it was a walk-up with an L-shaped balcony. It had gilded columns, mirrors and red flock wallpaper, and it held about 2,000 people—the same number as the Fillmore.

In return, Graham applied the usual music business pressure on the groups he hired, trying to insert clauses forbidding them from playing at the Avalon within a certain period of time. Jefferson Airplane, who had become more or less the house band at the Fillmore, had to agree never to play the Avalon again. On the other hand, Helms encouraged the bands to jam and to hang out where they liked. But the managers preferred dealing with Graham. They could understand where he was coming from, whereas with Helms they had to sit on a cushion on the floor— there were no desks or chairs—and Helms' fair wispy hair and beard almost reached his waist. Between the two of them though—and the

Matrix—San Franciscans had a choice of wonderful music on most weekends.

THE ART

1966 was the year that psychedelic posters really took off. The poster artists worked for both Bill Graham and Chet Helms. Helms gave them more suggestions and encouraged experimentation, whereas Graham just wanted the information, with maybe the name of a recent hit record, on the poster. Otherwise he pretty much left them alone, though he did sometimes complain if he couldn't read it easily. Wes Wilson, who did the first Family Dog posters, was employed largely because he had his own printing press. Helms provided most of the artwork and images—the Plains Indian and the Indian with the stovepipe hat—as well as the text. When Graham started doing posters for his dances he also used Wilson, though the posters done for each were so different that they could have been done by different artists. By May 1966 Bill Graham was realizing that, as fast as he could put up his posters, people would tear them down to take home for their walls. He began to offer free posters to those buying advance tickets, but that didn't work. He gave away free posters at the concerts. In August, Wilson stopped doing Family Dog posters because Graham gave him artistic freedom. Wilson's early posters were characterized by the blobby lettering, inspired by the sleeve lettering on the Beatles' Rubber Soul

and by Viennese *fin-de-siècle* expressionist Alfred Roller. The letters were often so distorted that they were very difficult to decipher—unless you were stoned. This made the posters and the events they were advertising even more appealing. When Wilson and Graham had a disagreement over royalties early in 1967, Graham's wife Bonnie MacLean took over until Mouse joined the team that December.

Stanley Miller, known as Mouse, had been on the scene for a while, making a living by painting strange monster dragsters on t-shirts at car shows. On June 17 Chet Helms hired him to do a poster for a dance featuring Captain Beefheart and His Magic Band; Mouse drew a bull's head. Mouse teamed up with Family Dog member Alton Kelly who had been at the Red Dog Saloon and for a while the two of them operated as Mouse Studios. Their first image was the famous Zig-Zag man, copied from the cigarette rolling papers that everyone used to roll joints and instantly recognizable to everyone on the Haight.

RIGHT: The Grateful Dead on the back stoop of the Dead House, 710 Ashbury. Clockwise from left, Phil Lesh, Bill Kreutzmann, Pigpen, Bob Weir, Jerry Garcia in the eye-catching sweater.

"Further is like the good ship Enterprise. Further will never die."

Ken Kesey

DOPE

A large number of hippies sold pot; usually just enough to make their own smoke free. The prices in 1966 were $8 to $10 for an ounce or "lid," though it usually weighed less. A key or kilogram went from $50 to $75 depending on how good it was, and how much was around on the street at that time. Most people rarely paid more than $65. There was a considerable saving in buying by the key as you could get at least 35 lids from that amount, giving a profit of $200 to $300 if you sold them all separately. Most dealers bought just enough to enable them to pay the rent, smoke themselves and cover day-to-day expenses. They were expected to allow people to try out the goods and much of their time was spent smoking with their clients. Many of their customers were students from State who were not prepared to take the risk of heavy dealing. A number of professional dealers quickly appeared. A kilo cost about $15 in Mexico, but it was only worth the expense of travel and accommodation, as well as the risk at the border, if you brought in a large quantity. The people who sold wholesale usually bought their supplies in Los Angeles, where a kilo cost about $35 or $40, but you had to buy a large quantity to get that price. Even so, in the mid-60s it was still a largely amateurish business, conducted by the same people who used the stuff. As Charles Perry pointed out, this was exemplified by the diminutive terms used: a nickel bag was $5, a lid was a dime or $10.

In the spring of 1966 Owsley moved his lab back to the Bay Area, to a secret location in the

woods. It was fully equipped with a pharmaceutical pill press complete with an indentation down the middle so that each pill, which contained 250 micrograms, could be split in half. He gave each new batch a different colour so that his competition couldn't flood the market with counterfeits; each new batch was announced by his agents walking down Haight Street or University in Berkeley, handing out free samples. That way, within hours, the new colour was established. He used his powerful position to establish the market price: $2 a tab. LSD was still legal and he was making an enormous amount of money.

TOP: Ken Kesey and Mountain Girl.
ABOVE: Psychedelic finery.
RIGHT: Ken Babbs and Ken Kesey decide to turn on the world.

MEDIA

THE SCENE

Though the local underground newspaper, the Berkeley Barb, listed events in the Haight and generally covered underground news from across the Bay, some people felt that the Haight-Ashbury scene was enough of a community to have a newspaper of its own. Ron Thelin from the Psychedelic Shop put up most of the money and after a series of increasingly divisive meetings, he insisted that they put something out and discuss it later. The first issue came out as the P.O. Frisco on September 2, 1966, standing for Psychedelic Oracle. It was a very amateurish affair, giving no indication of who had edited it or how to contact the paper to advertise, write for it or help in any way. It clearly used the Barb as a model with front page stories headed: "Viet GI Speaks Out" and "Concentration Camps Ready For 'Subversives'," stories more suited to the more politically aware students on Telegraph Avenue. There was a recipe for hash cookies and an obituary of Ron Boise, the sculptor, whose metal torsos had filled the woods at Kesey's La Honda retreat. Richard Alpert wrote on LSD and there was a report on Lenny Bruce, but apart from the listings the issue could have been produced anywhere in the US.

The next issue, the first published as The San Francisco Oracle, came out on September 20. The second was directed even more at the psychedelic community. It reprinted puzzles from a pre-war children's book in which figures were hidden in the drawings—ideal for stoned hippies.

RIGHT: Members of the Oracle Cooperative working on an issue of The San Francisco Oracle at their offices at 1542 Haight Street.

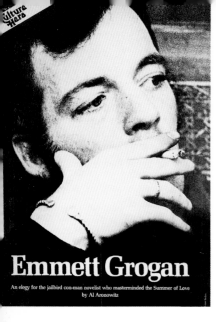

Emmett Grogan

An elegy for the jailbird con-man novelist who masterminded the Summer of Love
by Al Aronowitz

"Essentially, however, the Papers were an attempt to antagonize the street people into an awareness of the absolute bullshit implicit in the psychedelic transcendentalism promoted by the self-proclaimed, media-fabricated shamans who espoused the tune-in, turn-on, drop-out, jerk-off ideology of Leary and Alpert."

Emmett Grogan

THE DIGGERS

As the scene grew, many of the organizations underwent a split. A faction of the Mime Troupe felt more allied to the Haight-Ashbury community than they did to the Berkeley radicals and eventually broke away to form the Diggers. They were named after Gerard Winstanley, William Everard and about 100 of their supporters who, in 1649, took over the common land at Saint George's Hill, Surrey, as a protest against the high price of food in England, calling themselves the Diggers. The main agitator for this new direction was a recent recruit, a Brooklyn-Irish, ex-junkie called Emmett Grogan. It was not his real name; he changed it when he was dropped from the army after a self-induced psychotic attack. The Diggers liked what was going down on the Haight—not the psychedelic thing, but the fact that the members of the Haight community seemed to be trying to assert their individual freedom and do their own thing. The Diggers thought they could only be free by drawing the line and living outside the nexus of profit, private property and power that was the premise of Western culture. They did not believe you could change anything from within.

Meanwhile, the boutique and shop owners of Haight Street were doing very well and did not want to rock the boat. The police were cracking down heavily on the area and, rather than exacerbate conflict between the street people and the authorities, they wanted to calm everyone down. Ron Thelin and several other merchants (as the Haight Independent Proprietor, or HIP) put posters in their windows asking everyone to invite a policeman to share a meal with them; they wanted to show the police that hippies were good, quiet, rather religious, citizens. Comparing this to racketeers taking cops to dinner with pay-offs, the Diggers circulated a leaflet ending with the line: "And so, if you own anything or you

don't, take a cop to dinner this week and feed his power to judge, prosecute and brutalize the streets of your city." The two positions could not have been clearer.

Despite the conflict in attitude, beginning in their second issue the Oracle ran a notice which read: "Free Food: At Oak-Ashbury Panhandle. 4pm everyday. Bring a bowl and spoon. It's free because it's yours. The Diggers."

Billy and Emmett drove to the San Francisco Produce Market on the outskirts of town in Billy's '55 pickup. Emmett spoke fluent Italian and, despite his long hair, convinced the stall holders to give them unsold or day-old vegetables. At the only poultry plant in the market they got 50 lbs of chicken and turkey parts. They stole two twenty gallon milk churns from a dairy in the Mission and

by 8am they were making the stock for the stew. The stew was served at 4pm that afternoon. Billy and Emmett did it for about a week before a commune on Clayton Street consisting of six young women, most of them dropouts from Antioch College, took over the cooking indefinitely. Butcher Brooks and Slim Minnaux from the Mime Troupe took over the 4pm delivery and food serving, and each morning Emmett went to the Produce Market, the Farmers Market and the Ukranian Bakery.

On December 16 the Mime Troupe organized a street event to "celebrate the death and rebirth

ABOVE: Diggers distribute free food at Golden Gate Park.
RIGHT: Sculptor Le Mortadella, Emmett Grogan, Slim Minnaux, Peter Berg and Butcher Brooks at City Hall after charges of creating a public nuisance were dropped in court.

of the Haight-Ashbury and the death of money." They gathered 200 car mirrors from used car lots, bought or acquired 1,000 pennywhistles, incense, candles and several hundred lilies and printed up hundreds of posters with the word "NOW." The Mime Troupe split into two groups that walked up and down Haight on either side of Haight Street, chanting and handing out the posters and the pennywhistles to the crowd. Girls dressed in white sheets like togas gave out flowers and the car mirrors were used to reflect the sun from the sunny side of the street to the shaded side. People quickly moved out into the street, blocking the traffic. A bus driver stopped his bus and got out and danced while, to the sudden anxiety of the crowd, the San Francisco Hell's Angels drove down the central white line of the street, flying "NOW" flags from their sissy bars. Between 3,000 and 4,000 people eventually

took up the chant: "The streets belong to the people. The streets belong to the people."

The police gathered, but didn't know what to do. So they did what they always did and arrested the Hell's Angels, Chocolate George and Hairy Pete. All 4,000 people then marched to the police station demanding their release.

That same evening, Emmett Grogan was caught stealing meat from the Armour meat company, but when he came to trial the judge accepted the modern-day Robin Hood defense and only gave him a six-month suspended jail sentence, provided he paid for the 100 lbs of steak he'd stolen. As the Diggers came to represent the psychedelic-radical face of what was happening on the Haight, so Kesey and the Pranksters began to fade out.

On September 27 a white policeman shot a black youth in the Hunter's Point ghetto, precipi-

ABOVE: Graduation Day at the Pranksters Hippie High School, San Francisco.
RIGHT: Modern-day Robin Hoods: the Diggers feed the people at the Panhandle, Golden Gate Park.

tating six days of riots. Though San Francisco has relatively cold summers, the Indian summer that year was particularly hot. The rioting quickly spread to the Fillmore district, right next to the Haight, and a curfew was extended over the entire area. Police arrested 124 people on Haight. Kesey returned from Mexico and showed up at an event at State College, surrounded by Hell's Angels as guards, but the police were far too busy with the riot to bother about a fugitive from a pot bust.

LEFT: The San Francisco Mime Troupe.
BELOW: Hairy Henry just prior to his arrest.

"We want Chocolate George! We want Hairy Henry!"

4,000 people chanting outside the San Francisco police station for the release of two Hell's Angels

LEFT: Chocolate George, whose arrest, along with Hairy Henry, provoked 4,000 people to protest outside the station house for their release.
RIGHT: A key of grass, just over two pounds, cost $80 in 1966.
OVER (LEFT): Trips Festival poster.
OVER (RIGHT): The Trips Festival at Longshoremen's Hall.

TRIPS FESTIVAL

1966

LONGSHOREMEN'S HALL
(400 NORTH POINT)
JANUARY 21-22-23
8 TO 12 PM
(SEE OTHER SIDE)

"The Diggers, the Trips and the vibe of Haight-Ashbury was incredibly communal."

Neil Binder, San Francisco hippie

LEFT: Life in a San Francisco hippie commune.
OVER: The Anonymous Artists of America perform at the Acid Test Graduation, The Warehouse, Harriet Street, San Francisco, October 31, 1966.

117

"The bus trip ... communicates something that can't be bottled and sold so people don't think of it as valuable."

Ken Kesey

ACID TESTS

LSD became illegal in California, criminalizing half of the people on the Haight. Ken Kesey's last big public event was scheduled for Halloween. He wanted to hold an LSD Graduation party at Winterland, an old ice rink that held more than 5,000 people, located only two blocks from the Fillmore and asked Bill Graham to produce it for him. When Bill Graham heard that Kesey and

Owsley were planning to spike everything at Winterland, from the water supply to the door knobs and railings, he panicked and even went so far as to telephone Chet Helms to ask for his advice. Though Helms was not a friend of Kesey's, he knew the Prankster's dosemaster, who reported that Kesey intended to dose everybody. It was what the street people called "Acid fascism." When Helms reported this to Graham, Graham said, "Well, that's the end of it."

Graham cancelled the Winterland booking. Kesey had his LSD Graduation in a warehouse on 6th Street, at which various Pranksters received diplomas from Neal Cassady. Ken Babbs said, "It

was time not to do Acid Tests anymore. It was time to move on and do other stuff. So we did. We all moved up to Oregon." They became farmers.

LEFT: Janis Joplin in full flight.
ABOVE: Chet Helms, Gary Goldhill and Ken Kesey backstage.

Grace wanted a tighter, more professional outfit; the Great Society wanted a more spacey, Indian feel. Things came to a head when they were more or less blown off stage by the Blues Project. Jefferson Airplane got their girl.

LEFT: Grace Slick joins the Jefferson Airplane.

A condition of Kesey's parole was that he not associate with Pranksters, yet he was doing so openly. A second conviction carried a mandatory jail sentence.

LEFT: Preparing the bus for Halloween. When Bill Graham learned that Ken Kesey intended to spike everyone with acid he pulled out of the October 31 Acid Test Graduation, forcing them to move to The Warehouse.

Like twentieth-century San Franciscan Robin Hoods, the Diggers had no leader and didn't want one, either. They stole from those who had plenty—mostly shops and suppliers—and gave to those who didn't have any. Which meant the kids drawn to their city by the promise of a new way of thinking and living and being hippies.

They were a theatre group drawn to making grand public statements that usually confused and antagonized the authorities—any kind of authority, including the newly formed association of Haight Independent Proprietors (HIP). From whom they sometimes stole, of course.

HIGH TIMES

As Al Dente, Romney dealt LSD under the business name of Goon King Bros Dimensional Kreemo.

LEFT: Wavy Gravy showing off his button collection.
ABOVE: Lenny Bruce.

WAVY GRAVY

Early in 1966, with Kesey away, Babbs came into his own. The ex-Marine captain teamed up with comedian/ poet Wavy Gravy, loaded up the bus with Pranksters and took off to Los Angeles for a series of Acid Tests. Owsley had set up his lab there and was prepared to pay for accommodation for the Grateful Dead and the Pranksters and provide LSD for the Acid Tests.

The Dead moved into Owsley's house, taking over all the space except the part used as his lab. Owsley was making a huge amount of money dealing in LSD and it was his policy to always provide the bands with free drugs. In the case of the Dead, he also invested heavily in a huge, unwieldy PA for them—a great wall of speakers and amps that soon became their trademark. No other band on earth was so loud.

The first test was held in Northridge, at Paul Sawyer's Unitarian Church. The Pranksters prepared pineapple chili and handed out acid to the audience, a few of the regular churchgoers included. Neal Cassady and Wavy Gravy, each holding a microphone, stood before the congregation and rapped to each other and people later swore that Cassady knew what Wavy Gravy was going to say before he said it.

Wavy Gravy, real name Hugh Romney, studied acting at the Neighborhood Playhouse in New York City, but was first known as a poet; he had a poem in the seminal Beat Generation anthology The Beat Scene, published in 1960. He began to improvise in between poems and one day Lenny Bruce told him, "Skip the poetry." Bruce actually became his manager, booking him as the opener for jazz concerts by Thelonius Monk and John Coltrane. He shared a room over the Gaslight in Greenwich Village with Bob Dylan and became part of the early 60s folk music revival.

His act, meanwhile, became stranger and stranger. He put together a show at the Fat Black Pussycat which must have been extraordinary: the line-up consisted of Romney, Moondog—the blind multiinstrumentalist street musician who made the most of his own instruments and dressed like a Viking in robes and horned helmet—and Tiny Tim, who sang 30s love songs in a high falsetto to the accompaniment of a ukulele.

Around this time Romney took mescaline at Coney Island and bought $50 worth of roller coaster tickets: "I remember it got very scary every time I got off the roller coaster, and I've been fairly strange ever since." He was perfect for the Acid Tests.

The second LA test was held on February 5, at the Youth Opportunities Center on South Alemeda on the outskirts of Watts, which was still a shaky neighborhood after the riots of the previous summer. The Grateful Dead provided the music, slides of flowers were projected over the band and celebrants, acid-spiked Kool-Aid was served and parts of the bus movie screened. It was a nightmare for many people; instead of 80 mikes, the dosemaster got his figures mixed up and gave everyone 800. Los Angeles had not been exposed to the drug culture of San Francisco and many of them had bad trips. The Pranksters made things as edgy as possible by putting a microphone next to one woman who was screaming, "Who cares? Who cares?" at the top of her voice. Seven people were hospitalized and there were terrible transportation problems as people, high on LSD, attempted to drive home. It was a classic example of the carelessness that sometimes ensued as a result of the Pranksters' approach to taking LSD.

There was a third Acid Test held in Hollywood and a fourth in a Hollywood sound studio. As photographer Lawrence Schiller was photographing the Pranksters for Life magazine, Babbs took aside Mountain Girl and a few of the others and took off, leaving Cassady and the rest stranded in LA. "Never trust a Prankster!"

LEFT: Buffalo Springfield. Left to right, Bruce Palmer (bass), Neil Young (guitar, vox), Dewey Martin (drums), Richie Furay (guitar), Stephen Stills (guitar, vox).

"There was no leader. Everything was communally written, and if one person didn't agree about something, no matter how strongly the other three felt about it, it didn't go in. If one of us doesn't get it then something's wrong. But if we get it, then it doesn't matter who else does."

Peter Bergman

BREAK ON THROUGH

That summer all the folk groups went electric and the teenage girls switched from boots and bell-bottoms to something a little more freaky.

Los Angeles style was different, more show biz, more sophisticated than San Francisco. San Francisco had the Mime Troupe, who specialized in street theatre, whereas LA had the Firesign Theater, a self-contained four-man comedy troupe of actors and writers whose medium was radio and the recording studio. Using multitrack recording, they collaged together James Joyce and the found poetry of used-car salesmen, science-fiction and TV shows, mixed old movies with avant-garde drama and literature to make multilayered surrealist satire.

The Firesigns, in true 60s style, were so named because astrologically they were all fire signs. Peter Bergman, David Ossman, Phil Proctor and Phil Austin came together in 1966 as part of a free-form, late-night FM radio program called "Radio Free Oz," on the public subscription channel KPFK, Los Angeles. It was hosted by Bergman in his persona as the Wizard of Oz. He described the format as "a late-night talk show on FM just before FM got discovered." Austin said it was "on three or four hours a night and featured everybody who was anybody in the artistic world who passed through LA."

Bergman said, "I saw the Beatles in 1965, and right away I made a vow that someday I would have a four-man comedy group, although we wouldn't dress alike. Which of course would make us more like the Rolling Stones."

Between 1967 and 1975 they recorded thirteen albums for CBS in various group permutations, the most celebrated of which was their 1970 masterpiece, Don't Crush That Dwarf, Hand Me The Pliers. They worked with the Grateful Dead and Buffalo Springfield and their heavy promotion of the first-ever Los Angeles Love-In brought 40,000 hippies to Elysian Park. They were key members of the LA hippie scene.

RIGHT: The Firesign Theater prepare their props.
OVER: Love in action in 1965. Arthur Lee is at left.

"In walks this guy with chandelier droplet glasses, one lens was red and one was blue, like a prism. My goodness, I'd never seen anything like him before: he was a freak. Then they started playing and I'd never heard anything like that in my life."

Robert Rozelle (a member of Love in the 70s)

135

"Father, I want to kill you. Mother, I want to … Aaaaah!"

on the Doors self-titled debut album

Jim Morrison plays Oedipus on "The End," the closing track

LOVE

By 1966 Love had developed a large core of fans who jammed Bido Lito's and lined up down the street. With the success of the Byrds, the big New York record labels suddenly became very interested in the Los Angeles scene and Jac Holzman, the owner of Elektra Records, flew out to scout the Strip. In his book Follow the Music, he recalled the first time he saw Love play: "It was a scene from one of the amiable rings of Dante's inferno Bodies crushing into each other, silken-clad girls with ironed blonde hair moving the kind of shapes you didn't see in New York, to a cadence part musical and all sexual." Love were already onstage when Holzman arrived: "The band was cranking out 'Hey Joe' and 'My Little Red Book'. Inwardly, I smiled. 'My Little Red Book' was by Burt Bacharach and Hal David, and featured in the Woody Allen movie What's New, Pussycat? Hip but straight. And here were Arthur Lee and Love going at it with manic intensity. Five guys of all colors: black, white and psychedelic … My heart skipped a beat."

Holzman right away offered the band a deal and that night, at Bido Lito's, the group signed a standard Elektra three-album contract. Holzman stuck them in a studio and they recorded their first album, Love, in just four days. At that time the band was living together and with their advance money they moved into "The Castle," a mansion in the Los Feliz hills that once belonged to Bela Lugosi and that was to be the site of many of the band's promo shots. They lived and worked together, but, with the exception of his writing partner MacLean, Lee regarded the others essentially as sidemen.

Love's single "7 and 7 Is" reached No. 33 in

September 1966, but when it came time to tour Lee resolutely refused to leave Los Angeles—a move that had a profoundly negative effect on their career. Holzman also found his match in Lee as a businessman. Lee negotiated a new—and better—contract by stating that his signature on the original contract wasn't legal because he was a minor when he'd signed. "He treated the label as if we were trying to scam him," Holzman wrote. "He scammed us first!" Arthur Lee and Love were cool in a way that no San Francisco band could be. It was Hollywood cool—sex, drugs and rock 'n' roll—but there wasn't all that much in the way of peace and love.

THE DOORS

Love was not Holzman's only LA signing in 1966. His West Coast representative, Billy James, was a central member of the Laurel Canyon and Sunset Strip musician and freak scene. One band he had watched with interest was the Doors.

The Doors had a difficult time getting gigs, their material was seen as too theatrical, too over-the-top and just not cool enough for the Strip. They finally got exposure with a steady gig at London Fog, a small club between the Hamburger Hamlet and the Galaxy. Ronnie Haran, talent booker for the Whisky, managed to persuade a skeptical Elmer Valentine to hire them as a support act. Beginning that spring, the Doors could be seen trying to outdo Love, Captain Beefheart, The Byrds, The Lovin' Spoonful and Motown acts such as Marvin Gaye.

Ronnie Haran brought Holzman to see the Doors, but he was unimpressed. At Billy James' insistence he saw them a second time. He was

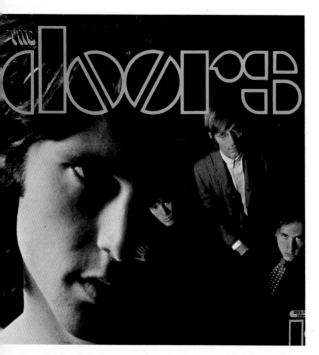

still unenthusiastic, but this time James convinced him that they were commercial and, in late 1966, he signed them. They made him a multimillionaire.

Elektra had an enlightened studio policy and the Doors had considerable freedom in recording their first album, which was ready for release by the following January. By then, however, the Doors were once more without a gig. Morrison's powerful song, "The End," ends with an Oedipal re-enactment where Morrison yells that he wants to kill his father. The song's last line was usually cut off at "Mother, I want to …" But one night Morrison had stared Mario, manager of the Whisky, in the eye and roared, "Mother, I want to fuck you!" After the set Mario came up to the stage: "Those guys are nuts—get them out of here." And they were fired. It was not unexpected. Some months earlier the Mothers of Invention had lost their gig at the Whisky because Zappa said "Fuck" on stage. They hadn't worked there since.

THE MOTHERS OF INVENTION

In January 1966 MGM Records A&R man Tom Wilson visited the Coast. One evening at The Trip he met up with Herb Cohen, manager of the Mothers of Invention. Somehow Cohen was persuasive enough to get him to leave the girl who had been sitting on his lap and go with Cohen to the Whisky to catch the Mothers. They were doing an extended boogie version of the "Watts Riot Song" when Wilson arrived. Wilson was black and might have appreciated the anti-racist sentiments of the song more than the average producer. At any rate, according to Zappa, "He heard us sing 'The Watts Riot Song (Trouble Every Day)'. He stayed for five minutes, said 'Yeah, yeah, yeah', slapped me on the back, shook my hand and said, 'Wonderful. We're gonna make a record of you. Goodbye.' I didn't see him again for four months. He thought we were a rhythm and blues band. He probably went back to New York and said, 'I signed me another rhythm and blues band from the Coast. They got this song about the riot. It's a protest song. They'll do a couple of singles and maybe they'll die out.'"

In fact Wilson—who also signed the Velvet Underground—heard several demo tapes before finally committing himself to signing the group. TT&G recording studio, at Sunset and Highland,

This is about the Mothers of Invention. We have watched them grow, and with their growth, we hopefully have grown. Their honesty has offended some and been provocative to many, but in any case, their performances have had a real effect on their audiences.

The Mothers' music is very new, and as their music is new, so is the intention of their music. As much as the Mothers put into their music, we must bring to it. The Mothers, and what they represent as a group has attracted all of the outcasts, the pariahs, the people who are angry and afraid and contemptuous of the existing social structure. The danger lies in the "Freak Out" becoming an excuse instead of a reason. An excuse implies an end, a reason a beginning. Being that the easiest way is consistently more attractive than the harder way, the essential thing that makes the "Freak Out" audiences different constitutes their sameness. A freak is not a freak if ALL are freaks. "Freaking Out" should presuppose an active freedom, freedom meaning a liberation from the control of some other person or persons. Unfortunately, reaction seems to have taken place of action. We SHOULD be as satisfied listening to the Mothers perform from a concert stage. If we could channel the energy expended in "Freaking Out" physically into "Freaking Out" intellectually, we might possibly be able to create something concrete out of the ideological twilight of bizarre costumes and being seen being bizarre. Do we really listen? And if we really listen, do we really think? Freedom of thought, conversely, brings an awesome responsibility. Looking and acting eccentric IS NOT ENOUGH.

A mad tea-party is valid only as satire, commenting ironically, and ending in its beginning, in that it is only a trick of interpretation. It is not creation, and it IS NOT ENOUGH.

What WE must try to do then, is not only comment satirically on what's wrong, but try to CHANGE what's wrong. The Mothers are trying.

Suzy Creamcheese

PREVIOUS PAGE (RIGHT): Jim Morrison in his famous
leather pants.
LEFT: Frank Zappa.
ABOVE: A paid ad in the LA Free Press—one of Frank Zappa's
attempts to steer his audience into the path of righteousness.

was booked for a four-day block from March 9 until March 12—enough time, in those days, for an album.

Wilson was so impressed with the first day's tapes that he negotiated a more or less unlimited budget for the project from MGM in New York: "You can do something big," he told Zappa.

Freak Out! was released in June and broke a lot of new ground. It was the first rock 'n' roll double album, it was the first rock "concept" album, the first to print the lyrics on the sleeve and the track "Trouble Coming Every Day" is arguably the first recorded rap song. It was enough to give Zappa and the Mothers very high street cred and, old and ugly as they were, they suddenly attracted the attention of groupies.

ABOVE: The proposed demolition of Pandora's Box was the final straw for the freaks of Sunset Strip who, on November 12, 1966, after months of police harassment, reacted by staging a riot.

WHISKY A GO GO
8901 SUNSET STRIP • 652-4202

THE Byrds
vs.
Byrds
&
THE DAILY FLASH

PSYCHEDELIC LIGHT SHOW

SEPTEMBER 1 – 11
ONLY

FOOD FUN till 2 A.M. AGE 18 AND UP WELCOME

RIGHT: Roger McGuinn of The Byrds set a fashion for small granny glasses that spread quickly in the rock 'n' roll community.

RIOT ON THE STRIP

Pandora's Box was a small coffee house, set on a traffic island at 8118 Sunset at the intersection with Crescent Heights, where the Strip proper begins. In the 50s it had been a beatnik hangout and, in 1966, it still featured poetry readings and folk music. The building was listed to be demolished as part of a road-widening scheme and was on a month-to-month cheap lease, but when the eviction notice arrived the whole Strip rose up in anger. All through the summer young people had thronged the sidewalks of the Strip—one of the few places people could walk in LA—blocking the doorways of stores and crowding out into the street, halting traffic. The more traditional shop owners complained to the police,

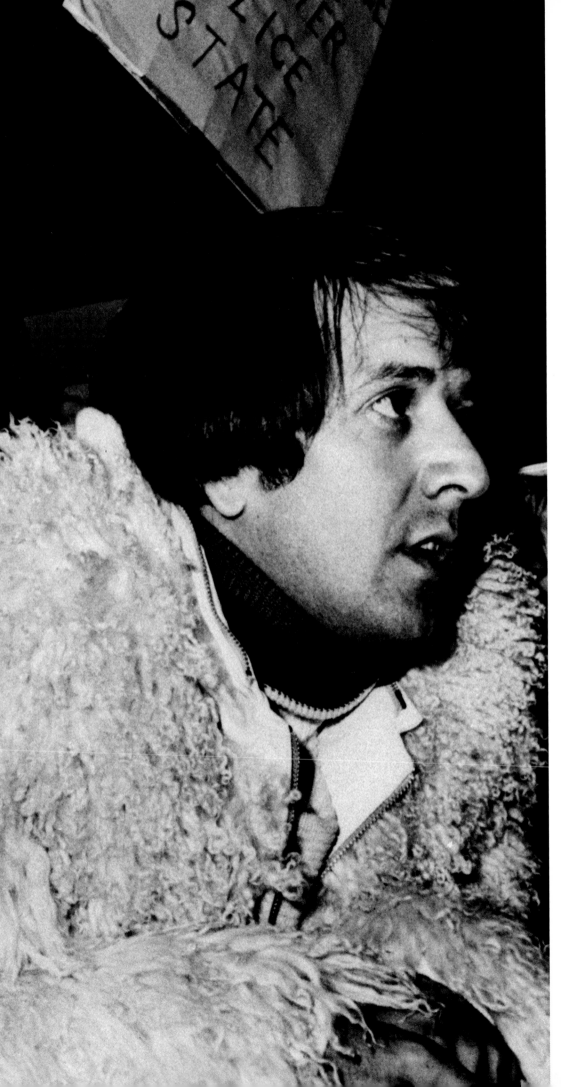

"For What It's Worth."

The song in which Stephen Stills captured the mood of the Strip, initially recorded by Buffalo Springfield and covered by Cher in 1971.

"Everyone would meet at Ben Franks' and Pandora's Box. That was a very important corner."

Mike Nesmith of The Monkees

VITO AND A CROSS-SECTION OF HIS DANCERS AND FREAKERS

Riot on Sunset Strip starred Aldo Ray, Mimzi Farmer and the Chocolate Watch Band.

provoking massive retaliation. Sometimes the traffic jams were productive. Neil Young had just arrived from Canada when he ran into Stephen Stills and Richie Furay in a traffic jam on the Strip. From this meeting, Buffalo Springfield was born.

The police raided Ben Frank's twice to arrest people for loitering and curfew violations. There had also been mass arrests at GeeGee's and at Cantor's 24-hour deli, where scores of innocent customers were beaten to the ground with night-sticks as they left the premises after paying their bill or collecting takeout food. The closing of Pandora's Box provided the spark necessary. The young people had finally had enough. On the night of November 12, 1966 about 1,000 demon-

strators dressed in psychedelic finery of beads, face-paint and fringed jackets, protested the tight enforcement of the curfew laws by blocking the street, causing massive traffic jams. Protesters including Sonny and Cher sat down in the road. The LAPD moved in from the west and the LA county sheriff's department sent in two bus loads of cops from the east, trapping the crowds. When someone was pushed through the plate glass window of the Liquor Locker the police, hearing the sound of breaking glass, assumed that looting was taking place and began arresting everyone. Peter Fonda and over 300 other freaks were led away in handcuffs and taken to the West Hollywood sheriff station in police buses. Outraged demonstrators began throwing rocks; they overturned a car and set it on fire and tried to set fire to a bus after chasing off all the passengers.

Not a lot was achieved. Some months later, on August 3, 1967, Pandora's was bulldozed and paved over. The site is now an access lane off Sunset where it curves into Crescent Heights. Out of these events came one of Steven Stills'most famous songs, "For What It's Worth"—it is about the riots and was released within a month. Frank Zappa also referred to it by name in "Plastic People" and Monkee Mike Nesmith wrote a song called "Daily Nightly"—in his words, a "rambling account on the Hollywood street scene at the time when people were meeting at Ben Frank's and Pandora's Box ... That was a very important corner where people would congregate." And someone put out a cheap exploitation movie called Riot on Sunset Strip, which starred Aldo Ray, Mimzi Farmer, and the Chocolate Watch Band. This was Hollywood, after all.

PREVIOUS PAGE: Sonny and Cher join the sit down protest.
LEFT: Joni Mitchell joined the Laurel Canyon community.
ABOVE: Karl Franzoni & Zsou, center, Vito on right with baby Godot.

Peter and Jane Fonda were the kids of Hollywood Royalty, but they wanted to be part of The People.

LEFT: Peter Fonda and Nancy Sinatra in The Wild Ones. The beautiful people of Hollywood embraced the psychedelic lifestyle, then introduced the ideas to a general audience with films such as The Trip and Easy Rider. **BELOW:** Jane Fonda.

VELVET UNDERGROUND

The hippie phenomenon was able to define a small town like San Francisco, but New York was too large and had too much happening for the hippies to make any kind of impact on the city. Very few New Yorkers even knew of their existence. However, in the mid-60s the record industry was still based largely in New York, along with virtually every advertising agency and large book and magazine publisher. New developments were quickly snapped up by the "straights," as the hippies called them, and the fashion and style magazines quickly jumped on Andy Warhol's activities in the realm of music.

Though they would have hated to be described as hippies, the Velvet Underground were probably the most influential 60s band after the Beatles and were central to the underground scene in New York. Unlike the hippies, they dressed entirely in black with sunglasses—except for one gig in Ann Arbor, Michigan, where they all wore white. Their drugs of choice were speed and, at least in Lou's case, heroin, which also set them apart from the laid-back, pot-smoking hippies.

The group first got together in New York in 1965 and played under a number of names, including the Warlocks—a name

ABOVE: L-R Nico, Mary Woronov, Andy Warhol and International Velvet at the New York premiere of Antonioni's Blow Up.
RIGHT: The Warhol-designed cover of the debut Velvet Underground album.

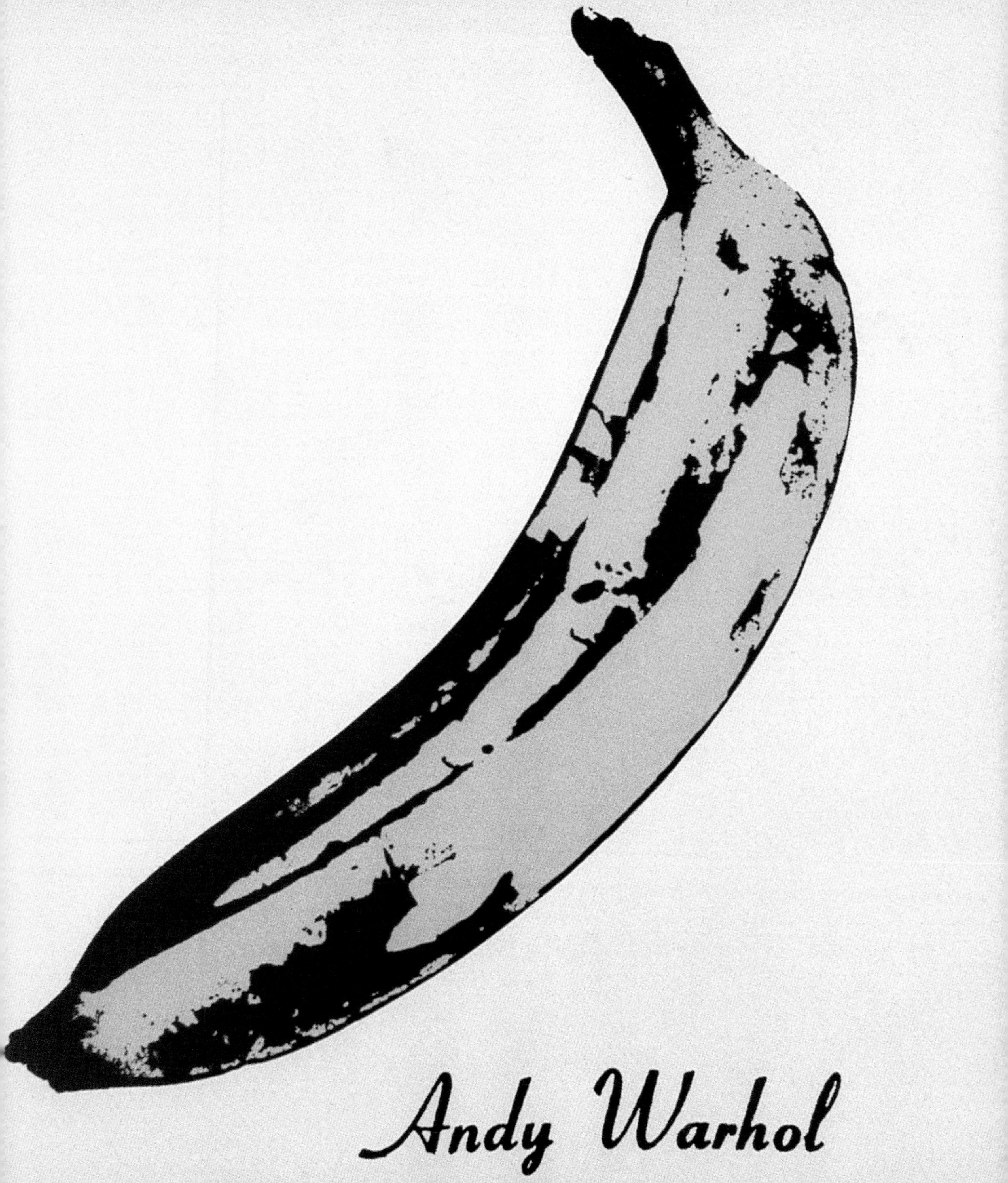
Andy Warhol

also used by the early Grateful Dead. The original line-up consisted of Lou Reed, John Cale and Sterling Morrison. Drummer Angus MacLise left rather than accept money for his art at their first gig on December 11, 1965, at Summit High School in New Jersey. They got $75 between them. They opened with "Venus In Furs" and ended with "Heroin," numbers which caused the students to stand, mouths open in disbelief. MacLise was replaced for the gig by Mo Tucker, who not only had a unique style but also owned a much-needed amplifier. The new line-up got a gig at the Café Bizarre in Greenwich Village at West 3rd Street near MacDougal, where they were seen by Warhol Factory regular Brigid Polk. She brought Andy Warhol down to see them and he asked them to work with him on his idea for a total light and sound environment. This was to be called the Exploding Plastic Inevitable and involved music, dancing, a light show and movies all at once. Andy Warhol said, "The pop idea was, after all, that anybody could do anything, so naturally we were all trying to do it all. Nobody wanted to stay in one category, we all wanted to branch out into every creative thing we could. That's why, when we met the Velvet Underground at the end of 1965 we were all for getting into the music scene too."

Paul Morrissey, manager of Warhol's Factory, put it rather more bluntly, "What really happened is that I had this idea that Andy could make money not only from underground films, but from putting the movies in some sort of rock 'n' roll context. Discovering the Velvets, bringing them up to the Factory and working with them was done for purely commercial reasons."

In January, Warhol was featured on a public broadcasting TV show called American Artists. He naturally brought along the Velvets, who shocked the TV executives with "Venus In Furs" and "Heroin." Then Nico arrived from Europe, where she had appeared in Fellini's La Dolce Vita and had made a single with Jimmy Page. Andy had arranged for poet Gerard Malanga to do his whip dance in front of the group, accompanied by Warhol superstar Edie Sedgwick. Edie left to join the Dylan camp and Nico was brought in as lead singer. They were ready for the Dom.

The Dom was a Polish dancehall on St. Mark's Place. Warhol took a one-month lease for April 1966, and the Warhol Factory moved in to paint the place and hang screens for the movies and projections. Someone stole Mo Tucker's tom toms so she went out to the street and found two garbage cans, put a mike under each one and used those for a week. Allen Ginsberg joined them onstage and sang "Hare Krishna." It was wide open.

Tom Wilson signed the band to MGM and, after recording some basic tracks in New York, took the group to Los Angeles to record the rest of the tracks for the album. They opened at The Trip, but the police closed it down and they did two nights at the Fillmore in San Francisco instead. Bill Graham was incensed when they arrived at the venue in a limousine (though Graham took plenty of them himself later on) and when they complained about his rudimentary lightshow—a projection of the moon onto a sheet behind the stage—Graham screamed, "I hope you guys bomb!" They set up their own multimedia projections and movies, but the San Francisco hippies couldn't understand what they were trying to do and they did not go down very well. There could not have been a wider rift between the two ends of the underground.

After making the album and touring the country, playing art galleries and boutiques as well as regular venues, the Velvets returned to the Dom, now renamed the Balloon Farm. All the amphetamine was taking its toll and relations within the group were getting very prickly, but they stuck it out, constantly trying new things to keep the show fresh.

PREVIOUS PAGE: The Velvet Underground with Nico. Left to right, Lou Reed, Mo Tucker, Nico, Sterling Morrison and John Cale. RIGHT: Andy Warhol.

"The rock 'n' roll music gets louder, the dancers get more frantic, and the lights start going on and off like crazy. And there are spotlights blinking in our eyes, and car horns beeping, and Gerard Malanga and the dancers are shaking like mad, and you don't think the noise can get any louder, and then it does, until there is one big rhythmic tidal wave of sound, pressing down around you, just impure enough so you can still get the best; the audience, the dancers, the music and the movies, all of it fused together into one magnificent moment of hysteria."

George English, writing about the Exploding Plastic Inevitable in Fire Island News

RIGHT: Nico's debut solo LP cover set the look for the intellectual hippie chick. Nico was only with the Velvets for their first album; she went on to make solo albums until her death in 1988.

THE FUGS

The Fugs could only have emerged from the literary protest scene of New York. Their name was taken from the euphemism for "fuck" used in Norman Mailer's The Naked and the Dead. Meanwhile, their three permanent members consisted of a Mid-Westerner poet, Ed Sanders; a Texan drummer, Ken Weaver; and a Hasidic pacifist-anarchist poet, Tuli Kupferberg, who was strictly from New York. Ed and Tuli were both publishers. Tuli's Birth Press published mostly poetry, though there was also a magazine written entirely by young children. Ed Sanders operated the Fuck You Press "from a secret location in the lower east side." This produced a number of mimeographed books, as well as the notorious Marijuana Newsletter and Fuck You/ A Magazine of the Arts, which had published Norman Mailer, William Burroughs, Allen Ginsberg and many other notable literary names since its beginning in 1962. All of these were available from Sanders" Peace Eye Bookstore, a former kosher butcher shop that still had "Strictly Kosher" painted in Hebrew on the window, located at 383 East 10th Street between Tompkins Square and Avenue C. Sanders had added the symbol of the eye of Horus and a notice reading: "Ed Sanders—book creep, grass cadet, fug poet, editor, squack slarfer, madman composer and poon scomp." The Peace Eye was Fugs' headquarters.

Describing themselves as "The Lower East Side's most fantastic protest rock 'n' roll peace-sex-psychedelic singing group," the Fugs played music with literary themes—William Blake's "Ah Sunflower!" and Allen Ginsberg's "Howl" with a musical setting, along with "The Swinburne Stomp." They sang many sexually

RIGHT: New York, 26 September 1966. Allen Ginsberg, in stars and stripes hat, marches with the Fugs and at his left poet Peter Orlovsky. More than 15,000 anti-Vietnam demonstrators paraded down Fifth Ave. as objectors carried Pro-Vietnam signs.

"We have to do what every group in this country did— we gotta take over the community where we outnumber people so we can have decent jobs."

Stokeley Carmichael

explicit numbers, among them "Group Grope," "Coca Cola Douche" and "Slum Goddess," as well as songs dealing with peace and war—"CIA Man," "Kill For Peace," "Strafe Them Creeps In The Rice Paddy Daddy" and so on. Ed Sanders summed up their aims by saying, "This is the era of the civil rights, sexual & consciousness expansion revolutions, & those are the banners under which the Fugs are going to present themselves to America."

Not surprisingly, the authorities soon noticed them and early in the morning of 2 January 1966 Sanders was telephoned by Kupferberg, who lived next door, to say that the Peace Eye was swarming with cops. The police were investigating a possible burglary, but while they were there they found hundreds of copies of Fuck You/A Magazine of the Arts, as well as copies of The Bugger Anthology, The Marijuana Newsletter and The Platonic Blow by W. H. Auden. Ed was hauled off down to the 9th Precinct station house. The police spent hours "screaming with glee" as Ed put it, but Ed knew it was a misde-

meanor—possession with intent to sell porn—and eventually he was set free on $500 bail.

The Fugs had begun in 1965 with an album called The Village Fugs, released on the folk music label Folkways, but it was in 1966 that they became an underground cult band. They had an eponymous album out with ESP, and introduced an element of theatricality into their act. At the Bridge Theater in the Lower East Side they held a "Night of Napalm," concentrating mostly on their political numbers about the Vietnam War. Screaming "burn those creepy gooks" and "Kill! Kill!" over the roar of feedback, they flung 50 pounds of gooey red-dyed spaghetti over themselves and their audience. They meant it. Kupferberg even told an interviewer that if they ever started to make any money he would quit. By the end of the year, Sanders had moved the Peace Eye to a safer neighborhood, to 147 Avenue A, next to Tompkins Square Park, near the Psychedelicatessen—supposedly the world's first head shop—and the offices of the East Village Other.

ABOVE: Martin Luther King (left) and Stokeley Carmichael (right) on the March Against Fear through the town of Philadelphia. The march went to Philadelphia to protest the unsolved murders of three civil rights workers in 1964.
RIGHT: A female anti-Vietnam War protester is arrested in New York, 1966.
OVER: The cover of Bob Dylan's seminal 1966 recording, Blonde On Blonde.

BOB DYLAN

New York's favorite song-writer poet was not seen much during 1966. On 5 February, he began a American tour of 27 cities and left from Honolulu on 9 April to play Australia. The tour ended at the Royal Albert Hall in London on May 27. This was Dylan's acid-rock period. On April 22 Columbia had released his first double album, Blonde On Blonde, confirming his new role as an underground poet and spokesman. Back in New York he bought a brownstone in the East 30s, but then, on July 29, tragedy struck and Dylan did not tour again for many years.

On August 2, 1966 the New York Times reported: "Bob Dylan, the folk singer and song-writer is under a doctor's care for injuries suffered in a motorcycle accident last Friday. A representative of Mr. Dylan said the injuries have forced the cancellation of a concert scheduled for Saturday night at the Yale Bowl in New Haven."

Dylan described the accident, which occurred near his home in Woodstock, NY. He was taking his Triumph 500 to be repaired when "the back wheel locked, I think. I lost control, swerving from left to right. Next thing I know I was in some place I never heard of—Middletown, I think—with my face cut up so I got some scars and my neck busted up pretty good."

His wife Sara was following him in the car to take him home after dropping off the bike. Dylan later told a friend that, as he was hurtling through the air, "I saw my whole life pass in front of me." Dylan was diagnosed by Middletown hospital as suffering broken vertebrae in his neck, internal injuries, concussion and lacerations of the face and scalp. He was hospitalized for a week and confined to bed for a month at home to recuperate, during which time old friends like Allen Ginsberg brought him books and magazines to cheer him up. Dylan withdrew from public while bizarre rumors circulated about him—he was a helpless drug addict, his brain had been mashed and he was in a lunatic asylum, totally insane, so badly scarred that he would never appear in public again.

Dylan was exhausted from the long American and world tour and from years of drugs and running around. There had been strong rumors that he was on heroin when he was in London. Three years later he spoke of the accident: "I had a dreadful motorcycle accident which put me away for a while ... and I still didn't sense the importance of that accident until at least a year after that. I realized that it was a real accident. I mean, I thought that I was just gonna get up and go back to doing what I was doing before."

"Songs are in my head like they always are … and they're not goin' to get written down until some things are evened up. Not until some people come forth and make up for some of the things that have happened."

Bob Dylan speaking from his hospital bed

featuring I WANT YOU and
RAINY DAY WOMEN Nos.12 & 35

SPONTANEOUS UNDERGROUND

The Spontaneous Underground afternoons at the Marquee in London began in January, Indica Bookshop and Gallery opened in February, independent filmmakers were starting the London Film-makers Co-op and, all through the spring, a mix of people talked earnestly about setting up the London Free School. These included Rhaunie Laslett, John Hopkins, Felix de Mendelssohn, Graham Keen, Michael De Freitas, Joe Boyd and many others. It opened in late spring, with some sessions in a rooming house of Michael X's large basement at 26 Powis Terrace. Previously he had used this space as an illegal gambling club and it was available, rent free, for another eighteen months. Michael had a somewhat seedy history before his involvement in community affairs, having been a pimp and then an enforcer for a notorious slum racketeer named Peter Rachman—he went in with the dogs if tenants didn't agree to be evicted. An encounter with Malcolm X converted him to Islam. He became first Michael X, then Michael Abdul Malik, and set about creating a black power movement in London to emulate the growing political consciousness of blacks in the States. As a very vocal member of the community in Notting Hill he soon came into contact with the London Free School crowd.

Michael taught a class in basic English, mostly to elderly Irish people. When world heavyweight champion of the world Muhammed Ali came to Britain, Michael somehow persuaded him to visit the fifty children in Rhaunie Laslett's Free School play group.

When the LFS first started, it was the endless discussions and meetings that contributed the most, because they brought together a group of people who went on to publish magazines, write for underground newspapers, organize poetry readings, promote concerts and create the beginnings of an alternative lifestyle in the capital. Pete Jenner described the London Free School as "possibly the first public manifestation of the underground in England."

In fact, the first stirrings were probably to be

RIGHT: John Hopkins, cofounder of the London Free School, IT, organizer of the 14-Hour Technicolor Dream and founder of the UFO Club. Seen with singer Julie Felix at a happening in Piccadilly Circus.

found in a basement in Wardour Street, Soho. Though the inchoate hip community had been identified at the Albert Hall poetry reading, there was nowhere for them to meet. This gap was filled by Steven Stollman, a documentary filmmaker who had recently arrived from New York. Steven hired the Marquee Club on Sunday afternoons, beginning January 30, 1966. The first invitation read:

SPONTANEOUS Underground at the Marquee this Sunday January 30th organized by Steve Stollman of ESP Disk with the aid of everybody. Among those taking part will be Donovan / Mose Allison / Graham Bond / Pop / Mime / Kinetic Sculpture / Discotheque / Boutique

THIS TRIP begins at 4.30 and goes on. Liquor license applied for. Costume, masque, ethnic, space, Edwardian, Victorian and hipness generally....face and body makeup—certainly

This is a spontaneous party, and profit will be held in trust by Louis Diamond, Solicitor, that such spontaneities may continue. Invitation only, donation at door 6/6.

The invitation was accompanied by six strips of paper: Burroughsian cut-ups, sliced from left-over pages from Alex Trocchi's sigma portfolio, Long Hair magazine and various Marvel comics.

People turned up wearing fancy dress, others made theirs in the club. The garment district was just on the other side of Oxford Street and until the mid-70s the streets were littered with the cast-off remnants of bolts of cloth and trimmings. A number of people arrived with arms full of these and set about improvising costumes on the spot. Mose Allison didn't show, but both Donovan and Graham Bond were there, the

former with each eye heavily made up with thick kohl to represent an Egyptian eye of horus extending down his cheeks. He sat cross-legged on stage, surrounded by six sitar players and engulfed in clouds of pot smoke, and was so out of it that he didn't remember the event at all the next day.

Most of the entertainment came from the audience themselves, as was the intention, with an improvised play/happening, and a number of poets showed up including Roger Jones and Pete Brown; the latter wrote a number of hits for Cream including "Wrapping Paper." Spike Hawkins and Johnny Byrne, who later cowrote Groupie with Jenny Fabian, performed magic tricks, most of which went wrong. Calling themselves Poison Bellows, they arrived wearing floor length overcoats and mufflers (nothing unusual about this—it's always a good idea to wrap up in London in February), pushing an old pram in which stood a wind-up gramophone and a bunch of old 78s, which they played while juggling with Pete Brown's father's collapsible silk top hat.

LEFT: Cream. Left to right, Eric Clapton, Ginger Baker and Jack Bruce try on western clothes prior to conquering America.
RIGHT: An acid party held in a communal flat in Notting Hill, London's equivalent of Haight-Ashbury.

"We were just having fun. We were not taking it seriously at all. Most of the time we were fooling around, drinking, and just having a good time."

Eric Clapton on Cream

> "I arrived around ten-thirty and there on stage was this strange band who were playing a mixture of R&B and electronic noises. In between the routine stuff like 'Louie Louie' and 'Road Runner' they were playing these very weird breaks. It was all very bizarre and just what I was looking for—a far out, electronic, freaky pop group."
>
> Pete Jenner

RIGHT: The original Pink Floyd line-up. Standing: Roger Waters. Left to right, Nick Mason, Syd Barrett, Rick Wright. Syd became an acid casualty and the group's sound changed radically as the group moved from psychedelic whimsy to architectural blocks of sound.

PINK FLOYD

Some sources say the Pink Floyd played that afternoon but it was more likely the March 13 session, when they followed AMM, a random sound group led by Stockhausen's pupil Cornelius Cardew, on stage. Pink Floyd would soon be London's premier psychedelic band. Like most British bands they played R&B standards, but they would improvise in a most unusual way, deconstructing the chord structure and sometimes playing around with the elements of one chord for twenty minutes at a time.

Lead vocalist and guitarist Syd Barrett moved to London in the summer of 1964 from Cambridge to attend Camberwell Art College. He arrived with Bob Close, a jazz guitarist with Cambridge band Blues Anonymous, who was taking a place at the Regent Street Polytechnic. Syd's school friend Roger Waters had moved from Cambridge two years earlier to study architecture at the Poly and they soon met up again. In Cambridge Roger and Syd had played together briefly in a local band called Geoff Mott and the Mottoes (they played one proper gig before disbanding). Meanwhile Roger had teamed up with roommates and fellow Poly students Nick Mason and Rick Wright, along with several others, to form a group known variously as Sigma-6, the Meggadeaths, the Abdabs, and the Screaming Abdabs.

Wright and Mason moved out the summer Syd moved to London, enabling Syd to share a room with Waters, and soon the embryonic Pink Floyd was formed with the line-up of Syd Barrett,

Roger Waters, Nick Mason and Bob Close, joined a few months later by Rick Wright on piano. In the autumn of 1964 Syd came up with the name Pink Floyd, composed by joining the Christian names of bluesmen Pink Anderson (1900–1974) and Floyd "Dipper Boy" Council (1911–1976). Syd later told reporters that the name was transmitted to him by a UFO while he sat on the ley line crossing Glastonbury Tor and by then he may have really thought that. Even as the Pink Floyd, the group never considered that they would make their careers in anything other than art and architecture; they were just playing for fun.

When Steven Stollman began to put on Sunday afternoon happenings at the Marquee, it was obvious that this was where the Pink Floyd Sound, as they were then called—the name was painted on the bass amplifier—belonged, a place where the audience was looking forward to experiment and innovation. Movies were projected directly onto the group through the thick clouds of pot smoke and incense while red and blue lights pulsated in time to the music, making it hard to make out the features of any of the musicians and rendering the band effectively anonymous. This they liked and, with a few exceptions, they kept their faces off their album sleeves, so that even at the height of their fame they could walk around London unrecognized except by the most hardcore fans.

Most of the West Coast groups did not record until the following year, and were something of a disappointment to the British groups when they did finally hear them after all the enthusiastic descriptions they'd received of their live shows.

SYD BARRETT

In 1965 Syd returned to Cambridge for the summer vacation and hooked up with his school friend Storm Thorgeson. That August they hitchhiked to St. Tropez with yet another old friend from Cambridge Tech, David Gilmour, a guitarist with his own R&B band called Jokers Wild. David and Syd had known each other since they were fourteen and had spent their lunchtimes hanging around the Art Department, teaching each other to play guitar. Though Syd was already smoking pot and writing songs, it was not until 1966, when he was 19, that he took his first trip.

Syd, along with Storm Thorgeson and Ian "Imo" Moore, was visiting his friend Bob Gale in his garden in Cambridge. Thorgeson and Imo had laid out hundreds of sugar cubes in rows and were treating each one with two drops of liquid LSD from glass bottles. The acid was very concentrated and as they licked the sugar granules from their fingers they became hopelessly confused, giving some cubes a double dose and others none at all. In a famous story told by Imo, Syd found three objects which he sat and stared at for twelve hours: an orange, a plum and a matchbox. The plum became the planet Venus and the orange was Jupiter. Syd travelled between them in outer space. His trip came to an abrupt end when Imo, feeling hungry, ate Venus in one bite. "You should have seen Syd's face. He was in total shock for a few seconds, then he just grinned." From then on acid became Syd's drug of choice.

THE HAPPENINGS

It was at the Spontaneous Underground of March 27, 1966 that the Pink Floyd met their future manager, Pete Jenner, who was one of those planning to start the London Free School. He had a full-time job as an assistant sociology lecturer at the London School of Economics, but his greatest interest was music, the more avant-garde and experimental the better. He was looking for a band to produce, something challenging but more commercial than the music he had recorded so far. He had already made a record with AMM, who were also playing at the Marquee that afternoon. It had been released by Joe Boyd, then head of the UK branch of Elektra Records, but AMM only received a 2% royalty, which didn't go very far.

Peter had been very impressed by the tapes he heard of the Velvet Underground, but by the time he got through to Lou Reed on the phone, Andy Warhol had already signed them. The Pink Floyd intrigued him.

Jenner realized that he could not manage a band by himself and discussed it with his friend Andrew King, an educational cyberneticist, who had recently left his job at the British Airways training and education department and was at a loose end. Andrew agreed to become his partner and together they visited the Pink Floyd's house in Highgate and offered to manage them. The band, in fact, was on the verge of breaking up. Gigs were hard to come by, they had no proper equipment and rehearsals were interfering with their studies. However, seeing that Peter and Andrew were serious, they went along with the game, though Roger and Nick secretly thought that Peter and Andrew were drug dealers. In the spirit of the times, Jenner and King formed Blackhill Enterprises—named after a cottage in Wales owned by Jenner—and divided the shares into six equal parts between the band and themselves. This was absolute anathema to the traditional Denmark Street managers, who usually creamed 25% off the top before expenses were paid. The papers were finally signed on October 31, 1966. Andrew invested £1,000 he had recently inherited in new amplifiers for the band and they set about getting them gigs. The Pink Floyd played the London Free School all through the autumn. One evening, an American couple called Joel and Toni Brown brought along a projector and began throwing strange images over the group, changing them in time to the music. It was a light show they had developed while

LEFT: The Pink Floyd were the first British band to develop their own light show. In America light shows were free agents who worked with specific dance halls, but in Britain the bands each had their own.

169

> "I am aware of adjustments to my essence … and then my 360 degree vision is swamped with lights. I am a figure of focus on a wide stage lit by light towers. A large rock festival audience stretches far & wide … I am overwhelmed … with the connection between souls … the QUALITY of intense LOVE."
>
> **Daevid Allen on his first Acid Trip**

living in Tim Leary's psychedelic community in Millbrook and, though not as mind-blowing as the descriptions people had heard of Californian light shows, it encouraged Pete Jenner to develop a light show of his own for the group. His first effort was very rudimentary: a row of household spotlights mounted on a piece of board with bits of colored perspex in front of them. They were operated by ordinary household light switches. It was the beginning of the Pink Floyd's famous light shows.

With all these experiments going on, the Floyd's regular set at the Free School was labeled the Sound/Light Workshop.

LIGHT SHOWS

The psychedelic light show developed differently in Britain than in the States. In America the light-show teams operated independently, as if they were groups themselves, and would be hired to provide a show for all the groups playing that evening, whereas in Britain, any band wanting a light show tended to develop their own.

By October the Pink Floyd had the best show in town, provided by Syd's new roommates, Peter Wynne-Wilson and his girlfriend Susie Gawler-Wright, along with 17-year-old Joey Gannon, who hung out at the lighting workshop of Hornsey College of Art and whose idea it had been to use powerful 500 and 1000 watt projectors to shine

ink slides on the band. They developed a system of pulsating blobs of colored ink, manipulated between glass slides so that they throbbed and moved and grew with the music; the shapes expanded when a blow-lamp was directed at them and contracted when cooled by a hair-dryer set on cold. The rhythm was applied by manually squeezing them. The spots worked on a series of microswitches that responded when Gannon waved his hand over them—far removed from Jenner's old manual light switches of a few months before.

They became a major part of the entertainment, as the ad for the October 14 London Free School showed:

Announcing Pop Dance featuring London's farthest out group, The Pink Floyd in Interstellar Overdrive, Stoned Alone, Astronomy Domini (an astral chant) & other numbers from their space-age book. Also Light projection Slides, Liquid Movies. . .

The next day, the Pink Floyd did their first large-scale gig, playing as the headline band at the launch party for Europe's first underground newspaper, International Times, known as IT. This was an event that entered London underground legend and became the template for many future underground activities.

INTERNATIONAL TIMES

IT was launched with an all-night rave, a "Pop op costume masque drag ball et al" held at the Roundhouse, a huge circular Victorian building in Camden Town that once housed the winding gear to pull steam trains up the hill from Kings Cross station. For your five shillings in advance, ten at the door, people were promised: "Strip trip/happenings/movies/Soft Machine/Pink Floyd/Steel band" and a "sur prize for the shortest-barest." The building had stood empty for fifteen years and had never been used as a venue before. It was owned by Arnold Wesker's Centre 42, but he was still raising money to convert it to an arts center. The IT organizers had no license, no insurance, no fire extinguishers or whatever else was needed for such events, nor was there an adequate power supply, or toilet facilities, or heating, or even a proper floor. There was a doctor in attendance, however.

Bits of twisted metal stuck up from a century of undulating grime, a balcony ran around the building originally used by Gilbey's Gin to hold storage vans decades before and condemned as unsafe. Huge doors opened onto the railway tracks, which were used by the bands to bring in equipment and served as emergency fire exits.

RIGHT: A private Acid Test held in a communal flat in London's Notting Hill Gate, complete with its own light show.

"There was a quote that used to be on the masthead of International Times for a while and certainly was one that you saw around a lot: 'When the mode of the music changes, the walls of the city shake.' It was a political statement to get stoned and listen to somebody improvise on an Indian modal scale for twenty minutes with an electric group playing around him."

Joe Boyd

Some 2,500 people queued up for an hour to climb the single-file staircase up from the street.

Marianne Faithfull won the "shortest-barest" contest in a nun's costume that didn't quite cover her ass. Paul McCartney, dressed as an arab, circulated without being hassled. Monica Viti and Michelangelo Antonioni seemed in a state of shock. Films by Antony Balch, William Burroughs and Kenneth Anger played continuously, and the lack of heating on the cold October night made everybody dance. It was the Pink Floyd's first large gig and they pulled out all the stops, ending the night dramatically by blowing the fuses on the entire building and plunging everyone into complete darkness. As they had a light show they received the most money: £15 ($36 at the then-current exchange rate).

In the middle of the hall was a mountain of jelly, which people ate at midnight. Next to it was a motorbike.

The parked motorbike belonged to the other band, the Soft Machine, named after William Burroughs' third novel. Their singer, Daevid Allen, remembered the event: "That was our first gig as a quartet. Yoko Ono came on stage and created a giant happening by getting everybody to touch each other in the dark, right in the middle of the set. We also had a motorcycle brought onto the stage and would put a microphone against the cylinder head for a good noise." When they weren't playing they used it to give attractive young women rides around the bumpy dark inside circumference of the Roundhouse.

After some cosmetic maintenance the Roundhouse became an established venue, and the Pink Floyd played there again on 3 December at a benefit organized by the Majority Rule For Rhodesia Committee called "Psychodelphia Versus Ian Smith." Ian Smith had seized control of the country and declared independence from Britain in order to preserve white rule. The event organizers promised underground films, poets and happenings and suggested that the audience "bring your own happenings and Ecstatogenic substance." When the right-wing Daily Telegraph asked organizer Roland Maldoon what these were he told them, "Anything which produces ecstasy in the body. Alcohol was not allowed for the rave-up, unhappily, nor were drugs … All it really means really is that you should bring your own bird."

UFO

UFO was to the Floyd as the Cavern was to the Beatles. They were unknown when it started and famous when it closed, less than a year later.

UFO was held every Friday night, all night, beginning at 10pm in the Blarney Club, an Irish Ballroom in a basement on Tottenham Court Road. The club was run by Hoppy, cofounder of International Times and organizer of the All Saint's Hall Pink Floyd gigs, who saw it as a way of paying the staff of IT as the paper was already deeply in debt. UFO's musical director was Joe Boyd, also from the LFS, who had always thought

that they should have moved the All Saint's Hall gigs to the West End. He gave the Pink Floyd the contract to provide the lights and music for the first two UFOs. He and Hoppy had decided to try two gigs—one on either side of Christmas—and, if they were a success, to continue on a weekly basis. UFO immediately became the "in" club of the London underground scene and the Pink Floyd its resident house band.

The other house band was the Soft Machine. In many ways they were more committed to hippie ideas than the Floyd. The Soft Machine had their origins in Canterbury. Drummer Robert Wyatt was a central figure in the development of the scene, partly because his parents had a huge house that became the main hanging out place. His parents were part of a group of bohemian intellectuals who went to Majorca in the 30s, where they were friends with the poet Robert Graves. Robert grew up listening to Virgil Thompson, Shostakovich, Bartok, Webern, Monteverdi and Hindemith. His elder brother played Cecil Taylor, Mingus, Ornette Coleman and Duke Ellington. Other members Daevid Allen, Hugh Hopper and Brian Ratledge were equally musically eclectic and were tuned toward the avant-garde.

RIGHT: As the 60s progressed, artists absorbed psychedelic style. This is the cover of Texan psychedelia band the 13th Floor Elevators OVER: A flyer for the Scotch of St. James's club and the Beatles' proto-LSD album cover, Revolver (as in RPM).

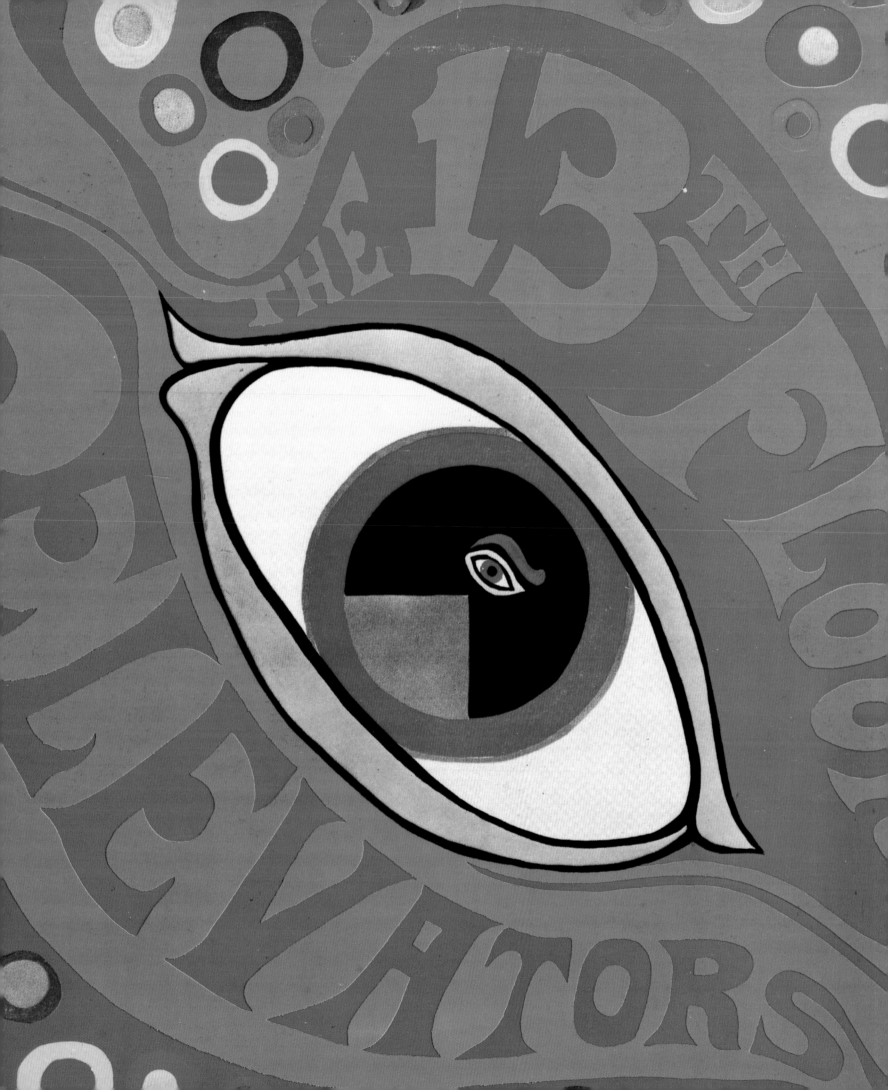

"It's a funny thing, but when you're dealing with your information second-hand, it all gets very distorted. You produce a very strange version of the thing that inspired you. Little elements of Haight-Ashbury and things like that did occur in Britain, but in a very odd way."

Pete Brown

LEFT: The Soft Machine in Kings Road psychedelic finery. Left to right, Kevin Ayers, Robert Wyatt, Mike Ratledge, Daevid Allen.
ABOVE: London clothes boutique, I Was Lord Kitchener's Valet. London psychedelic style embraced Victorian uniforms. Jimi Hendrix was arrested for impersonating an officer by wearing a dragoon jacket.

The fashion scene in London was centered around Chelsea's Kings Road until Biba opened in Kensington. The fashionable hippies of Europe would dress themselves almost entirely in clothes bought at one London boutique or another. Granny Takes A Trip, Hung On You, Lord Kitchener's Valet and in 1967 the Beatles' Apple boutique made extraordinary, psychedelic outfits to suit any trip.

LEFT: A Biba hat.
RIGHT: Two pairs of identical twins model fashions at Biba Fashion. Biba made boutique fashion available to the general public, and was often so crowded that there was a line outside.
OVER (LEFT): A Kings Road hippie couple model the look, 1966. OVER (RIGHT): The Who's A Quick One sleeve used LSD-inspired graphics in an effort to appeal to hippies as well as mods.

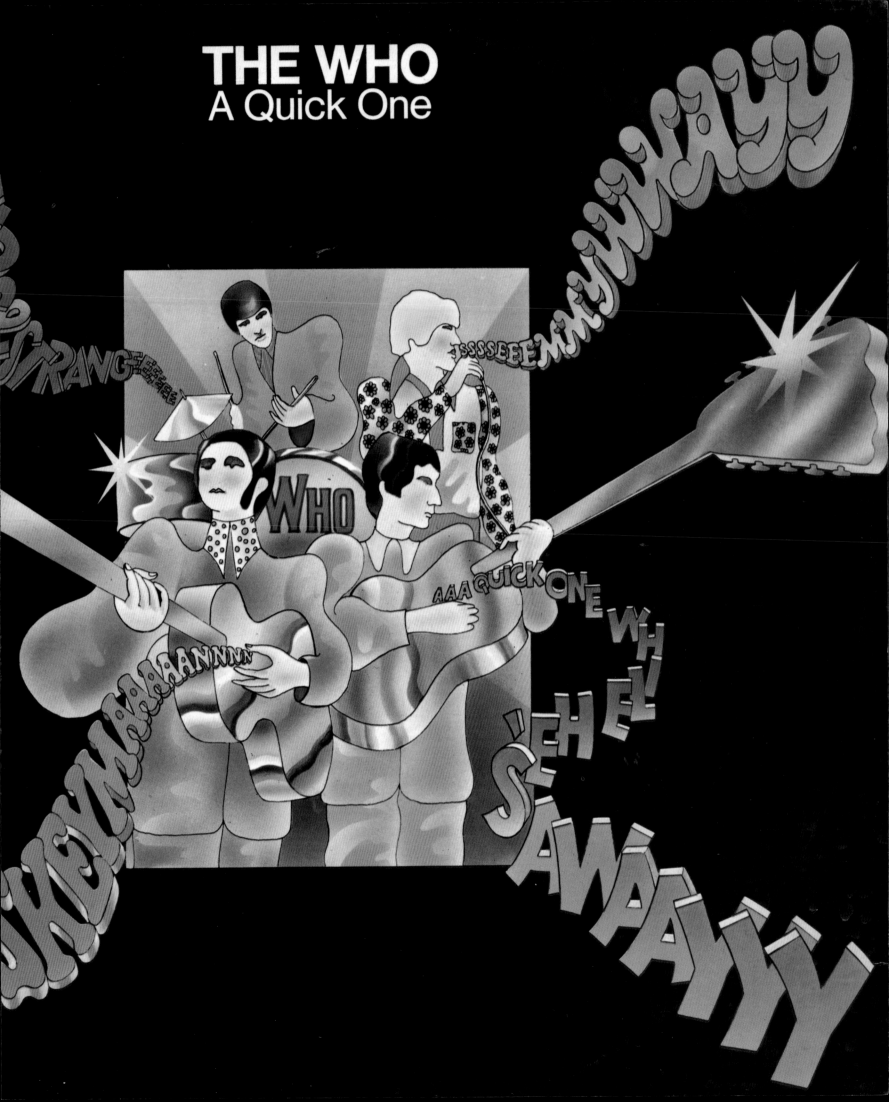

This was the year of the Summer of Love, but it also saw the beginning of a massive police clampdown on hippies and the counterculture. It opened with Be-Ins in San Francisco and Los Angeles, and saw tens of thousands of young people arrive in Haight-Ashbury, looking for love and peace and beautiful people.

6566 67 686970 71

It was the year of Sgt. Pepper, Surrealistic Pillow, Satanic Majesties, and dozens more psychedelic classics; it was the year that Jimi Hendrix first astonished London then took on America at the Monterey Pop Festival, the festival that also launched Janis Joplin beyond the Bay Area, introduced the Who to the West Coast and Wilson Pickett to a white audience.

It was also a year of protest as American involvement in Vietnam continued to grow. The black community was also in uproar and 43 people died, 2,000 were injured and 5,000 made homeless in a week of riots in Detroit, Michigan.

As waves of tourists, dropouts and runaways descended on San Francisco, the Diggers opened up crash pads, a free store and began a soup kitchen in Golden Gate Park while the Family Dog at the Avalon Ballroom and Bill Graham at the Fillmore both opened all week through the summer to cater to the crowds of young people. Owsley became a multimillionaire by selling LSD, then other, more dangerous drugs. Jack Casady tried some of Owsley's new STP at Monterey Pop and finished up in jail after police found him sitting in a mud puddle, baying at the moon. The Haight became more tripped out and Berkeley more radical.

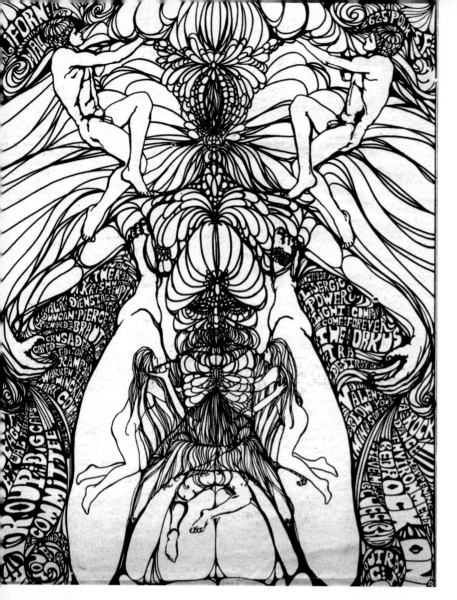

GROOVIN' ON A SUNNY AFTERNOON

HUMAN BE-IN

The Diggers were still at Frederick Street when the Human Be-In was planned. Even though they were suspicious of the event, which they saw as a calculated way of getting publicity by the HIP merchants on the Haight, they nonetheless supported it. The HIP merchants had not helped out with the free food or free store programs at all, but before the Be-In, Owsley sent round ten thousand tabs of acid. The Diggers saw this as a test. As the pills were pure white, and had not yet been released on the market, it would be easy to see if they appeared on the market. True to their word, the Diggers gave them all away. Everyone on the street got five each, to take, sell, throw away or

eat all at once. Having passed the test, Owsley sent round some more—it was his famous powerful White Lightening batch—and also 75 twenty-pound turkeys to cook for the Be-In.

The Be-In was organized with a press conference, three different posters, press releases and by word of mouth. The Berkeley Barb, normally a bit sniffy about Haight-Ashbury, enthused over the idea: "The spiritual revolution will be manifest and proven. In unity we shall shower the country with waves of ecstasy and purification. Fear will be washed away; ignorance will be exposed to sunlight; profits and empire will lie dying on deserted beaches; violence will be submerged and transmuted in rhythm and dancing."

Known alternatively as "A Human Be-In," "Pow Wow" and "A Gathering of Tribes," the event was held on January 14, 1967 in the polo field of Golden Gate Park. All day long people drifted to the park. The crowd was not there to protest anything, they had no demands to make, it was simply a celebration of being together. Some aspects of the event have been criticized: the Diggers objected to the stage full of self-appointed gurus and leaders, and others pointed

PREVIOUS PAGE: Inside the Fillmore, dancers enjoy a psychedelic light show.
RIGHT: A huge crowd had assembled at the Human Be-In, but no one was making speeches, they were just having a good time.

out that, of the 30,000 strong crowd, there were very few nonwhite people. Allen Ginsberg was there in his white Indian pajamas, accompanied by his then girlfriend Maretta Greer, as were Gary Snyder with a conch, Timothy Leary in guru mode and Berkeley politico Jerry Rubin in full radical garb, calling for a marriage between the Berkeley and Haight-Ashbury tribes. Lenore Kandel read from the Love Book and Ginsberg chanted the Hari Om Namo Shivaya mantra to Shiva, the god of hash smokers. In fact, very little of the poetry or speeches could be heard in the field, but few people were actually that interested. The crowd wanted to see and be with each other.

And in the field girls were in long dresses and miniskirts, mothers were with babies, fathers were with babies, people wore masks, fancy dress, leather capes, feathers, body paint and see-through tops. There were people with tarot cards, astrologers, sufi dancers, Hare Krishna chanters, jugglers, stovepipe hats, porkpie hats, soap bubbles, balloons, people carrying kittens, people high on marijuana, people high on acid. A single-engine plane flew overhead and someone parachuted out of it into the meadow; thousands of people thought they had seen God. Many people claimed it was Owsley, but the unknown parachutist managed to slip quietly away.

The Diggers had crushed up the new supply of acid pills given to them and added it to the bread mix for the turkey sandwiches that were distributed by John-John, who handed them out to those that looked like they needed them. Owsley's White Lightening was also being distributed free by his agents, who circulated through the crowd. The stage and generator truck were guarded by the Hell's Angels after someone tried to cut the power lines. The best entertainment was the music, which went well with the turkey sandwiches. The names of the bands alone gave a perfect idea of the event: The Hedds, Moby Grape, Earth Mother and the Final Solution, Sopwith Camel, The Freudian Slips, the Jefferson Airplane, the Chosen Few,

RIGHT: More than a dozen local bands donated their services for free at the Human Be-In in Golden Gate Park, the first—and almost the last—of the great hippie community events.

"What I have to say can be summed up in six words— tune in, turn on, drop out."

Timothy Leary

the Grateful Dead, Big Brother and the Holding Company, the Only Alternative and his Other Possibilities. At the end of the day at 5pm, Gary Snyder blew his conch and Allen Ginsberg led the crowd in chanting Om Sri Maitreya, the mantra of the Buddha of the Future. Then he led a house-keeping team to clean up the trash. As the sun neared the horizon, thousands of people turned east and walked towards the Pacific Ocean. They crossed the highway and watched the sun go down from the Ocean Beach strand, where they built fires and walked along the beach. It was a beautiful event and one that was subsequently repeated in cities all over the world. It was also the last day of innocence for the Haight.

According to Allen Ginsberg it was the last idealistic hippie event.

THE LOVE GENERATION

That night the police swept down Haight Street, arresting 50 people. When a group of concerned friends showed up at the Fillmore, where the Doors and the Grateful Dead were playing that evening, Bill Graham refused to let them make a collection to get people out on bail. At the Avalon they managed to raise $50. All the soft drug dealers were driven off the scene or arrested and

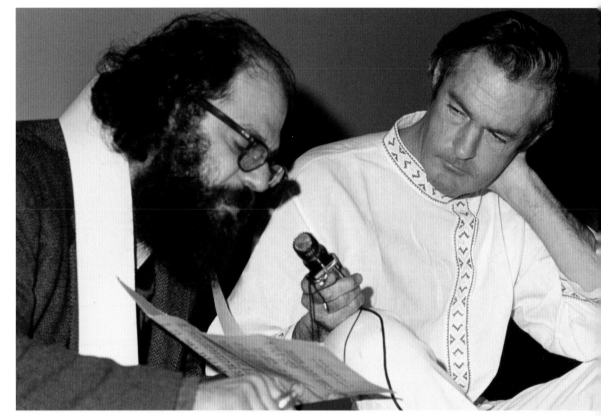

LEFT: The cover of Jefferson Airplane Takes Off, the band's debut album release.
ABOVE: Allen Ginsberg and Timothy Leary.

within weeks the area was flooded with heroin and amphetamines. So much so that even the most skeptical reporter admitted that it looked planned. The communal nature of drugs such as LSD and pot—as manifested by the cleaning up of the park after the Be-In—was destroyed and replaced by amphetamine culture.

The HIP merchants, concerned by the Be-In night police raids and continual police pressure, handed out police whistles so that, in the event of further police harassment, everyone would blow their whistles in order to attract a crowd. It had been noted that they didn't like photographers around when they roughed people up.

On January 29 Ron Thelin and a number of other HIP merchants had a meeting with the police department. They pointed out that 26 new businesses had opened in the area in the previous nine months and asked for police support and protection, rather than harassment. They tried to explain their philosophy to bemused police chief Thomas Cahill, telling him how acid trips had changed their view of life and made them better people. After a while Chief Cahill said, "You're sort of the Love Generation, aren't you?" Previously they had used the terms "New Generation," "Hip Community" and others, but now the chief of police, of all people, had found the right name. Like the Lost Generation of the 20s and the Beat Generation of the 50s before them, they were the Love Generation.

Tim Leary, apolitical except when regarding his own busts, held up copies of the Berkeley Barb—in black and white—and the San Francisco Oracle, in full psychedelic rainbow color, and proclaimed that if Buddha were here today he'd read the Oracle. The Barb slagged him off in the next issue.

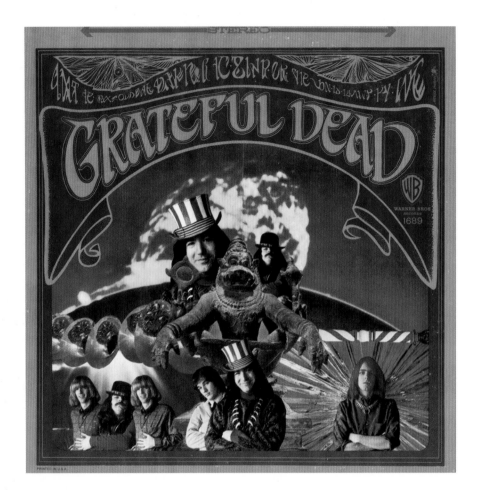

GROOVIN'

The soundtrack to Haight was from Los Angeles and London—the Dead, Quicksilver, Big Brother, Jefferson Airplane and the other groups had not yet released any records. On the turntables in the old Victorians were Revolver, "Strawberry Fields Forever," Dylan's "Rainy Day Woman No 12 & 35," the Byrds, Buffalo Springfield, the Doors, the Mothers of Invention and the Rolling Stones" Between The Buttons album. In the Haight, they mostly got their music live at the Fillmore, the Avalon and the Matrix. Other promoters tried to break into the market, but were quickly rebuffed.

That spring there were two new rumors: one, spread by Country Joe Macdonald, was that smoking banana peel could make you high. The other that LSD could scramble your chromosomes and cause damage to future children. The banana scam spread fast, every grocery store in the Haight sold out as people scraped and baked, liquidized and toasted. It was harmless fun: anthropologists wrote scholarly monographs in the underground press claiming it was ancient knowledge and chemists discussed chemical formulae. Donovan released "Mellow Yellow" with its line about "electrical banana" and, responding as usual to the latest craze, Warhol put a peel-off banana on the sleeve of the Velvet Underground's first album. All through the summer, the hippies ate lots of fruit which was very good for them, even if the skins didn't do a thing except in their imagination. The story about acid damaging your chromosomes originated in Science, a scholarly journal, where it had been noted that large doses of acid did damage the chromosomes of rats. There was no evidence that it affected humans and there still isn't.

LEFT: The debut LP by San Francisco's Grateful Dead.
RIGHT: Though hippie stores operated pretty much like any other shop, they didn't necessarily have to look the same and many were painted and decorated in psychedelic designs.

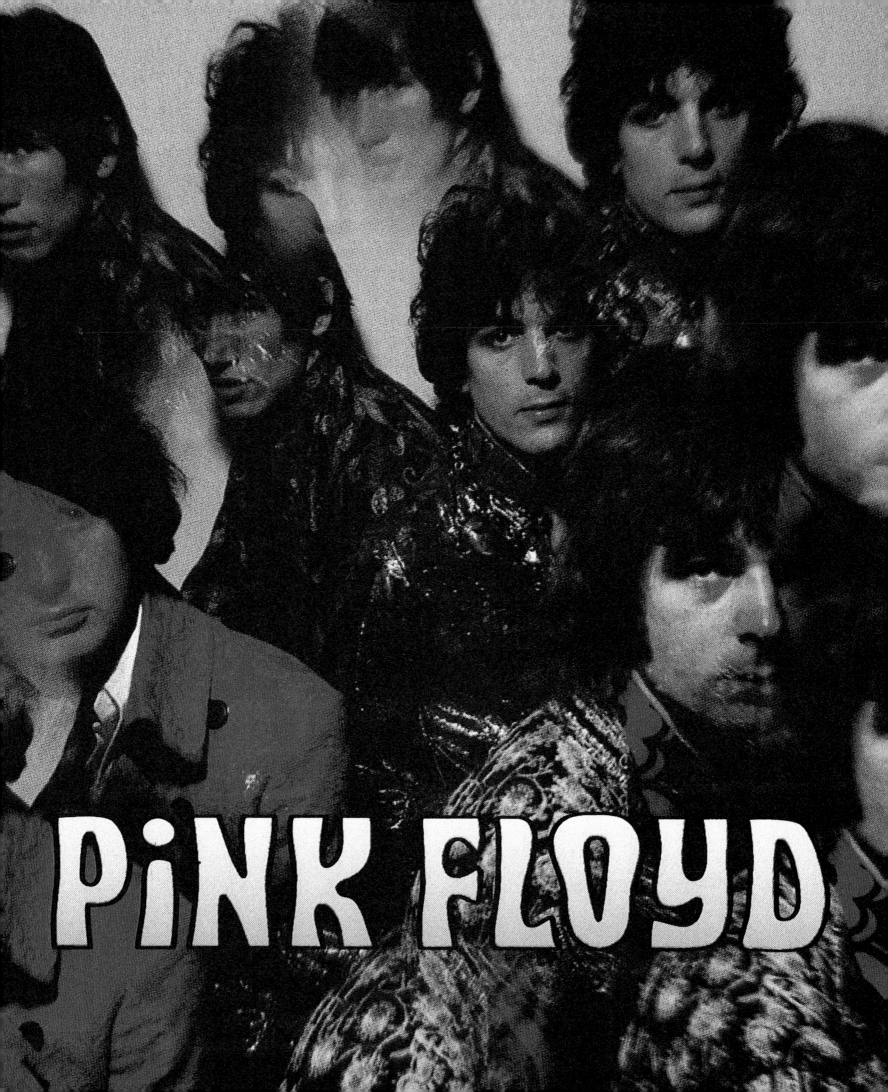

"You're sort of the Love Generation, aren't you?"

LOST LITTLE GIRL

After the Easter weekend, the visitors didn't go away. Haight Street was packed with people, many of them in standard high school gear with short hair, some of them obvious runaways, some artists, some poets. People competed for the oddest and strangest outfits—Haight Street never had the fashion sense that London did. Most of them looked like beggars, and in fact most of them were, but were happy to be so. There were many evangelists on the street as well—people proclaiming themselves to be the one true saviour, people with UFO cults to promote, and dozens of Christian missionaries toting the Bible. Some of them were in for a surprise when Hindu hippies tried to convert them

LEFT: The cover of Pink Floyd's seminal 1967 album Piper At The Gates of Dawn.

instead. The atmosphere was much as a medieval street fair must have been, and with the same undercurrent of violence and danger. On April 16 a Communication Company flyer read:

Pretty little sixteen-year-old middle-class chick comes to the Haight to see what it's all about & gets picked up by a seventeen-year-old street dealer who spends all day shooting her full of speed again & again, then feeds her 3000 mikes & raffles off her temporarily unemployed body for the biggest Haight Street gang bang since the night before last. The politics & ethics of ecstasy.
Rape is as common as bullshit on Haight Street.

Three thousand micrograms was twelve times the usual dose of acid. Rape was common, as were beatings and drug burns, but it was only the

Diggers and the All Saints first aid station that saw what was really happening on the street. Hardly anyone smoked pot any more, and speed, STP and heroin were rapidly overtaking acid as the drugs of choice. Speed freaks, particularly if they were eating badly and had nowhere to live, often turned violent or crazy. And junkies had no morality at all, they would do anything to get the money for the next hit. In May the Communication Company issued a flyer which said, "An Armed Man Is A Free Man." And into this, dozens of wide-eyed young people arrived each day from small-town America or from - protected middle-class environments.

That April there was another mass bust on the Haight. At 609 Ashbury, near the corner with Haight, a group of guitar players set up their equipment on a balcony and played an impromptu Rain Festival to the wet Sunday crowds. About 400 people gathered, some of

"Our smiles are our political banners and our nakedness is our picket sign!"

Jerry Rubin at the Be-In, San Francisco

LEFT: Thousands of young people arrived in Haight-Ashbury with nowhere to live and no money. Beggars became as common on the street as in Calcutta.
OVER: Inside a hippie poster shop on Haight-Ashbury.

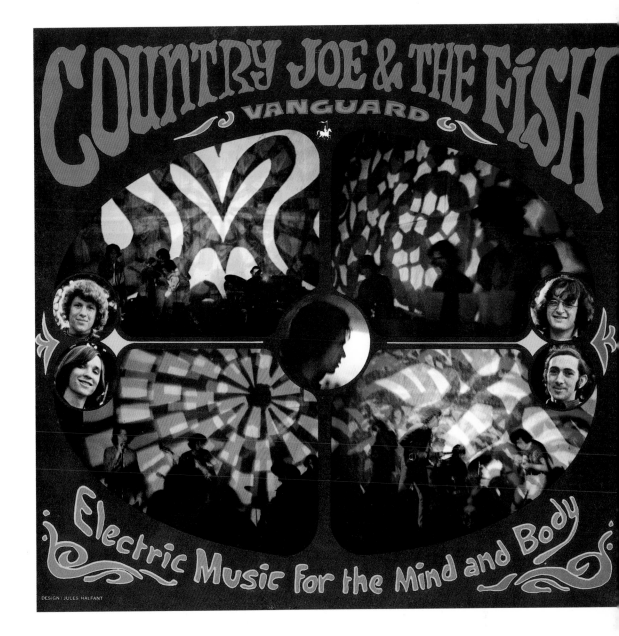

DESIGN / JULES HALFANT

them dancing naked in the rain, and when the police arrived to put a stop to the music, the crowd threw eggs and vegetables at them. Police reinforcements arrived and a phalanx of cops six abreast swept down the street making 50 arrests. Someone broke the valves off three of the tires of the lead paddy wagon, which slowed the arresting procedure down quite a bit as they couldn't pump up the flats.

In May, Country Joe and the Fish celebrated the release of their first album, Electric Music For the Mind and Body on Vanguard, which included the strange "Not So Sweet Martha Lorraine" but the crowd-grabbing "Feel Like I'm Fixin' To Die Rag." The Fish Cheer had to wait for their second album. Electric Music was launched with a free party at the Fillmore, during which five kilos of joints were given away. For that evening, at least, the Haight returned to the good old days.

ORANGE SUNSHINE

That spring the Jefferson Airplane appointed Bill Graham as their manager. Matthew Katz had proved too egotistical and unstable for them to work with any longer. (He made sure that his next group, Moby Grape, were utterly unable to ditch him by writing in ownership of the name and the publishing on virtually every contract they signed. It was only with difficulty that Columbia Records dissuaded him from calling the group Matthew Katz's Moby Grape on their first album, and got him to settle for his own logo instead.) Graham's first action, naturally, was to deal with the law suits that Katz had launched against the group. Though Graham was about as unpsychedelic as you could get, he nonetheless loved the group's music and presumably turned the other way when they threw LSD tabs out into the audience. Owsley's latest batch—called Orange Sunshine—was first introduced to the public that way.

On April 4 Paul McCartney and Beatles roadie Mal Evans flew into San Francisco in Frank Sinatra's Lear jet. They had flown from London to Los Angeles the previous day and were a little shaky from jet lag. San Francisco had just had its first snow in 42 years and they found it much colder than they had been expecting. After driving around and doing the sights such as the Golden Gate Bridge, they went to check out the Fillmore Auditorium. The Jefferson Airplane were rehearsing there and invited them back to the apartment that Marty Balin, Jack Casady and Bill Thompson shared on Oak Street. Paul had acetates of some of the tracks from Sgt. Pepper with him, including "A Day In The Life," which suitably impressed the band. They offered him some DMT, but when he asked what it was and was told it was nerve gas he politely declined and just smoked pot. They tried a jam session, but even after restringing Jack Casady's bass, Paul had great difficulty playing it upside down—he is left-handed. In the end jet lag won out and

In the week after Easter, the police staged a mass bust and headbreaking on Haight, making 32 arrests for such serious offenses as walking in the gutter.

Casady took Paul and Mal back to their hotel. The next day they took the Lear on to Denver, where Paul made a surprise appearance at his girlfriend Jane Asher's 21st birthday party.

As the Jefferson Airplane's "Someone To Love" and Scott McKenzie's saccharin "San Francisco (Be Sure To Wear Flowers In Your Hair)" filled the airwaves, world attention was fixed on San Francisco. In June a headline in the London Times read: "Flower Children Invade San Francisco." "The big 'hippie' summer invasion is about to begin, and San Francisco officials don't know what to do about it," they reported. "The hippies call themselves the love generation or the flower children. Theirs is a nonviolent, apolitical, gentle, altruistic, communal, thoroughly alienated

existence in which sex, 'dope' and self-exploration are what is happening."

Then, on June 16, 17 and 18, there was the Monterey International Pop Festival. This was the event that brought the San Francisco groups to the attention of the world and also introduced two major new British groups: the Jimi Hendrix Experience and the Who.

HALO

Organizations were coming into being to look after the crowds. Brian Rohan and Michael Stepanian were lawyers who opened HALO—the Haight-Ashbury Legal Organization—at 715 Ashbury, directly across the street from the Dead

house at 710, and there was a lot of traffic between the two. Most of the problems they dealt with concerned drug busts and runaways. By May, the Juvenile Justice Commission was returning 200 runaways a month to their parents from the streets of Haight-Ashbury and some of them tried to fight it.

There was also The Switchboard, a 24-hour help service that started up in May. They received about 100 calls each day, mostly from people looking for somewhere to stay or to get help for bad drug trips. Switchboard tried to find beds in crash pads for new arrivals—in fact they did more than any other organization to provide for the naive youngsters that flocked to San Francisco with flowers in their hair, looking for the beautiful

"Law, order, and health regulations must prevail. Any encouragement through the mass media tending to attract still more undesirables to the problem areas of San Francisco is a disservice to the community."

Police Chief Thomas Cahill, San Francisco PD

PREVIOUS PAGE: Police presence on Haight-Ashbury increased throughout the summer of 1967.
LEFT: Many of the kids arriving in Haight-Ashbury were very young and the street scene often looked more like recess at a high school than the streets of a city.

"How long did it take you to grow your hair that long, Danny?" Rifkin smiled. "We always figured that if we ever held a press conference, the first reporter to ask a stupid question would get a cream pie in the face, and you're him."

A Grateful Dead press conference

people. It was also somewhere that the parents of runaways could contact to leave messages. Papers like the Berkeley Barb then printed lists of names of parents who had left messages. There were a number of other, similar outfits that tried to find temporary jobs and places to live for people. One of these was called the British Embassy, and was run by a 21-year-old Englishman called Paul McCarthy (no relation).

On June 9 Dr. David Smith opened a 24-hour free medical clinic at 558 Clayton, on the corner with Haight Street. America had no free medical care and the hippies were in sore need of some. Smith was studying clinical toxicology and the patients at the Haight Street clinic gave him ample subjects for study, as they managed to poison themselves on an extremely wide variety of drugs, medicines and toxic substances. The Haight-Ashbury Free Medical Clinic was staffed by 30 part-time doctors, as well as scores of

medical volunteers, all of them donating their skills and time. The clinic provided free treatment for venereal diseases, which were rife, foot ailments and, of course, adverse drug reactions.

COMMUNAL LIVING

The Morning Star Ranch now housed scores of people and the Santa Rosa Press Democrat ran a series of articles about it, resulting in a local petition to close it down. In the spirit of independence for all, on July 4 Lou Gottlieb was given 24 hours to close down his "camp." Three days later Time magazine, in a story headlined "The Hippies," described Morning Star as "perhaps the most encouraging development of the hippie philosophy." According to Charles Perry, they were impressed by the neat rows of cabbages and vegetables in their garden. There were still a lot of Diggers living and working there—although

on July 5, the Diggers formally changed their name to the Free City Collective.

Meanwhile Ken Kesey had been through the courts for his rooftop bust and on May 2, after two hung juries, he was finally allowed to plead "nolo contendere"—"I'm innocent but I can't afford the legal fees to defend myself"—to a diminished charge of "knowingly being in a place where marijuana is kept." This had a maximum sentence of 90 days in prison. He was found guilty, and on June 22 he went to jail. They allowed him to serve his 90 days concurrent with the six months for his first grass bust.

Busts were occurring all the time. On July 9 a street incident in which some hippies tried to stop traffic on Haight escalated into violence, when someone threw a bottle at a policeman and hit a hippie girl instead. Twenty police cars sped to the scene and in the fight that ensued four people were seriously injured, nine arrested, and a woman who screamed, "Revolution, Revolution, Get the cops!" had her jaw broken in two places by a cop's nightstick. One man out walking his sheepdog was arrested and his dog killed by a policeman wielding a riot stick.

Two days later there was a bust that made news all around the world. On July 11 police

ABOVE: The front of the Haight Free Medical Clinic at 558 Clayton.
RIGHT: A typical family scene at the Morning Star Ranch Commune.

responding to a noise complaint arrived at 42 Belvedere Street at 3.30 in the morning. For the police it was a good haul: twelve joints, two suspect pills, two reels of suspected pornographic film and eighteen arrests. Among those arrested were two hairdressers, the assistant manager of the Seattle Symphony Orchestra, the Russian ballet star Rudolph Nureyev and his English dancing partner, Dame Margot Fonteyn, who was found hiding on the roof wrapped in her white mink coat. Nureyev and Fonteyn were in town to perform at the Opera House and police jubilation quickly turned to panic when they realized just how famous these people were. That afternoon the charges against all eighteen people were quickly dropped, the Assistant District Attorney saying that the evidence was insufficient to show who exactly was disturbing the peace and who had possession of the drugs. That evening, 200 hippies did a snake dance in front of the opera house, knowing that the world's most famous ballet dancers were on their side—even if only in secret.

GEORGE ON THE HAIGHT

It was just as the Haight reached its nadir that George Harrison decided to visit. On August 7 George and his girlfriend Patti Boyd, accompanied by Patti's sister Jenny (who was then married to Mick Fleetwood of Fleetwood Mac and living in San Francisco), ex-Beatles publicist Derek Taylor (soon to work for them again) and Beatles roadie Neil Aspinell, arrived by limo at Haight and Masonic. They had just flown up for the day from Los Angeles in a private Lear jet. After lunch they had all taken acid before setting off on their walk to see the famous Haight-Ashbury. George was wearing a blue denim jacket and heart-shaped shades. They walked up to Hippie Hill, at first attracting little attention, then as more and more people saw who it was, a crowd gathered. George was horrified by what he saw. To him it looked like a bunch of bums on the Bowery. "I thought it would be something like Kings Road [London] only more. Somehow I expected them all to own their own little shops. I expected them all to be nice and clean and friendly and happy." Instead he found himself surrounded by what he described as "hideous, spotty little teenagers." Someone asked him what he thought of Haight-Ashbury. "It's all too much," said the mystical one, quoting one of his own songs. Someone pushed a guitar in his hand and demanded that he sing something. The acid was really kicking in and he strummed a few chords as they strolled along, desperately trying to remember the words to "Baby You're A Rich Man," but they wouldn't come. He handed back the guitar and the crowd turned hostile and began to boo him. They turned and ran back to the waiting limo, surrounded by jeering hippies. So much for Haight-Ashbury. "They were all terribly dirty and scruffy," he said privately. Nonetheless, George supported the hippies—after all, he too was an acid freak.

GOIN' UP THE COUNTRY

In September Bill Graham reverted to opening at three-day weekends only, and most of the kids drifted back to their high schools and colleges for the new term. On September 16 the park officials announced that the hippie invasion was over and the police estimated that about 75,000 had visited the Haight that summer. To many people, the Haight was now like a burned-out battlefield, and many of the old-time residents began thinking of moving out, possibly to the country. Unfortunately, many of the places normally open to them were being closed down. Lou Gottlieb was still fighting the closure notice at Morning Star Ranch, for example. The court had enjoined him not to allow the public on to his property or to operate it as a camp, which would have required costly upgrading of the facilities. He was now allowing people to visit by claiming they were "prospective buyers" who were just trying the place out before parting with the seven-million-dollar asking price. It didn't work and in October the courts imposed a fine of $500 for each day that "guests" were on the premises. His "guests" refused to leave so he reluctantly had to ask the police to arrest the remaining fifteen of them. So much for Time magazine's "most encouraging development of the hippie philosophy."

Among the people looking to leave town were the Grateful Dead, who sent their "old ladies" on a property prospecting trip to New Mexico. Beautiful as it was down there, they returned saying that they preferred to remain near to San

RIGHT: George Harrison visits the Haight: "I expected them all to be nice and clean and friendly and happy."
OVER: The Death of Hippie march. It was a procession along Haight-Ashbury by local residents designed to show their displeasure at the increasing commercialization of a lifestyle choice that, to them, eschewed commerce.

"The hippies are a good idea—love, flowers, and that is great—but when you see the other half of it, it's like anything. I love all these people, too, those who are honest and trying to find a bit of truth and to straighten out the untruths. I'm with them one hundred percent, but when I see the bad side of it, I'm not so happy."

George Harrison

Francisco and began to look closer to home. To a certain extent they were being hounded out of town by the police. On October 2, 710 Ashbury was busted, along with two other houses.

Not all was lost in San Francisco, however. The four original members of the Family Dog had been working since May to restore and reopen the old Haight Theater, right on Haight Street. It was larger than either the Fillmore or the Avalon, with a higher legal capacity, and was right in the center of the scene. Big Brother, Quicksilver and Owsley all put money into the scheme. The building inspectors made their work as difficult as possible, waiting until work was done before revealing yet another requirement that meant it had to all be torn out, but eventually—many tens of thousands of dollars later—it was complete and met all legal requirements. All it needed was a permit, and this of course was rejected. After their second appeal was rejected, their lawyers came up with a way around the law. Dance schools did not need the same certification as

dance halls. There was already a modern dance school in the Masonic Hall, next door to the Straight Theater; this now relocated to the Straight Theater and became the Straight School of Dance, offering public dance instruction. Ann Halprin, the nationally famous dance instructor, was among the instructors, along with Neal Cassady and members of the Grateful Dead. The poster read: "The Board of Permit Appeals Presents: Dance Your Misery Away. Professional Dance Lessons—5 Hours For Only $2.50. Instructors Include Jerome Garcia, Dr. P. Pen." It seemed that everyone wanted to learn how to dance and 2,000 people immediately enrolled in the student body.

Chet Helms' Family Dog was also showing confidence in the future, though Helms himself was less than confident in some of the plans. His partner Bob Cohen had been out to Denver and liked the scene so much that he signed the lease on a huge former factory in order to start a Denver Dog. But as usual the forces of reaction

soon closed in and Detective John Gray, the Denver equivalent of Cahill, vowed to drive the hippies out of town. After a program of systematic police harassment, in February 1968 they pulled out, but only after some spectacular false arrest and harassment court cases, one of which resulted in the firing of the police chief.

THE DEATH OF HIPPIE

The commemorate the anniversary of making LSD illegal, an alliance of Haight organizations including the Free Clinic, the Switchboard, the Free City (Diggers) and others, announced a Death of Hippie ceremony for October 6. The medical section of the Free Clinic had already closed and someone had embezzled the Switchboard, so it was deeply in debt. The Free Store had been damaged in a night-time burglary—they could have come in the day and every-thing would have been free, but junkies and speed freaks will do anything—and even the

Psychedelic Store, one of the leading HIP merchants, was $6,000 in debt. The Matrix was in financial trouble because they had given up their liquor license in order to let in minors. When police arrived in the early hours of October 6 to investigate yet another noise complaint and threatened to arrest Big Brother and the Holding Company, the Matrix management led the Death of Hippie ceremonies by closing in protest.

There was a wake at All Saint's Church, but the main ceremony began the next morning at dawn when about 80 candle-carrying people gathered at the top of Buena Vista Hill and ceremonially burned hippie artifacts, including bells and beads, marijuana (supposedly) and copies of underground newspapers, as well as the daily newspapers to get the fire going. They played Taps before setting off down Haight Street bearing a cardboard coffin containing a "representative hippie." They passed under a banner stretched across Haight that read: "Death of Hippie Freebie, i.e. Birth of the Free Man." The destination of the procession was the Psychedelic Shop that had filled its windows with signs reading: "Nebraska Needs You More," "Be Free," "Don't Mourn For Me, Organize." Inside the shop a girl was on a bad acid trip and the record player was turned up loud to cover her screams, which nonetheless cast a pall over the proceedings. That afternoon the police swept down Haight in the first of their regular daily searches for runaways. These were particularly bothersome for young men, who risked being picked up if they were not in possession of a draft card. If they didn't have one, they were assumed to be either underage or a draft dodger.

The hippie era was over. It had lasted little more than two years.

ABOVE: The Death of Hippie march held on the first anniversary of making LSD illegal. The coffin contained a "representative hippie" and the march was in many ways a closure of the hippie era. Nothing was ever the same again on the Haight as hard drugs decimated the community.

MONTEREY

"It was the first time many bands met and saw each other perform, so we were all really marvelling at each other. It was just one good group of people after another, and different kinds of music— Jimi Hendrix to Ravi Shankar, the Mamas and the Papas to the Who. They had a backstage area where there was food being cooked and served 24 hours a day, so everybody was wandering around meeting each other. It was just amazing."

Grace Slick

The Monterey International Pop Festival was first thought up by Alan Pariser, a Sunset Strip veteran who had put on a benefit for the people arrested after the Strip riots that had featured the Byrds and Buffalo Springfield. He and booking agent Benny Shapiro raised $50,000 and hired Derek Taylor as publicist. Taylor approached the Mamas and the Papas as the headline act. John Phillips, head Papa, loved the festival idea and, together with his producer and label owner, Lou Adler, ousted Pariser and Shapiro in a complicated manoeuvre by making the festival a charity fund raiser, with the groups all appearing for free.

In all 32 bands appeared from June 16 to 18, including the Who, Otis Redding, Janis Joplin, Jimi Hendrix, Country Joe and The Fish, Simon and Garfunkel, Canned Heat, Al Kooper, Steve Miller, Moby Grape, Paul Butterfield Blues Band,

Mike Bloomfield, the Byrds, the Blues Project, the Mamas and the Papas and Electric Flag. It was the first time many of the bands had been exposed to a large audience; some of them bombed like Laura Nyro, who couldn't handle it, and some of them, notably Hendrix, the Who and Janis Joplin, exploded onto the world scene with their performances at Monterey. It was the Jimi Hendrix Experience's American premier and no one knew what to expect; they certainly were not prepared for him to set his guitar on fire! The love and peace crowd did not really know how to react to the violence of the London bands, but were soon convinced that they were in the presence of something special and gave them a great reception. Janis Joplin was determined to make her name with her performance and pulled out all the stops. Unfortunately her thick-headed man-

ager refused to allow her first set to be recorded and so what was regarded by many people as one of the greatest moments in rock history was not preserved. After tremendous pressure from the group and from D. A. Pennebaker, who was filming the entire festival, she came on again the next day. Though it was a stunning set, the first is regarded as her lost masterpiece. Backstage she was approached by Dylan's manager, Albert Grossman, and soon joined him as a solo artist.

SUMMER OF LOVE

"How often have you taken LSD?" "Um, four times."

Paul McCartney being questioned on primetime television, June 19, 1967

By 1967 Los Angeles had established itself as the major music city. The Byrds, the Doors, Love, the Mothers, the Mamas and the Papas, Buffalo Springfield (whose "For What It's Worth" reached No. 7 in the charts in February 1967) and the Turtles (whose "Happy Together" topped the charts that year), had all transformed the former pop music capital into the rock music capital. Along the way it threw up dozens of minor 60s groups, such as the Association, who had hits with "Along Comes Mary" and the weird "Pandora's Golden Heebie Jeebies." There was also Sagittarius, the Peanut Butter Conspiracy, the Electric Prunes, the Bees, the West Coast Pop Art Experimental Band and—one of the best—the United States of America, featuring the pure clear voice of Dorothy Moskowitz.

One of the first LA psychedelic bands was the Seeds, which blossomed at Bido Lido's on the Strip in 1965. They had played lots of clubs before under other band names, but at Bido Lido they developed their own material and built a following. With Sky Saxon on lead vocals, Rock Andridge on drums, Daryl Hooper on keyboards and Jan Savage on lead guitar, they were an archetypal LA psychedelic band. Hooper claimed, "We were the first group to make an album of all original material, first to use a keyboard bass, and the first with really long hair. We coined the term 'flower power' for the peace and love movement, 'flower children' for the kids with the long hair and the beads, and 'flower music' for our particular sound." Their 1967 album Future was a psychedelic classic, with such tracks as "March of the Flower Children" and "Travel With Your Mind." They represented a naive, hedonistic side to the movement particular to LA, with Sky Saxon holed up in his Malibu pad overlooking the Pacific with a giant pool, waterfall, jacuzzi and all the psychedelic toys needed for a Hollywood dude to appear cool.

The Byrds, meanwhile, were going through line-up changes. With the departure of Gene Clark they released two albums as a foursome—Fifth Dimension and 1967's classic Younger Than Yesterday—but Clark's vocals were missed and the band that once dominated the LA music scene was in trouble. The pressures of fame, groupies and too many drugs did not help, but the band were together enough to release an ironic comment on their situation: "So You Want To Be A Rock & Roll Star?" One of the problems was that David Crosby was not a happy Byrd; he would rather have been in one of the Bay Area groups and spent a lot of time in Haight-Ashbury, hanging out with the Jefferson Airplane and other San Francisco groups. These tensions within the group were apparent from their ragged playing at the Monterey Pop Festival.

PEOPLE ARE STRANGE

The Doors were building and consolidating: their first album, The Doors, and the single "Break On Through" were released in January to a unique advertising campaign: they were the first rock act to have a billboard on Sunset Strip, which from then on became de rigueur for any group with clout. They played third on the bill at the Fillmore Auditorium after the Young Rascals and Sopwith Camel, and blew them both off stage. They arrived early in order to attend the Be-In in Golden Gate Park. They didn't play in the park—no one had asked them—but felt right at home. They did a week at Hullabaloo and a week at Gazzari's, their following growing all the time.

They then returned to San Francisco, this time to play at the hipper Avalon Ballroom, where they headlined over Country Joe and the Fish.

The venues got larger and larger. Elektra brought out a second single, "Light My Fire," which climbed the charts until, on July 25, they received the telephone call that informed them that they were No. 1 in the Billboard charts. By August both the single and their first album had gone gold.

They were now stars, with managers, lawyers, accountants and huge amounts of money. Morrison celebrated by buying a skin-tight black leather suit and in August they began recording a second album, titled Strange Days, with Paul Rothchild as producer. Jerry Hopkins' Morrison biography gives a good idea of the atmosphere in the studio at the time: "Paul suggested that Jim get some girl to go down on him while he was singing 'You're Lost Little Girl' … Paul liked the idea so much he said he'd even pay for a hooker. But Pamela liked the idea too, and she stripped right where she stood in the control room and padded softly into the vocal booth with Jim. Paul waited for a slow count of 60, then said, 'Uhhhhh … you let me know when, uhh you're ready, Jim.' About twenty minutes later Jim entered the control room and Paul shrugged his shoulders. 'Well,' he said. 'You can't win 'em all.'"

By the end of the year the press were clamoring for interviews with Morrison, who was seen as a new James Dean or Brando. Time, Newsweek, Look, the Saturday Evening Post,

RIGHT: In Los Angeles the freaks had their own stylish version of psychedelic fashions, which the Doors parodied with this, the sleeve to their second album, Strange Days.

forever changes

"Forever Changes finished what Da Capo began—Arthur Lee's insane mutation of Mick Jagger into Johnny Mathis."

Sandy Pearlman on the first two Love albums

LEFT: David Crosby of the Byrds on stage, soon to fly the nest.
OVER (LEFT): Public smoking of dope increased through the summer.
OVER (RIGHT): Singer Barry "Eve of Destruction" MacGuire feels the love all around him with a friend at an open-air gig.

Vogue and the New York Times all notched up column inches on this good-looking new star, and the Sunset Strip groupies were now complemented by society ladies and movie stars.

Love also released an album in January 1967 called Da Capo. It was an ornate masterpiece unique to Los Angeles that quickly became part of the psychedelic canon. They returned to the studio and recorded the even more orchestral Forever Changes.

"The doors of perception were flung open and everybody in the rock scene was liberated. They would no longer conform."

Jack Good, television producer of the 60s

Being part of Big Brother & the Holding Co. gave Janis a family, and the close-knit community of musicians in San Francisco provided friendship and occasional lovers.

LEFT: A poster advertising the first LA gig for Big Brother & the Holding Co. Janis Joplin was not a big enough star to warrant a mention at the time.
OVER (LEFT): Hippie fashion became more ethnic on the West Coast of the USA than in Europe.
OVER (RIGHT): Psychedelic design of a British poetry anthology, It's World That Makes The Love Go Round.

POEMS FROM BREAKTHRU

IT'S WORLD THAT MAKES LOVE GO ROUND

SUMMER IN THE CITY

"There wasn't too much going on in the Village that interested me. The people who came to see us at the Garrick mostly had short hair, they came from middle-class white Jewish environments, mostly suburban. They came to see our show because we were something weird that was on that street and we were a sort of specialized recreational facility."

Frank Zappa

Whereas the summer of love in California was a time to frolic in the parks, in New York the high temperatures simply revealed the terrible squalor of the Lower East Side: the burnt-out cars, the overflowing garbage cans, the backyards filled with trash. The area was dangerous at the best of times, but in the summer, with everyone out on the stoops, the incidents of rape and muggings increased alarmingly. Most hippies tried to get out to the country or, even better, to go to California, and this left a large, hardcore community centered around Tompkins Square Park and the surrounding blocks.

New York had its heroes: Timothy Leary, Allen Ginsberg and many other Beat Generation figures were still around, and the Hotel Chelsea was filled with writers and poets, filmmakers and musicians, from Harry Smith to Leonard Cohen, Viva to Arthur C. Clarke. Arthur Miller still lived there, having moved in after breaking up with Marilyn Monroe; it was also where Dylan lived when he wrote "Sad-Eyed Lady of the Lowlands" and where Andy Warhol made Chelsea Girls. Lots of Warhol superstars were still living there, Nico among them. The Chelsea was to New York what Laurel Canyon was to Los Angeles. If you could afford to live in the Chelsea you were automatically accepted into a free and easy scene. Josie on the switchboard always knew which room the party was in and in the summer great gangs of people gathered on the roof to sunbathe and smoke pot.

FREAK SCENE

In March, the Mothers of Invention arrived in town for an Easter gig at the Garrick Theater on Bleeker Street, which was so successful that the promoter decided to hold them over through the summer. After expenses they each received

RIGHT: The famous Hotel Chelsea at 222 West 23rd Street. Its rooms have been home to Janis Joplin, the Jefferson Airplane, Bob Dylan, Dylan Thomas, William Burroughs, Arthur Miller, Thomas Wolfe and other artists, writers and filmmakers for over a century.

about $200 a week, which was not bad money and it was regular. Zappa and Gail took an apartment at 180 Thompson Street, just around the corner from the Garrick, and settled in. Most of the time there were at least four people sleeping on the living room floor, their sleeping bags in a neat row.

The Garrick was upstairs from the Café a-Go-Go, next door to the Bleeker Cinema, in what had been the center of the folk music scene just a few years before. Now the clubs were switching to rock 'n' roll. With a long steady gig, the Mothers were able to relax and experiment. Zappa called the show Absolutely Free: Pigs and Repugnant, and pushed it to the limit.

"One time we brought 30 people up on stage and some of them took our instruments and the rest of them sang 'Louie, Louie' as we left."

Frank Zappa

When the suburban kids had finished being insulted by Zappa, they could always go around the corner to the Players" Theater, where the Fugs also had a summer-long gig. The Fugs were even more anarchic. There was one show, called "The Night of the Great Spaghetti Death," when they dumped 200 lbs of warm spaghetti over the audience. Not the best thing to happen if you were out on a first date.

Bob Dylan remained sequestered in his Woodstock home for most of 1967, recuperating from his accident. Michael Iachetta visited him in May, and Dylan told him, "What I've been doing mostly is seeing only a few close friends, reading a little about the outside world, poring over books by people you never heard of, thinkin' about where I'm going, and why am I running, and am I mixed up too much, and what am I knowing, and what am I givin' and what am I takin'. And mainly what I've been doing is working on getting better and making better music, which is what my life is all about."

He spent time jamming with his friends Robbie Robertson and other old members of the Hawks in the house that they called Big Pink on a mountaintop in the West Saugerties a few miles from Dylan's home. That summer he also recorded about a dozen new songs in his basement, which, after years of being bootlegged, were released as the Basement Tapes. Then in October, just after Blonde On Blonde went gold, Dylan travelled to Nashville and, accompanied by

three country musicians—Charlie McCoy on bass, Kenny Buttrey on drums and Pete Drake on steel guitar—he cut Nashville Skyline; about as far from the old Dylan psycho-babble as you could get.

LSD

Tim Leary was often away from Millbrook, providing a welcome escape from the police harassment. As he fought his Mexico bust through the courts, the local police, led by Assistant District Attorney G. Gordon Liddy (who was later jailed for his role in the Watergate break-in) staged two raids on the Big House in 1966, both of which were thrown out of court on technicalities.

Leary became more spiritual. He had started his own religion, the League for Spiritual Discovery (LSD) the previous summer, and on the last day of 1966 it took over all the duties of the previous Castalia Foundation. Leary now referred to himself as a "prophet, a spiritual teacher. In other times I might have been called a messiah, or a guru, or a shaman or a medicine man ... how ironic that an American Irishman should be forced into sainthood!" Thousands of young acid heads lapped it up. To reinforce the religiosity of the place, sixteen members of the Adanda Yogic Ashram moved into Millbrook during the summer of 1966, making it the headquarters of three religious organizations—the third being Art Kleps' Neo-American Church, an acid religion which had

him set up as Chief Boo-Hoo, whose slogan was "Victory Over Horseshit").

The summer of 1967 saw Leary having fun because he had made some remarkable discoveries: "The conclusion I have come to after seven years of utopian living is that the basic problems are familial and sexual and that unless the individual has his sexual energies harnessed and harmonious, so that they're not spinning him off center, unless he has some enduring, growing family set-up, anything he does ... I see group sex as a very, almost necessary stage."

In July 1967 the police began systematic harassment once more, stopping every car in and out of the estate and making over 40 arrests for such crimes as "dirty number plate," and "obscured windshield." Wendy, Art Kleps' wife, was arrested for "lack of identification" when she rode into town on her bicycle. Tim and Rosemary moved to Berkeley, where Leary still had the house on Queens Road and, with them gone, Billy Hitchcock gave everyone else four months to get off the premises. On December 9 the Millbrook police raided once again, with warrants for "Conspiracy to Create a Public Nuisance." It was just another day in court in the "land of the free" for most of them.

RIGHT: Hippies prepare for the New York Be-In by painting their faces.
OVER: Hippies at the Central Park Be-In, New York.

"We rented a flat-bed truck and a sound system, and we chanted 'demons out.' It's on the Tenderness Junction album. The idea was for a formal exorcism that would exorcise the evil spirits from the Pentagon. It didn't work because the war went on for another seven years. We hoped it would work but we weren't prepared to crawl under if it levitated."

Ed Sanders of The Fugs on their attempt to levitate the Pentagon

FLOWERS IN THE RAIN

The year opened in London with the rapid growth of the UFO Club. The Pink Floyd, the Soft Machine and the Crazy World of Arthur Brown were the house bands. Brown always entered wearing a flaming headdress that more than once had to be put out with a pint of beer emptied over his head when his cloak caught fire. (There was no alcohol sold, but the bands had some backstage.) Procol Harum played their second ever gig there, the Move made an attempt at underground credibility by playing there, but the audience didn't like their mohair suits and aggressive act and booed them. The rest of the country, however, seemed convinced by their nods to flower power with "I Can Hear the Grass Grow" and "Flowers In the Rain." The latter was the first single to be played on BBC's new Radio One pop channel, but the publicity campaign, consisting of a psychedelic postcard involving a drawing of the prime minister, Harold Wilson, naked in the bath assisted by his secretary, attracted a winning libel suit and they received no royalties from this, despite it being one of their biggest hits. Jimi Hendrix, whose manager, Chas Chandler of the Animals, now also managed the Soft Machine, used to come down in the early hours and jam with whoever was on stage.

UFO was more than just music. There were full-length movies screened at the side—everything from Marilyn Monroe to avant-garde work by Kenneth Anger or William Burroughs—and there were several different light shows to watch, including one by Fireacre Lights, a psychedelic nudist colony near Watford that consisted mostly of local teachers living in caravans. The clubhouse had a "trip machine" made up of an electrically powered wheel on the ceiling, from which strips of silver Mellonex hung down to the floor. As the wheel slowly turned, the assembled tripping nudists watched the flashing colors.

The food at UFO was by Greg Sams from the macrobiotic restaurant and was very welcome at 3am. Acid and pot were easily obtainable from any number of the dealers there. International Times was on sale, as were other underground publications. The Kings Road clothes shops— Granny Takes A Trip, Hung On You and Dandy Fashions—were always represented in case anyone fancied ordering a frilly shirt or a pair of yellow crushed velvet loon pants. Later you could buy UFO posters there, but transporting them home intact was a problem.

The posters were by Michael English and Nigel Weymouth, who were known collectively as Hapshash and the Colored Coat, a derivative of Queen Hatshepsut who organized the legendary journey to Punt. They were published by Joe Boyd's company Osiris, which quickly branched out to make posters for other venues, such as Brian Epstein's Saville Theatre, or to promote boutiques and announce the launch of new records. Every two weeks there was a new UFO Club poster and people tried to collect them all, just as Fillmore and Avalon posters were col-

lected in the US. In fact very few of the American posters had reached Britain at that time and Hapshash evolved a style very different from their American counterparts. They had heard that the Americans used rainbow printing and, as they were using silk-screen, they soon produced work with coloring running from silver to gold one way, and from crimson to green on a second screen pass. But this proved very expensive to do and eventually the posters were produced by offset, like the American ones. Their influences were flying saucers, English children's stories, the art nouveau movement, Beardsley, the pre-Raphaelites and blobby psychedelic light shows.

When UFO became hopelessly overcrowded Brian Epstein offered the use of the Saville Theatre, which he owned, but Joe Boyd and Hoppy decided that the Roundhouse, where it all started, was a more appropriate venue.

The Roundhouse was now in much better condition, with toilets and a proper entrance, and it was already in use for events. In fact there was a "Giant Freakout" there on New Year's Eve, but the overheads were enormous.

PREVIOUS PAGE: Central Park Be-In. In New York even the hippies refused to smile.
RIGHT: Birmingham's The Move pose in full psychedelic gear in Soho Square. They played the UFO to little acclaim, yet their debut album (left) cover was designed by The Fool. Band member Roy Wood (left of picture) would later become a Glam star as Wizard.

"Do you think you have encouraged your fans to take drugs?" "I don't think it will make any difference. You know, I don't think my fans are going to take drugs just because I did."

Paul McCartney answers questions

THE EXPERIENCE

The year 1967 saw a number of big concerts and dances in London. On January 6 there was "Freak Out Ethel" at the Seymour Hall, with Pink Floyd, Ginger Johnson's African Drum Band, Alexander Trocchi and Karma-Sigma, as well as light shows, films and slides. On January 17 the Pink Floyd played the Commonwealth Institute and on January 28 there was "A Million Volt Rave" at the Roundhouse, with lights by Binder Edwards and Vaughan and featuring a random sound, free-form electronic tape made by Paul McCartney and played by all four Beatles.

The greatest new sound heard in London, however, was Jimi Hendrix. He had arrived in Britain the previous September and quickly made a name for himself jamming at the late night clubs, but his manager, Chas Chandler, often had to spirit him off stage because he had no work permit and was not allowed to play, paid or otherwise. Within a month they had hired Noel Redding on bass and Mitch Mitchell on drums, and the Jimi Hendrix Experience was in rehearsal. After a short tour of France they went into De Lane Lee Music studios on Kingsway and recorded "Hey Joe." Decca turned it down (just as they did the Beatles). Rehearsals continued and Jimi and his new English girlfriend, Kathy Etchingham, moved into Ringo's old basement flat at 34 Montague Square, along with manager

LEFT: The Soft Machine took their name from the novel by William Burroughs, who used it to mean the human body. Here a Soft Machine fan uses it both ways. The lettering is from their second album.

Chandler and his girlfriend Lottie Lexon. Jimi was working hard rehearsing and writing during these few months—this was the period of "Purple Haze," "Stone Free" and "The Wind Cries Mary." Jimi loved to jam and was frequently seen down at the Speakeasy on Margaret Street, which had opened the previous December and had rapidly taken over from all the other clubs as the place to be if you were a rock star. Jimi didn't restrict himself to fashionable in-clubs. There was one memorable night at the UFO Club when he got on stage and played bass with Tomorrow.

Joe Boyd, the club's musical director, described the circumstances: "We had the Smoke booked in, but they got stuck in Germany. I rang up the agency and they sent down the In Crowd. I was pretty nervous at the thought of some group called the In Crowd playing at the UFO. But when they arrived at the club, we were informed they had changed their name to Tomorrow. Jimi Hendrix leapt up on stage and played bass and it was all very amazing."

With Keith West on vocals, Twink on drums and Steve Howe on guitar, Tomorrow became firm favorites with the UFO crowd, particularly when Twink wriggled along the top of the speaker stacks in his crushed velvet loon-pants and still managed to play drums at the same time. Their single "My White Bicycle" was one of the underground hippie anthems, always guaranteed to get the crowd up and dancing.

International Times ran out of money almost as soon as the first issue hit the streets, and the staff tried all means possible to make more. On January 29 they held an "Uncommon Market" at the Roundhouse, with fortune tellers and stalls

selling incense and hippie clothing. It was essentially a psychedelicized jumble sale, but a good time was had by all. More or less the same crowd could be seen that evening at the "Sunday At The Saville" show with the Koobas, the Who and the Jimi Hendrix Experience. It was the first big gig for the Experience and people were amazed.

TECHNICOLOR DREAM

The "14-Hour Technicolor Dream"—a fund-raiser for the fledgling International Times underground paper—was held on 29 April and featured the Pink Floyd, Alexis Korner, the Pretty Things, the Purple Gang, Champion Jack Dupree, Graham Bond, Yoko Ono, Savoy Brown, the Flies, Ginger Johnson's Drummers, the Crazy World of Arthur Brown, Soft Machine, the Creation, Denny Lane, Sam Gopal, Giant Sun Trolley, Social Deviants, the Block, the Cat, Charlie Brown's Clowns, Christopher Logue, Derek Brimstone, Dave Russell, Glo Macari and the Big Three, Gary Farr, the Interference, Jacobs Ladder Construction Company, Lincoln Folk Group, the Move, Mike Horovitz, 117, Poison Bellows, Pete Townsend, Robert Randall, Suzy Creamcheese, Mick and Pete, the Stalkers, Utterly Incredible Too Long Ago To Remember, Sometimes Shouting At People, Barry Fantoni, Noel Murphy and various others. Many of these were poets or dance groups, but still there were so many bands that two performed at the same time, one at each end of the giant hall, creating a strange neutral zone between them where both could be heard at equal volume. Many of the more than 10,000 people who attended hung around the neutral zone,

entranced by the stereo possibilities. Huge canvases had been hung on either side of the galleries for the light shows and the whole thing was controlled from a huge gantry in the center of the hall, where Hoppy and the UFO staff took care of lights and sound.

There was a fairground helter skelter and an igloo where you could smoke banana skins—that year's harmless scam. Skinheads who'd arrived hoping for a bit of trouble were seen skipping hand in hand with girls in lace and velvet dresses, out of their heads on acid. John Lennon saw it on the BBC TV news, jumped in the Rolls and arrived high on LSD. As the dawn broke through the giant rose window the Pink Floyd came on stage, having just arrived after playing a gig in Holland. Syd Barrett was on acid but he never sounded better. As people left, Hoppy stood at the entrance shaking hands with everyone. The skinheads, having now come down again, stole a ten-foot papier-mâché joint from some hippies and spent a happy hour kicking the monster to pieces on the parkland outside.

LEFT: Left to right, Michael English and Nigel Weymouth, working as Hapshash and the Colored Coat, were the premier psychedelic poster designers in London. They were first introduced to each other in order to make posters for the UFO Club, but soon branched out into other areas, developing a unique style involving silk-screen rainbow printing. Here they are surrounded by their work. They formed a rock group using the same name, which included record producer Guy Stevens (standing).

ALL YOU NEED IS LOVE

Talk of drugs filled the air. On May 19, weeks before the release of Sgt. Pepper, the BBC, in its self-appointed role as guardian of public morality, banned the track "A Day In The Life" in case it was about drugs. Sgt. Pepper was released on June 1 and became the supreme psychedelic album of the era.

From San Francisco to Moscow, where copies were smuggled in, every note and every word was dissected and played over and over. Then, as if to confirm their support for the hippie movement, on June 25 the Beatles appeared live on the BBC's Our World Live—the first international live telecast linking television stations around the world—and with an audience of 200 million, they sang "All You Need Is Love" dressed in their psychedelic finery.

EMI's massive studio was filled with flowers and potted plants and among the guests were Keith Richards, Eric Clapton, Graham Nash and Gary Leeds and the Faces, dressed up in new Granny Takes a Trip clothes. Keith Moon fooled around on the drums with Ringo during the long wait before transmission. Mick Jagger sat on the floor with Marianne Faithfull, smoking a large joint. Two days later, Jagger was sent to jail.

STONE FREE

This was the year the Rolling Stones had their greatest media exposure, most of which they would rather have done without. On February 5 the News of the World reported that Mick Jagger had taken LSD at the Moody Blues' house in Roehampton. Typical of the News Of the World, the story was a year old and their reporter had mistaken Brian Jones for Jagger. Mick over-reacted and foolishly announced on ABC-TV's Eamonn Andrews Show that he was suing the News of the World for libel.

Jagger's writ was issued on February 10. Two days later, Redlands, Keith Richards' house in West Sussex, was raided by police tipped off by the News of the World that a drug party was taking place. It was widely believed that an American called David "Acid King" Sneidermann was acting as their informer in the Stones camp; certainly he was the one who suggested the party and who provided the drugs. He was also the only one not searched and was allowed to leave the country immediately afterwards. Everyone else was searched and police seized suntan lotion, Earl Grey tea and other suspect substances for analysis. Marianne Faithfull had just taken a bath and was wrapped in a large fur rug when police arrived, something they regarded as somehow degenerate. Though the police did not make the raid public, that weekend the News of

SUNDAYS AT THE SAVILLE
A NEMS PRESENTATION

OCTOBER 8: 6 p.m. and 8 p.m.

JIMI HENDRIX EXPERIENCE

CRAZY WORLD OF ARTHUR BROWN

JOHNS CHILDREN
CRYING SHAMES

BOOK TEM 4011

THERE ARE SUNDAY SHOWS EVERY WEEK-END
AT THE SAVILLE
ASK FOR FULL DETAILS AT THE THEATRE BOOKING OFFICE

the World carried a carefully worded report, headlined, "Drug Squad Raid Pop Stars' Party"—information no other paper had.

The police waited for George Harrison and Patti Boyd to leave the party before going in—at that point the Beatles were still untouchable. The police had noted, however, that the Beatles and Stones were best of friends, and this was true. On the day the writ was issued Mick, Keith, Marianne and Donovan had attended the Beatles' recording session at Abbey Road to see the Beatles and a 40-piece orchestra record "A Day In The Life," and they saw a lot of each other socially.

The Stones escaped the depressing atmosphere caused by the drug bust by going to Tangier, but en route Brian Jones' girlfriend, Anita Pallenberg, left him for Keith.

On March 16, in Marrakesh, the painter Brion Gysin took Brian to the great Djemaa el Fna public square to record Moroccan trance music and smoke hashish with the Mejdoubi brothers who, in Gysin's words, "go into their long drawn out mint tea routine which can take a whole afternoon." But while Brian was away from the hotel, Keith and Anita Pallenberg, accompanied by Mick and Marianne, flew back to London, leaving him stranded in Morocco without even a note to say where they were. A distraught Brian Jones flew back two days later. The splits within the group were showing.

On May 10 Mick Jagger and Keith Richards, along with art dealer Robert Fraser—also known as "Groovy Bob"—appeared in court at Chichester, Sussex and were released on bail of £100 each, to be tried on June 22. The police drove their message home by raiding Brian Jones' London flat that same day and arresting him along with Stash de Rollo (Prince Stanislaus Klossowski) for unlawful possession of drugs. Brian was remanded on £250 bail.

WE LOVE YOU

Mick Jagger was found guilty of having four anti-air sickness pills, bought over the counter in Italy but requiring a doctor's prescription in Britain. His doctor knew he had them, but couldn't issue a prescription because he already had them. Judge Block, one of the old-style reactionaries of the period, was determined to get the Stones. Mick's codefendant, Keith Richards, was found guilty of allowing his Sussex house to be used for

LEFT: Art dealer Robert Fraser and Mick Jagger are taken from the court in handcuffs after being sentenced at Chichester Crown Court. Jagger was freed on appeal but Fraser served four months of a six-month sentence in Wormwood Scrubs.

"The establishment was still very much the establishment."

Nigel Weymouth

LEFT: The 14-hour Technicolor Dream held at Alexandra Palace was the biggest and best of the British underground events.
OVER: The Rolling Stones" attempt at psychedelia, Their Satanic Majesties' Request (left) paled in comparison to American first wave psychedelic exponents such as the Red Crayola. The sleeve to their 1967 classic Parable of Arable Land is shown.

smoking hemp. The jury at West Sussex quarter sessions took six minutes to reach their verdict. They had retired after a ruling by the chairman, Judge Block, that Jagger had no defense to the charge. They were remanded to Lewes jail.

Reaction from the underground and the musicians' community was swift. The following day a host of newspapers, including the Evening Standard, carried an advertisement placed by the Who, which read: "The Who consider Mick Jagger and Keith Richards have been treated as scapegoats for the drug problem and as a protest against the savage sentences imposed upon them at Chichester yesterday, the Who are issuing today the first of a series of Jagger/ Richards songs to keep their work before the public until they are again free to record themselves."

If the Establishment wanted to confirm the hippies' belief that the law was prejudiced and corrupt, Judge Block could not have done a better job. Mick and Keith were granted bail in the High Court on June 30 in the sum of £7,000 each, but Robert Fraser remained in the Scrubs, where he served four months for possession of heroin.

The hippies were not the only ones who thought that Judge Block was making the law look like an ass by issuing draconian sentences for minor drug offenses by first offenders. On July 1 The Times, risking contempt of court as an appeal was pending, published a leader headed "Who Breaks A Butterfly On A Wheel?" by editor William Rees Mogg. It was a damning criticism of the sentences given to Mick Jagger and Keith Richards and was echoed by most of the other newspapers in their later editions.

On July 31 the Appeals Court lifted the sentences against Mick and Keith.

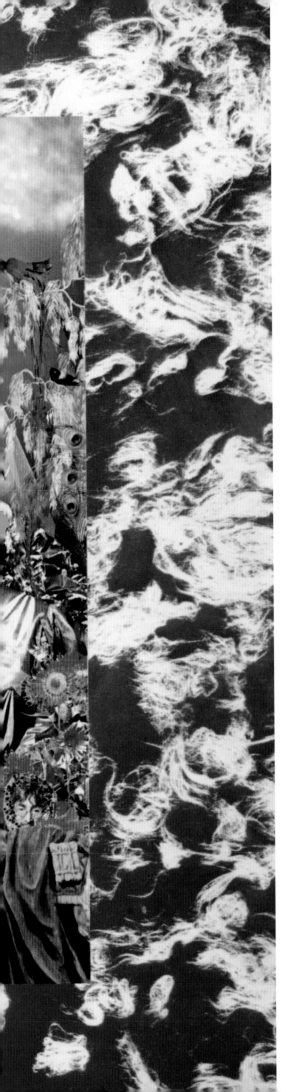

The Rolling Stones' contribution to psychedelia, Their Satanic Majesties' Request, was released on December 8. It went straight to No. 3 on the charts. The publicity had done some good.

"The use of cannabis is widespread among junior members of the university and the custom is also gaining favor among the dons."

Steve Abrams, Oxford University, 1967

LEGALIZE POT

Not only the rich and famous were being busted. In February Hoppy was busted at his communal flat in Queensway and in June he came up in court. Hoppy explained to the jury that marijuana was nonaddictive and in fact safer than alcohol. "You are a pest to society," said the judge, giving him nine months in Wormwood Scrubs for a tiny quantity of pot. Also jailed was Black Power leader Michael X for calling some Fleet Street reporters "white monkeys." Michael, who wrote regularly for IT, thus became the first person charged under the Race Relations Act, designed to protect black people. William Burroughs volunteered to be Michael's interpreter in court, but Michael opted to represent himself and did twelve months.

"Our entire lives have been affected lately by socio-political influences."

Brian Jones

Advertised on posters by Martin Sharp and Michael McInnerney, a Legalize Pot Rally was held at Speaker's Corner on 16 July, featuring Allen Ginsberg and assorted London policemen. When a policeman asked Ginsberg to stop playing his harmonium Allen politely quit and handed the man a flower. Not knowing what to do with it, he stood and held it. That night even the BBC-TV newsreader gave an Indian namasti sign as he signed off.

On July 24 a full-page advertisement headed "The law against marijuana is immoral in principle and unworkable in practice" appeared in The Times, calling for a change in the law regarding marijuana so that smoking cannabis on private premises would no longer constitute an offense. It demanded that cannabis be taken off the dangerous drugs list and controlled, rather than prohibited, that possession of cannabis be either legally permitted or at most be considered a misdemeanor, and that everyone now imprisoned for possession of cannabis or for allowing cannabis to be smoked on private premises should have their sentences commuted.

It was signed by 65 eminent people, including Nobel Laureate Francis Crick, the codiscoverer of the DNA molecule, novelist Graham Greene, Members of Parliament Brian Walden and Tom Driberg and future MP Jonathan Aitken, as well as all four Beatles and Brian Epstein. The £1,800 advertisement was paid for by the Beatles at Paul McCartney's instigation and caused a full-scale debate. Questions were asked in the House, setting off a chain of events that actually did result in the liberalization of the laws against pot in Britain.

LEFT: Beatles Paul McCartney and George Harrison sit with Jane Asher at the feet of the Maharishi in India.

A DAY IN THE LIFE

There was a pecking order in the higher reaches of the underground, and if the Rolling Stones were princes on the scene then the Beatles were kings. Remote, rarely seen, they nonetheless exerted a powerful presence. Sgt. Pepper was the anthem of the whole movement, and when they decided to investigate the Maharishi Mahesh Yogi, Mick Jagger, Marianne Faithful, Donovan and others all went along for the ride. The Maharishi was giving a weekend seminar in Bangor, Wales, and the Beatles, with full security, all went to hear him speak.

John Lennon found himself impressed and inspired by the experience. "Bangor was incredible, you know, Maharishi reckons the message will get through if we can put it across," he said, continuing, "What he says about life and the universe is the same message that Jesus, Buddha and Krishna and all the big boys were putting over. Mick came up there and he got a sniff and he was on the phone saying, 'Keith, send Brian, send them all down.' You just get a sniff and you're hooked.

"There's none of this sitting in the lotus position or standing on your head. You just do it as long as you like. (In a heavy accent) Twenty minutes a day is prescribed for ze workers. Twenty minutes a morning and tventy minutes after verk. Makes you happy, intelligent and more energy. I mean look how it all started. I believe he just landed in Hawaii in his nightshirt, all on his own, nobody with him, in 1958.

"The main thing is not to think about the future or the past, the main thing is to just get on with now. We want to help people to do that with these academies. We'll make a donation and we'll ask for money from anyone we know with money, anyone that's interested, anyone in the so-called establishment who's worried about kids going wild and drugs and all that. Another groovy thing: Everybody gives one week's wages

when they join. I think it's the fairest thing I've heard of. And that's all you ever pay, just the once."

That Sunday, August 27, the Beatles" manager Brian Epstein was found dead of alcohol and barbiturate poisoning in his London house. The Beatles gave a brief press conference then departed for London.

John Lennon explained, "We were in Wales with the Maharishi. We had just gone down after seeing his lecture first night. We heard it then. I was stunned, we all were, I suppose, and the Maharishi, we went in to him. 'What, he's dead' and all that, and he was sort of saying oh, forget it, be happy, like an idiot, like parents, smile, that's what the Maharishi said. And we did.

"I had that feeling that anybody has when somebody close to them dies: there is a sort of little hysterical, sort of hee, hee, I'm glad it's not me or something in it, the funny feeling when somebody close to you dies. I don't know whether you've had it, but I've had a lot of people die around me and the other feeling is, 'What the fuck? What can I do?'

"I knew we were in trouble then. I didn't really have any misconceptions about our ability to do anything other than play music and I was scared. I thought, 'We've fuckin' had it.'

"We'd never have made it without him and vice versa. Brian contributed as much as us in the early days, although we were the talent and he was the hustler. He wasn't strong enough to overbear us. Brian could never make us do what we didn't really want to do."

The first the public knew of Epstein's death was during a concert by the Jimi Hendrix Experience, Tomorrow and the Crazy World of Arthur Brown at Brian Epstein's Saville Theatre. Someone came on stage and announced his death. Rather than stop the concert, Jimi Hendrix played a beautiful set in his memory, including his version of "Sgt. Pepper's Lonely Heart's Club Band." The second show was cancelled.

"Mick was a delicate and beautiful creature. Brian was sturdier and into straight fancy dress and flouting all perceived wisdom about what to wear. He was into ethnic clothes much earlier than most people."

Christopher Gibbs

LEFT: Brian Jones in ethnic shirt and beads with photographer Michael Cooper in the back of a car.

BRIAN JONES

Of all the Stones, Brian Jones was the worst affected by the police harassment and on July 6 he was hospitalized, suffering from strain, but six days later was well enough to join the others in the studio.

After spending ten days on the Costa del Sol to get himself in shape, Brian Jones appeared in court on October 30. He admitted possession of cannabis and allowing his flat to be used for smoking it, but pleaded not guilty to possession of cocaine and methedrine. He was found guilty, sentenced to nine months in prison, and was taken to Wormwood Scrubs. Fans demonstrated in the Kings Road and seven, including Mick Jagger's brother Chris, were arrested for obstruction. The next day Brian was released on £750 bail, pending an appeal.

On November 12 the Rolling Stones PR Man, Leslie Perrin, released a statement, objecting to the contents of a speech made by Judge Leslie Block at a formal dinner given by the Horsham Ploughing and Agricultural Society where he said, "We did our best, your fellow countrymen, I and my fellow magistrates, to cut these Stones down to size, but alas, it was not to be, because the Court of Criminal Appeal let them roll free … I can only suppose that the Court of Criminal Appeal was influenced by the words of Shakespeare when he wrote his own epitaph in these words, 'Blest be the man who spares these stones.'" In view of Brian's upcoming appeal, Perrin questioned whether the Judge's words were helpful and suggested that an unbiased hearing might now be very hard to achieve.

On December 12 magistrates set Brian's sentence aside when three psychiatrists described him as "an extremely frightened young man," one of them even saying he had suicidal tendencies. Brian was fined £1,000 and given three years on probation. Two days later Brian collapsed and was rushed to hospital after an ambulance answered a 999 call to his London flat, but he was allowed home that night.

"With Acid there was an emergence of young people who dressed to die for."

Christopher Gibbs

FAR LEFT: Dutch artists, designers and clothing designers The Fool in their boutique, which was funded by the Beatles at 94 Baker Street in London. Founders Simon Koger and Marikje Posthuma are seated, cofounder Josje Leeger is standing. The Fool had painted psychedelic designs on John Lennon's piano and George Harrison's fireplace when they suggested opening a clothes shop to the band. The Apple Boutique opened in the summer of 1967 and closed in July 1968, with the Beatles giving away the last of the very expensive stock. Since a lot of stock had been stolen during its brief life, this was considered to be an ironic action by the band.
LEFT: A model shows off a Fool outfit behind a psychedelic light gel. Such gels had first been used as light slides to accompany performances by psychedelic bands in the UK such as Pink Floyd. The patterns, suitably enough, were created by the burning of acetate colored slides with acid. The clothes of the like-minded Fool were representative of such acid-burned slides. Colors and materials floated, crossed over into one another and seemed to expand and blur as the wearer danced.

les **hippies**

Qui sont vraiment ces hippies dont on parle tant ? Leurs mœurs, leurs idées et leur musique ne peuvent que passionner les lecteurs de Rock & Folk. C'est donc un véritable dossier que nous vous présentons. Vous pourrez lire, dans les pages qui suivent, le premier reportage d'Alain Dister, description objective et approfondie du phénomène. En outre, vous trouverez l'opinion de Philippe Rault, qui revient des États-Unis, et une prise de position carrément contre par Philippe Constantin qui se place sur un plan purement philosophique. Nous avons voulu aborder le sujet sous tous ces aspects. A chacun de se faire son idée.

It was the year of political activism and violence and the year of the great retreat to the country. It was the year that a commercial, superficial idea of the hippie lifestyle spread to the suburbs—through the medium of glossy magazines and pop music—and each town began to have its own genuine dropouts.

666 / 68 69 70

Every college town in America and most in Europe had a store where you could buy posters and rolling papers and the local underground paper. There were now more than 100 underground papers, ranging from the purely spiritual and psychedelic to the extreme radical, such as New York City's Rat.

Each major city now had hippie areas, or at least a hippie high street, but with high rents in the city centers hippies tended to live in groups, many of which became communes. There was a gay commune of 30 men living above a popular gay bar on Market Street, San Francisco, and hundreds living in geodesic domes in the original Drop City. There were subsistence farms, religious communities, ashrams, sex communes, covens and groups of followers of various gurus—most of whom were self-proclaimed. Most of them wore long hair, most of them smoked dope; to the general public they were all hippies.

In France, a real revolution was played out along the lines of the Paris Commune, resulting in more than half the working population going on strike. Hippies were generally more politicized in Europe and a network of like-minded activists grew across the Continent. In England, however, most didn't even notice.

POLITICS OF ECSTASY

"Paranoia is probably good because it's the recognition that everybody is part of a giant conspiracy."

The Digger Papers, August 1968

The spirit of Haight-Ashbury continued into 1968 with the Carousel Ballroom on 1545 Market Street, near Van Ness, which was owned by the Jefferson Airplane and the Grateful Dead. The initial money was raised by the Jefferson Airplane, who contributed the proceeds from a series of concerts. The Hell's Angels combined to manufacture a Carousel chopper that they were planning on giving away there—they always had free admittance to the Carousel. The hall held 2,500–3,000 people and the prices were kept as low as possible. The dances were initially free, then $2.50 with a free poster thrown in, in contrast to the $3.00 charged at the Fillmore. Brian Rohan, the pot-bust lawyer from HALO (Haight-Ashbury Legal Organization), was on hand and there was free food courtesy of the Diggers. The dances featured American Indian dancers and magicians, as well as the usual three-day weekend dances. The Hell's Angels held a dance every Wednesday with a $1.00 admission fee—the Angels only ever charged $1.00 for anything they did—usually with Big Brother and the Holding Company playing. During the other days there were dancing classes, and once a boxing ring was set up with two mattresses so that people could take out their aggression.

In March 1968 the Grateful Dead reluctantly gave up 710 Ashbury. It had become so public that the tourist buses were stopping outside for slack-jawed tourists to take photographs. Every mad person in the Haight felt it was their right to show up and be entertained or to explain their latest crack-brained scheme to Jerry Garcia. Many of the people were funnelled off into HALO, which had legal offices both there and across the street, but the days of the small close-knit community of musicians and psychedelic freaks were long gone. The band played a farewell concert from the back of a flatbed truck, with power lines running from the Straight Theatre, before moving out to Marin County on the other side of the Golden Gate Bridge and joining a widespread move into the country. Mickey Hart already had a ranch in Novato and the others moved nearby. Jerry, Mountain Girl and Sunshine, along with Robert Hunter and his lady, rented a place in Larkspur. Bob Weir moved to Nicasio, Phil Lesh to Fairfax and Rock Scully moved in to Dan Healy's place in Sausalito. The extended Dead Family of roadies and entourage spread out all across Marin.

BLACK PANTHERS

The KSO-3 soul station always advertised what was happening at the Carousel and it was one of the few dance halls where blacks felt welcome, the Black Panthers making a point of checking their guns in at the door. The Panthers had established a working relationship with the hippies, albeit a tentative one. After all, most of the black community in Fillmore wanted precisely what the hippies were dropping out of, but they had been welcomed at the Diggers' Free Store and now they set up one of their own at the Fillmore Auditorium, run by Ray Ballard and the Panthers. In addition to the Black Man's Free Store they swapped information with the hippies. The black welfare mothers counseled the hippie girls on the bureaucracy of how to get welfare checks and the Diggers helped the Panthers establish black communal housing. Some of them even pooled their welfare checks like the hippie communes. The result of these was an alliance between the black residents of the Fillmore and the hippies, which resulted in the blacks keeping straight whites out of the area. All this was to change, however, on April 4 , when Martin Luther King was assassinated in Memphis, Tennessee and riots and looting swept across every city in America, including San Francisco.

Bill Graham's Fillmore Auditorium was in the Fillmore, which was a black neighborhood, and though he had always allowed the community to put on their own evenings, relations had sometimes been strained—even with the Black Free Store in the building and Black Panther benefits. Following King's death there had been violent incidents and many whites were scared to go into the neighborhood. Many concerts that should have been sell-outs were half empty.

PREVIOUS PAGE: A sign of the times—nudity among the flowers in the sunshine. A hippie take on Adam and Eve.
RIGHT: American psychedelic posters were much more wordy than their British counterparts. Mint copies of any of them now cost hundreds and sometimes thousands of dollars.

GIMME AN F . . .

The Bay Area bands were developing in very different directions. The Jefferson Airplane were now wealthy from chart success and in May they bought a $70,000, four-story mansion, with mahogany paneling, crystal chandeliers and a grand staircase, located at 2400 Fulton, right across from Golden Gate Park. They had become traditional rock superstars with all the toys and money they wanted.

The Grateful Dead had done the opposite, but their commitment to the community meant that they were $40,000 in the red—in fact it wasn't until the early 70s that they paid off their debts. They were also having musical differences: Pigpen's drinking was getting in the way and Bob Weir was not up to playing the advanced material that Garcia and Lesh were writing for the group. As they were recording the band's third album, it was Rock Scully's unfortunate duty to fire them. But when the band next played live, at the Avalon, for three nights Pigpen and Weir were still there. Somehow the information had not sunk in and no one was about to enforce it.

Country Joe and the Fish essentially destroyed their chances of a commercial career with their famous FISH cheer. The band were in New York to appear on the Ed Sullivan Show—still the way to reach middle-America—and also play the Schaefer Beer Music Festival at the Wollman Rink in Central Park, which was one of the main New York summer events. Drummer Chicken Hirsh had the bright idea of changing the cheerleader introduction to "Fixin' To Die," so that instead of chanting out "Gimme an F," "Gimme an I" to spell their name, they got the

RIGHT: Black Panthers outside the Fillmore Auditorium, San Francisco.
OVER: The Fillmore assailed all the senses, with the music, the lights and the smell of so many people.

massive audience to spell out "FUCK" instead. The New Yorkers really went for it, they cheered and screamed and it was a great success, but the Schaefer Beer people told them they would never appear at the festival again and Ed Sullivan cancelled their appearance on the show. Promoters across the country got to hear that they used four-letter words on stage—illegal in most states—and gigs dried up. The group never really recovered.

Janis Joplin was preparing herself for a solo career and tensions within Big Brother were running high. The Charlatans split up, with Dan Hicks forming his own band, Dan Hicks and His Hot Licks, and the Quicksilver Messenger Service decided that their first album was not good enough, so started over from scratch. When the new album was finally released in June, they were all too laid back to bother with a tour to promote it. But there were new bands emerging, in particular Creedence Clearwater Revival from the East Bay. They made so much money for their record company, Fantasy, that it had to give them shares in lieu of royalties because they owed them so much and the cash flow from distributors and foreign territories was not paying up quickly enough.

BROTHERHOOD

Timothy Leary still owned the luxurious house in Queens Road, Berkeley, where he lived when he was a straight psychologist in pre-Harvard days. In April, with the closure of Millbrook, he returned

to Queens Road accompanied by his entourage. The lower level consisted of a huge living room with a plate-glass west wall, which opened out to a large wooden sundeck and faced out over San Francisco Bay. There were usually a dozen or so young people there, some naked, hanging out while Tim identified the stars in the zodiac, or read poetry, or simply rapped. Max Scherr, owner-editor of the Berkeley Barb, reported: "They were dropping acid constantly, and he drank a lot of wine. But the thing is, you see, he also dropped acid just the same as if he was drinking, you know. And there was no timing to it. He'd just drop acid. He didn't want to deal with anything like reality."

Despite evicting them from Millbrook, Billy Hitchcock remained a friend and, in order to be near Tim, he bought a luxurious house in Sausalito and quietly financed several major LSD manufacturing operations. One of them, called D & H Research and run by Nick Sand in the Bay Area community of Windsor, was able to make a million tabs on a single cycle. It produced Orange Sunshine, constantly endorsed by Leary as "pure gold." D & H made 10 million tabs before being closed down the summer of 1969. That August, Tim and his family helped to set up Mystic Arts Enterprises. Many of the people involved were also a part of the Brotherhood of Eternal Love. This was a nonprofit religious organization set up back in October 1966 on Leary's instructions. The Brotherhood had bought and fitted up a 300-acre ranch in Idlewild, California, and late in 1968 Tim, Rosemary and Jackie Leary (Tim's son) moved

out there, with other Mystic Arts friends.

The small farmhouse was surrounded by a circle of seven canvas tepees and a large lavender-painted barn. The community was more or less self-sufficient, as the 35 to 40 residents were mostly vegetarians and the surrounding land was fertile. The nearest road, Highway 74, was five miles away; the ranch could only be accessed through several locked gates and an approaching car could be seen ten miles away. Anyone who got too close was approached by lookouts. Nonetheless, they were being watched all the time and their car was known, so it was incredibly foolish of Leary to drive to Laguna with drugs in the car on December 26, 1968. They stopped to drop Jackie Leary off but, as a police car was across the street, he didn't want to get out of the car. The cop thought the car looked suspicious, standing in the middle of the road without moving, and investigated. When Leary opened the window to speak to him a cloud of pot smoke hit him in the face. Jackie had some pills and a chunk of hash and Rosemary had a purse filled with pot, 24 tabs of acid and a brick of hash. There were two roaches in the ashtray. They were in Orange County, California—one of the worst places in America to be busted.

ABOVE: The American Breed 1968 LP Bend Me, Shape Me.
RIGHT: Cream take the stage at the Fillmore East. The American psychedelic bands were always more blues based than the British ones, so Cream had a ready-made audience awaiting them.

Eric Clapton

"There you are on stage with thousands of little girls screaming their head off. Man, it's power! ... Whew!"

Eric Clapton

RTET

RANCISCO

PRETTY THINGS PRESENT

TWO SIDES OF "SORROW"

PRIVATE SORROW

c/w

Baloon Burning

Released Nov 1st on COLUMBIA D.B 84

"Music thrives wildly in England because they are jealous of someone else's success. [In San Francisco] you're encouraged. Everybody digs everybody else and they don't hide it. In England they could use a little more maturity."

Eric Clapton, May 1968

COMMUNES

"We are 50 people on a perpetual trip … [with] our pet pig, Pigasus."

Wavy Gravy on the Hog Farm Commune

In Los Angeles it has always been possible to live among the trees and mountains in the Hollywood Hills or in Topanga Canyon, as if you were in the country. Wavy Gravy spent two years working at Cal State by day and running a pig farm on a mountaintop in the San Fernando Valley in the evenings and weekends in exchange for rent. More people began to arrive and colonize the nearby shacks and put up tents, and the Hog Farm was born. They had been providing the light shows for Cream, Jimi Hendrix and the Grateful Dead at the Shrine Auditorium, and every Sunday they were holding open days for the people of Los Angeles. Then, in 1968, they decided that it was time to take it on the road.

Wavy Gravy: "The Hog Farm is an expanded family, a mobile hallucination, a sociological experiment, an army of clowns. We are 50 people on a perpetual trip, with six converted school buses, some vans and pickups, one for our pet pig, Pigasus."

Remembering his time with the Pranksters in the Kesey bus, Wavy Gravy's first move was for them all to go to Oregon to pick up Ken Babbs to take with them on the journey.

They wandered through New York, New Mexico and Vermont, hopped the Atlantic and started again in London. Financed by a benefit at Implosion, they bought a bus and set off to Germany, where they acquired another, and from there they drove overland to Kathmandu, Nepal, putting on the Hog Farm show wherever they went. They were on the road for six years and travelled a million miles.

RIGHT: The Hog Farm became a mobile commune, turning up at festivals and events to provide food and entertainment. They covered a million miles in their travels, from LA to Kathmandu.

THE MANSON FAMILY

Another commune, a little further out in the desert, in the old Spahn Movie ranch in Chatsworth, about twenty miles north of Beverly Hills, was Charlie Manson's Family. One of the girls, Dianne Blustein, had been a member of the Hog Farm where, at the age of thirteen, she had been given LSD and introduced to group sex. She was still thirteen when she joined The Family, astonishingly, with her hippie parents' permission. Charlie didn't find her submissive enough and whipped and beat her, but she stayed on.

Charlie Manson was just five foot two and of slight build, but his years in prison had taught him how to control and dominate people. He was born in 1934, the illegitimate son of a sixteen-year-old girl and a much older man called William Manson. His mother often disappeared for days or weeks and he was mostly raised by his grandmother or an aunt. When he was five, his mother and his uncle held up a service station and were sentenced to five years in the state penitentiary. Charlie went to live with an aunt until 1942, when his mother was paroled, but at the age of twelve the court sent him to the Gibault School for Boys in Terre Haute, Indiana. He ran away and by the time he was thirteen he had committed a series of robberies, including two armed heists, which landed him in the Indiana School for Boys. He ran away eighteen times, but they always brought him back. At the age of sixteen he stole a car and headed for California, robbing gas stations en route, until he was stopped and sent to the National Training School for Boys in Washington, DC. His aunt offered to have him if he was released on parole, but just before the hearing he held a razor blade

"Manson definitely has homosexual and assaultive tendencies. He is safe only under supervision."

Charles Manson's Reform School report, 50s

at another boy's throat while he sodomized him. (He had been involved in several other homosexual rapes as well. In addition, Manson was still more or less illiterate.)

He was finally released at the age of nineteen. He married a local waitress and began stealing cars. He and his new wife travelled to California in a stolen car, but within three months Manson was arrested. Though his chances of probation were very good, he skipped his hearing, was re-arrested and was back in jail, serving a three-year sentence in Terminal Island, when his son was born. By the time he got out his wife had divorced him. Charlie took up a new profession as a pimp, beginning with a sixteen-year-old girl called Judy. After a series of arrests and probationary sentences, he spent a year in the LA County Jail while appealing various convictions for robbery and running prostitutes. In July 1961 he was sent to McNeil Island on a ten-year term.

In jail Charlie studied Scientology and played the guitar. On March 21, 1967 he was released and headed straight for Haight-Ashbury. The scene there suited a hustler like him perfectly and he was soon living in a Digger crash pad and assembling a group of followers. There were a lot of self-proclaimed gurus in the Haight who had very little trouble in finding followers, as the streets were filled with spaced-out runaways from dysfunctional families, looking for love and attention. Charlie soon found a number of girls prepared to feed and clothe him and, in the manner of the times, Charlie got himself an old school bus, painted it black and spent the next year and a half roaming around the country with a dozen girls. He liked pre-pubescent girls but, failing that, fifteen- and sixteen-year-olds were fine. Charlie thought girls were inferior to men, good only for sex and babies. He had already fathered two children in the past and several

more were to follow. By the time he arrived at the Spahn Ranch in the summer of 1968 he had about 30 young women with him who were servicing four or five men, including 82-year-old George Spahn.

While in jail, Charlie had become an obsessive Beatles fan. The November 1968 release of the White Album was to have terrible repercussions, as his crazed brain deciphered secret apocalyptic messages hidden in its many tracks and addressed only to him.

EROTIC MINORITIES

1968 was the year of communes. Hundreds, if not thousands, opened up across the country, espousing different "ideals": group marriage, celibacy, religion, agriculture. Many of them could be found in the Santa Monica Mountains. There was Ed Lange's nudist colony, Elysium Fields, which occupied nine acres on Robinson Road at the top of Topanga Canyon, next to the State Park. There were many nudist societies in Southern California, but Elysium Fields, founded in 1960, was solely devoted to spreading the sexual revolution. Unlike the older AANR (American Association for Nude Recreation) nudist colonies, Elysium allowed hugging between couples, allowed same-sex couples to join, permitted the wearing of jewelry and ran very popular massage training workshops. There were saunas, a Jacuzzi, hot tubs and meditation rooms—though in practice these were more likely to be used for orgies than anything contemplative, with anything up to 100 people in there at one time.

In 1960 Elysium had begun publishing Sundial magazine. In 1968 it was replaced by Sundisk because, according to Lange, the time was over for publishing nudist propaganda; there were now hundreds of nudist clubs in America and the idea was accepted. Now it was time for a magazine which represented "the Erotic Minorities." The cover headline was "The Sexual Revolution Smiles." The magazine featured lots of attractive nude women and articles on sexual liberation,

LEFT: A peaceful commune eat dinner in the open air.
RIGHT: The mad stare of self-styled cult leader and murderer Charles Manson, whose "commune" lived in the desert outside LA.

with a Swedish doctor attacking the hegemony of the missionary position and monogamous heterosexuality and an article in favor of the polygamous "varietism" practiced by the Sexual Freedom League of Berkeley. (Founded by Jefferson "Fuck" Poland, they promoted the nude "wade-in" in San Francisco Bay in 1965 and had been active throughout the Bay Area ever since.) Sundisk led its readers towards the golden dawn of sexual liberation: "The water is over the dam. If the rapids below are turbulent and dangerous, they are also beautiful and exciting. And they lead to the sea."

In fact, perhaps more than the widespread use of drugs, it was the sexual freedom promoted by the hippies that the authorities and "establishment" objected to the most, particularly in the American Midwest—the Bible Belt—and in conservative areas like Orange County south of LA. But it was an unstoppable phenomenon. Censorship was eroded first in books, then sex magazines began publishing explicit photographs and films began to show the odd glimpse of pubic hair, culminating in 1972 when two hardcore porn films, Deep Throat and the Devil In Miss Jones, both screened at regular cinemas across the USA.

THE MOVIE TRIP

This same crossover meant that the underground 60s philosophy made its impact on regular Hollywood too. This was the year of all the Mondo films: following in the wake of the success of Mondo Carne, Robert Cohen released Mondo Hollywood, a low-rent documentary featuring Vito and the Freaks and a brief clip of The Mothers. Peter Perry's Mondo Mod—about the Sunset Strip riots, LSD and life on the Strip—was also released, as were Mondo Teeno (Teenage Rebellion) and, in 1968, Mondo Daytona, about teenagers on Daytona Beach.

There was The Trip by Jack Nicholson, which was literally that—an LSD session seen through the eyes of an advertising salesman with Peter Fonda and Dennis Hopper and featuring spec-

LEFT: Hollywood quickly embraced the psychedelic lifestyle.
A still from The Trip, a film by Jack Nicholson, one of the better examples of the psychedelic movie genre.

tacular hallucinogenic special effects by Peter Gardener. The Monkees proved that they too could be psychedelic and made Head, a surreal fantasy directed by Bob Rafelson and Jack Nicholson, with walk-on appearances by Sonny Liston and Frank Zappa.

That same year saw Richard Rush's Psych-Out, a film about a seventeen-year-old deaf girl searching for her brother who has become a religious fanatic in Haight-Ashbury, featuring the ubiquitous Jack Nicholson. There was also Roger Corman's The Wild Angels, with members of the Venice Hell's Angels Motorcycle Club, as well as

Peter Fonda and Nancy Sinatra. It managed to get itself banned all over the country, guaranteeing instant cult status.

For all the films that did get made, there were hundreds that remained stoned dreams, which wasted thousands of dollars of development money as the potential directors and actors tripped out in the hills, envisioning the ultimate hip film that would blow everybody's mind. The best example of this was actually made: millionaire heir Conrad Rooks made the self-indulgent free-form Chappaqua in 1967, starring everyone he admired, from Allen Ginsberg and the Fugs to

William Burroughs, who played the Doctor. He commissioned two complete movie scores, one by Ravi Shankar and other by Ornette Coleman. At one point during shooting it was decided that they really needed a shot of a sunset in India, so the entire crew packed up and flew off to India. Some of the visuals were very beautiful, but it was an expensive flop.

ABOVE: The GTOs (Girls Together Outrageously), a groupie group of ex-Frank Zappa babysitters who toured with the Mothers Of Invention. Zappa produced their album Permanent Damage.

REVOLUTION

"My name is Abbie. I am a cultural revolutionary."

Abbie Hoffman, 1968

"1968," wrote Allen Ginsberg, "was the year when the standoff between the generations finally erupted into the open, worldwide warfare which completely transcended the antique battles of Cold War and Race." In February that year, Abbie Hoffman had been to see Ginsberg to tell him that he and Jerry Rubin wanted to hold a Festival of Life in Chicago in August, to coincide with the Democratic Party Convention, as an example of an alternative lifestyle to the one being promoted by the assembled politicians. They planned to launch a Youth International Party—Yippies—and run their own candidate, the Hog Farm pig named Pigasus. The idea was to have a Be-In with yogis, poets, musicians and anti-war speakers. Naturally, like every young hustler with an idea for an event, Abbie wanted Allen to contact the Beatles and Bob Dylan.

Ginsberg was supportive of the general idea, but was too overworked to take an active role. America was in turmoil. Two thousand US troops were killed in the Tet Offensive and less than a quarter of the population approved of how Johnson was handling the war. On April 4, 1968 Martin Luther King Jr. was assassinated, provoking widespread rioting. In Chicago, Mayor Richard Daley gave riot police his infamous instructions to "Shoot to kill"—an ominous warning of what was to come. In New York, students at Columbia University occupied the campus and found papers in the Dean's office connecting the university to big business war suppliers. This was followed by a wave of college protests against the Vietnam War on nearly every campus in the country. On June 4 Sirhan Sirhan killed Robert Kennedy, provoking more fears that the country was out of control and that violence ruled the day.

FILLMORE EAST

By 1968 Bill Graham had expanded his empire by opening a Fillmore Auditorium in the old Village Theatre on 2nd Avenue, right where the hippies lived, on the Lower East Side. The huge space above the auditorium was given to the East Village Other rent free as part of Graham's attempts to keep in with his audience. Being in New York meant that he could attract major British groups on American tours more easily. He found that the underground music of a few years before was now dominating the charts—Electric Ladyland by Jimi Hendrix reached No. 1 in the US album charts that November—and, as a long-time supporter of that music, he was getting the best acts. The Fillmore was next to Ratner's deli restaurant, which featured the rudest waiters in town and which quickly became a hippie favorite because it was always open. The surrounding blocks soon filled with hippie boutiques and little specialist import shops. There were lots of small storefronts for rent and it became quite common for people to run a head shop or a dress shop in front and sleep in back.

For serious hippie goods, however, you still had to go further east. The Psychedelicatessen on Avenue A had now become the biggest head shop in the city. One of the more amazing items for sale was a gigantic dope-smoking machine that actually pumped the smoke into your lungs to save you the trouble of having to inhale it. It stood three feet high in the middle of the store and comprised an air compressor and a large traditional water pipe, with eight flexible tubes attached so eight people could smoke at once.

The underground newspapers had also grown, and in New York the East Village Other now had competition. There was the New York Free Press, a community newspaper owned by Upper West Side liberals and published uptown. Jeff Shiro's Rat, a hard-core radical underground rag that had expunged every trace of spirituality from its pages, was published from a storefront near Cooper Union. The Avatar, the magazine of Mel Lyman—another self-proclaimed megalomaniac guru and leader of a large commune in Boston—had now opened a chapter in New York.

RIGHT: Abbie Hoffman took Emmett Grogan and the San Francisco Mime Troupe's street theatre and playful political activism and applied it first to New York City and then to Chicago.

FRIDAY & SATURDAY, FEB. 7 & 8

CANNED HEAT
THE PENTANGLE
RHINOCEROS

TUESDAY & WEDNESDAY, FEB. 11 & 12

JANIS JOPLIN
And Her Group
GRATEFUL DEAD

FRIDAY & SATURDAY, FEB. 14 & 15

JEFF BECK GROUP
WINTER

FRIDAY & SATURDAY, FEB. 21 & 22

MOTHERS
OF INVENTION
BUDDY MILES EXPRESS
CHICAGO TRANSIT AUTHORITY

FRI., FEB. 28 & SAT., MAR. 1

TEN YEARS AFTER
JOHN MAYALL
AND AT EVERY SHOW
JOSHUA LIGHT SHOW

FILLMORE EAST
SECOND AVENUE AT SIXTH STREET

2 SHOWS EACH NIGHT—8 & 11:30 P.M. ALL SEATS RESERVED: $3, $4, $5. BOX OFFICE OPEN MON.— SAT: 12 NOON TO 9 P.M. INFO: 777-5260.

MAIL ORDERS: CHECK OR MONEY ORDER PAYABLE TO "FILLMORE EAST," 105 2nd AVE., N.Y.C. 10003. ENCLOSE SELF-ADDRESSED STAMPED ENVELOPE & SPECIFY DAY, DATE & 8 OR 11:30 SHOW. ORDERS RECEIVED 3 DAYS BEFORE SHOW WILL BE HELD AT BOX OFFICE.
TICKETS AVAILABLE (thru Thurs. preceding show): Manhattan-DIFFERENT DRUMMER, Lexington at 61st, NEW YORKER BOOK SHOP, Broadway at 89th; VILLAGE OLDIES, 149 Bleecker (Upstairs); Brooklyn-PRANA-132 Montague, Bkln. Hts.; Westchester-SYMPHONY MUSIC SHOP, 28 Palisades Ave., Getty Square, Yonkers; Bronx-COUSINS RECORD SHOP, 382 E. Fordham Rd.; Queens-REVELATION, 71-20 Austin, Forest Hills; DISKINS, 135-26 Roosevelt Ave., Flushing; New Jersey-RED BARN, Garden State Plaza; THE LAST STRAW, 317 Glenwood, Bloomfield.
SPECIAL DISCOUNTS FOR GROUPS OF 30 OR MORE WHEN AVAILABLE. CALL MR. O'CONNOR: 777-3910.

"Life in this society is, at best, an utter bore ..."

The SCUM Manifesto begins

SCUM

1968 was a year of violence for many people. On June 3 the radical lesbian Valerie Solanas, head of the one-woman organization Society for Cutting Up Men—SCUM, acted on her own manifesto and gunned down Andy Warhol. Warhol had used her in his movie, I, A Man, but he refused to film her play Up From The Slime (alternative titles: Up Your Ass, The Big Suck or, in case it became a Broadway hit, From the Cradle to the Boat—in itself a lesbian joke). Warhol, in his paranoid state, thought she was trying to get him to make an obscene film and get him busted. He accused her of being a cop. "Sure I'm a cop," she said, unzipping her fly to show him her cunt.

The SCUM manifesto opens: "Life in this society being, at best, an utter bore and no aspect of society being at all relevant to women, there remains to civic-minded, responsible, thrill-seeking females only to overthrow the government, eliminate the money system, institute complete automation and destroy the male sex."

Among the craziness, her lengthy manifesto contained a lot of good arguments, and many of her grievances were later articulated by the women's movement, which began a year or so later. She certainly identified the central flaw in the commune movement—one which caused hundreds of them to fail:

"A true community consists of individuals—not mere species members, not couples—respecting each other's individuality and privacy, at the same time interacting with each other mentally and emotionally—free spirits in free relation to each other—and cooperating with each other to achieve common ends. Traditionalists say the basic unit of "society" is the family; 'hippies' say the tribe; no one says the individual.

"The "hippie" babbles on about individuality, but has no more conception of it than any other man. He desires to get back to Nature, back to the wilderness, back to the home of the furry animals he's one of, away from the city, where there is at least a trace, a bare beginning of civilization, to live at the species level, his time taken up with simple, nonintellectual activities—farming, fucking, bead stringing. The most important activity of the commune, the one on which it is based, is gangbanging. The "hippy" is enticed to the commune mainly by the prospect of all the free pussy—the main commodity to be shared, to be had just for the asking, but, blinded by greed, he fails to anticipate all the other men he has to share with, or the jealousies and the possessiveness of the pussies themselves.

"Men cannot cooperate to achieve a common end, because each man's end is all the pussy to himself. The commune, therefore, is doomed to failure: each "hippy" will, in panic, grab the first simpleton who digs him and whisk her off to the suburbs as fast as he can. The male cannot progress socially, but merely swings back and forth from isolation to gangbanging."

One can detect an element of levity in her words when she wrote this from the comfort of her room in the Hotel Chelsea, but then things got tough. She was thrown out of the hotel for not paying the rent and went in desperation to Warhol's Factory. He was in a meeting when she barged in brandishing a .36 and a .22—she was sure the .36 would jam so brought along a backup. Warhol did not die, but was very badly injured by the attack and had tremendous physical problems for the rest of his life. Mario Amaya, the editor of the London magazine Art and Artists, was also injured in her attack, but not badly. It was another example of achieving redress by the use of violence. Valerie went to jail, but not for long.

PREVIOUS PAGE: Relaxing in Central Park at a Be-In.
LEFT: Valerie Solonas, founder of the Society for Cutting Up Men, (SCUM) is arrested after shooting and seriously wounding Andy Warhol at the Factory.

CHICAGO

"In 1968 marijuana became rampant in the army. In 1969 low morale, even civil disobedience, became rampant in the army. 'Why does grass inspire the Viet Kong and kill the fighting spirit of the American GI?' Any pot-smoker can understand it: marijuana is a truth serum. The Viet Kong are defending their parents, children and homes—their deaths are noble and heroic. The Americans are fighting for nothing you can see, feel, touch or believe in. Their deaths are futile and wasted. 'Why die on Hamburger Hill?' asks the pot-smoking American soldier, as he points his gun at the head of the captain who ordered him to take a hill that only the Viet Kong want. If the Pentagon tries to stop pot in the army, she'll end up destroying her army in the process. But if the army brass leaves grass-smokers alone, army bases will soon be as turned on and unstoppable as college campuses. What's going to happen when all those American GIs come home? 'What do you mean, we're old enough to fight and die but not old enough to smoke?'"

Jerry Rubin

Mayor Daley's office refused to give the Yippies a permit to hold their Festival of Life in Lincoln Park, Chicago, but even if they had cancelled the festival, thousands of people would have still gone. Many anti-war groups had come to Chicago specifically to protest against LBJ, but after President Johnson decided to withdraw from the presidential race they had to rethink their position. David Dellinger, Rennie Davies and Tom Hayden assembled a large coalition of anti-war groups and planned marches and demonstrations. The Yippies coordinated their festival with the coalition.

Mayor Daley placed 11,500 police on twelve-hour shifts, mobilized 5,500 National Guardsmen and even had 7,500 troops airlifted in from Fort Hood, Texas, under the president's direct command. A Festival of Life with dancing, poetry and music seemed very unlikely to happen. Rennie Davies and Tom Hayden started training their people in karate and a number of other forms of self-defense. After someone (some suspected Jerry Rubin) sent the mayor a postcard suggesting they were going to spike the Chicago water supply, fully armed troops were deployed throughout the conference to guard the reservoirs and water treatment facilities.

On Saturday August 24 thousands of young people began converging on the city and heading for Lincoln Park. The police declared that the park was to close at 11pm. The Yippies had no permit and no contingency plans. Violent confrontation was inevitable but, as it later turned out, this was what Jerry Rubin had wanted all along. In fact the police entered the park and began beating people up at 9pm, even though they had every right to be there.

The next day, Sunday, a PA system was set up in Lincoln Park and John Sinclair and the MC5 worked the crowd up with their "Up against the wall, motherfucker" rhetoric. Allen Ginsberg came on next and chanted "Hare Krishna" for about fifteen minutes, then sang William Blake's "The Grey Monk" to try to calm the crowd. The MC5 came back on and worked them up again, though when the police appeared on the scene shortly afterwards, the band disappeared fast.

Ginsberg had teamed up with William Burroughs and Jean Genet, who, along with Terry Southern, had been sent to cover the convention by Esquire magazine. They were walking in the park around closing time the next night when they saw a mob of police burst out of the trees in pursuit, not of kids, but of news photographers. The police had taken off their badges and name plates, and some had even removed their unit patches. The club-swinging mob advanced on the crowd and, at the end of the incident, seventeen media reporters—pressmen from the Washington Post, the Chicago American, The Chicago Sun-Times, Life, Newsweek and cameramen from ABC, CBS and NBC—had to be taken to Henrotin Hospital for emergency treatment.

The main battle of Chicago occurred outside the Hilton Hotel on 28 August. The National Mobilization Committee organized a pacifist rally and march that was to start at the band shell in Grant Park, but the police and troops had sealed off the park. Nonetheless the march moved off, preceded by someone carrying a portable PA

RIGHT: Jerry Rubin on the steps of the Cannon House Office building in Washington, DC at the House Of Unamerican Activities subcommittee hearings, wearing the revolutionary chic combination red and blue Viet Cong flag cape and plastic machine gun.

"I can't wait for this city to rot. I can't wait to see weeds growing through empty streets."

Jean Genet to William Burroughs in Chicago, August 1968

system, who was then followed by NMC organizer David Dellinger and by a group of marshals. The march itself was led by Allen Ginsberg, William Burroughs, Jean Genet, Terry Southern, Richard Seaver from Grove Press and the British photographer Michael Cooper, their arms linked together, all holding flowers—an obvious target for press photographers who were delighted by the line-up. After a couple of blocks the march reached the edge of the park, where national guardsmen blocked the way with machine guns and jeeps equipped with barbed-wire shields. The march was not allowed onto the city streets.

After a long standoff, David Dellinger announced that the march was over; the government had forced them to abandon their citizen's right to have a peaceable assembly for redress of grievances. The march broke up but no one could leave the park because the troops were still blocking all the bridges, which were the only exits. The police, nevertheless, tried to clear the park by firing teargas at the marchers. One large group of marchers managed to force a lightly guarded bridge and get back to the city across Michigan Avenue, only to run straight into the

LEFT: The Yippies present their presidential candidate, Pigasus, at the 1968 Democratic Party Convention in Chicago.

Reverend Abernathy's Poor People's Campaign march, complete with mules and wagons, which was just then progressing up the avenue. Mayor Daley had had no choice but to grant the Reverend a permit for his march, lest the press and cameras focus on a full-scale riot in Chicago's black South Side as well. It was like an episode in a science fiction book, with the mules making a stark contrast against the troops in battledress and gas masks, and the thousands of ragged, long-haired kids breaking through the armor to join in.

Just before the Hilton Hotel, the mules and wagons were allowed across the intersection. Then, as the Poor People's Campaign marched out of sight, the others found themselves surrounded on three sides by rows of angry cops. The police, moving in arcs of twenty or thirty men, sliced into the crowd with their clubs and with Mace, beating people indiscriminately. Tourists, newsmen and people on their way home from work were all attacked and beaten.

So many people were injured that the Eugene McCarthy campaign headquarters on the fifteenth floor was turned into a makeshift hospital, but the police even burst into that and swept through clubbing people, leaving great pools of blood on the floor.

PARIS

Though there was a lot of talk about "the revolution" in hippie circles by people such as Abbie Hoffman and Jerry Rubin, the real revolutionary activity was all happening in Europe, with the actions in France almost toppling the government. French students were, for the most part, unaware of the activities of the hippies, largely because of the language problem—if no one translates Tim Leary then his ideas remain unknown. The ideas that did get through were largely transmitted by rock 'n' roll, with glossy magazines like Rock et Folk giving great coverage to the new psychedelic music and trying to explain the drugs and the message. The same Beat generation influences that shaped the hippies were also known in France, largely thanks to Claude Pelieu and Mary Beach, who translated Burroughs, Ginsberg, Bob Kaufman and others into French.

However, the events of May 1968 were sparked not by a hippie uprising, but by a combination of frustrations. It was a time of full employment so there was plenty of money around, but something was lacking. French students were intellectual and traditionally left wing, usually divided into numerous warring factions. The Cuban revolution had inspired many of them and had shown that it was possible to transform a society. The French had fought a colonial war in Vietnam and students were very opposed to the war being continued by the Americans. This was a major rallying cause.

RIGHT: It was the closest thing ever to a reenactment of the Paris Commune. The student strikes and activism at the Sorbonne spread throughout the country until more than half the population was on strike and the government was threatened.

"Cours camarade, le vieux monde est derrière toi."
"Soyons réalistes, demandons l'impossible."
"Prenez vos désirs pour la realité."

Situationist slogans printed on posters and pasted across Paris, May 1968

Student frustrations were magnified by massive overcrowding at lectures. Up to 1,200 students tried to attend some of the lectures at the Sorbonne.

The events began with student unrest led by Daniel Cohn-Bendit at the University of Nanterre—one of the divisions of the University of Paris—when, on January 8 , at the inauguration of a new swimming pool, the Minister for Youth and Sports was forced to leave by demonstrating students. On February 7 there was a counter-demonstration against supporters of US Vietnam policy that resulted in violent exchanges with the police in Paris. It was followed by pro-North Vietnam demonstrations. The next day there were incidents at universities throughout France with students demanding freedom of speech and movement.

On March 22 the administrative tower of Nanterre University was occupied by 150 students led by Cohn-Bendit, who told the press they were anarchists. Courses were suspended until April 1.

Meanwhile, in parallel developments in Germany, an attack on student leader Rudi Dutschke by the police resulted in riots, which were followed by supporting demonstrations in France. On April 27 Daniel Cohn-Bendit, who is German, was arrested at Nanterre. Massive demonstrations followed throughout the university and on May 2 courses at the faculty of letters in Nanterre were suspended. The courtyard of the Sorbonne was occupied, but the police were able to clear it the next day. That evening violence erupted throughout the Latin Quarter, resulting in

LEFT: Students, workers and socialists lined up together against the State—in the form of the gendarmes and later the army—in Paris, May 1968. Across the city slogans would appear on walls painted by Situationists—followers of Guy Debord—after each street battle.

more than 100 people getting injured and 596 arrested. On May 4 all courses at the Sorbonne were suspended.

On May 5 the courts convicted fifteen demonstrators, giving four of them jail terms. Naturally this was followed by more demonstrations. On May 6 345 police and about 600 students were injured in battles in the Latin Quarter. There were 422 arrests. Students at universities throughout France pledged their support. On the night of May 10 riots broke out throughout the Latin Quarter. Students tore up the cobblestones to use as ammunition, trees were felled and cars and buses were overturned to make more than 60 barricades. The police attacked the barricades with teargas and were beaten back by a fusillade of missiles. The battle of rue Gay-Lussac lasted for twelve hours. By the end of the night, 1,500 people were injured. 367 were hospitalized (of which 251 were police) and 468 arrested. As usual the police overreacted and the public support was largely for the bloodied students.

On May 11 , seeing an advantage to themselves, the three major unions—the CGT, the CFDT and the FEN—sided with the students and called for a general strike. In an attempt to defuse the situation, Prime Minister George Pompidou announced the re-opening of the Sorbonne on May 13—the day of the strike. It didn't work. The general strike filled the streets of Paris with hundreds of thousands of students and workers and, in the midst of the confusion, students occupied the Sorbonne.

The walls and trees of Paris were adorned with posters, consisting of what were often brilliant graphics and revolutionary slogans. Though they seemed spontaneous, in actuality they were carefully thought up by the International Situationists—a radical group that began at Strasbourg, whose goal was total liberation from

the old hierarchical organization of society.

Strikes spread rapidly and, on May 16 , air transport, the metro and SNCF were closed. There were no newspapers and factories began closing down all over France.

By May 20 an estimated 10 million workers were on strike—more than half of the working population. France was practically paralyzed. Battles with the police became a nightly ritual: students, their faces painted with white zinc-oxide paste to resist tear-gas, would man the barricades and the police would charge into a hail of ball bearings and cobblestones.

On May 22 an amnesty for demonstrators was passed by the National Assembly and union confederations said they were now willing to negotiate with the employer's association and the government. Demonstrations were held in Paris to protest the withdrawal of Daniel Cohn-Bendit's residence permit for France.

The night of May 24 saw the worst violence to date, with barricades appearing outside the Latin Quarter and in other cities. Overnight rioting in Paris resulted in 795 arrests and 456 injured. An attempt was made to burn down the stock exchange, but though all the papers in it were burned, the building was occupied instead and a large white flag with a joint drawn upon it was flown from the roof.

By May 27 an end was in sight, as an agreement was reached between the unions, employer's associations and the government. The minimum wage was to be raised, working hours cut, the age of retirement reduced and the right to organize extended. But workers at Renault and other big factories refused to return to work. The Minister of Education finally resigned and President de Gaulle secretly visited General Massu, head of French troops stationed in Baden-Wurttemberg, to see if he still had the

"The spectacle is capital accumulated to the point where it becomes image."

Situationist Guy Debord

support of the army. On May 29 the CGT—the biggest union—brought several thousands of members to demonstrate in the streets of Paris as a show of strength.

The next day, President de Gaulle announced the dissolution of the National Assembly on the radio. New elections would take place. Georges Pompidou would remain Prime Minister. He also implied that, if necessary, force would be used to maintain order; clearly the army was still behind him. The minimum wage was raised to three francs an hour. The cabinet was reshuffled and elections announced for June 23 and 30. By now the right wing and the middle classes were organized and demonstrations of support for the government began throughout France.

The crisis ended on June 1 , the long Pentacost weekend and a traditional holiday in France. Gas stations were opened again and the roads were blocked with huge traffic jams as people filled their tanks and set off for the coast or country. Workers drifted back to their jobs. Not that the election campaign was free from violence: on June 11 1,500 people were arrested, 400 injured and a demonstrator was shot and killed at Montbéliard. The next day, demonstrations were banned in France. On June 13 students were evicted from the Odéon and two days later, amid clouds of tear gas, from the Sorbonne.

The fragility of the state had scared many people and the right wing gained a lot of seats in the elections. Georges Pompidou resigned and Maurice Couve de Murville became Prime Minister, warning that it would take six months to implement the "grands réformes."

President de Gaulle held a referendum in April 1969 to ask voters to decide whether he was to continue as President of France. He was voted out and, on June 16, 1969, Georges Pompidou was elected president in his stead.

RIGHT: Every night the students and revolutionaries would battle for control of the Left Bank, the police used tear gas and batons, but the barricades held and the Latin Quarter remained a free zone.

REVOLUTION #9

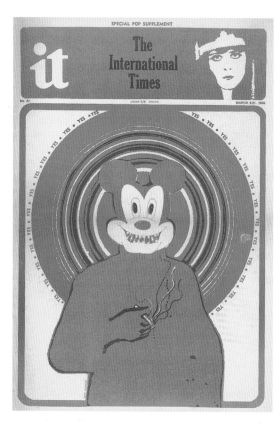

"There's no point in dropping out because it's the same there and it's got to change. It all comes down to changing your head and, sure, I know that's a cliché."

John Lennon

Psychedelia was spreading. In January the Cream Cheese club opened in Cologne, Gandalf the White Wizard head shop opened in Stockholm, in March an Arts Lab opened in Berlin and by the spring there were four underground newspapers in Amsterdam, the main one being Witte Krant.

In London drugs were now in such widespread use that IT began reporting on the price. In March not very good "red" acid was £1 a tab or £400–£500 a gram; hash was £8 an ounce or £85–£95 a pound. Pakistani, Lebanese, Afghani and Nepalese temple sticks were all available.

The Free University of London was due to open on February 12, on Rivington Street, with courses by Ronnie Laing, Steve Abrams, and others. However, the day was filled with bickering and a shouting match between Joe Berke and others developed over how it was to be structured: should it emulate traditional educational structures or was the whole point to experiment? International Times devoted a page to three of the differing arguments, and in the same issue published J. G. Ballard's prescient poem: "Why I

Want To Fuck Ronald Reagan," who was years away from the US presidency.

Middle Earth on King Street, Covent Garden, had now taken over completely from the defunct UFO club. Traffic, Blossom Toes, Dantalion's Chariot, Fairport Convention, Family, Jeff Beck, Tyrannosaurus Rex, Peter Green's Fleetwood Mac and the Pink Floyd all played there in the first three months of 1968. At 2am on March 3 it was raided by 150 police—apparently the biggest paramilitary operation since the war. They took more than five hours to search over 750 people. There were only seven drug arrests, plus three for unnamed "offensive weapons" and one "assault" of a policeman.

The evening was saved by the nearby Arts Lab. Ex-IT editor Jack Henry Moore and his resident theatre company, the Human Family, organized an emergency station for over 200 Middle Earth "refugees" who couldn't get home, as there was no public transport at that time of night. The Human Family acted as runners between Bow Street police station, Middle Earth and the Arts Lab, letting people know they were welcome at

the Arts Lab, making them tea in the restaurant, caring for sick junkies and calming people who had been badly roughed up by the cops, as well as keeping everyone posted on the arrests and releases. IT reported, "Whatever else, the Middle Earth raid provided an opportunity for the community to work together and come together in a spirit of love." In his "Perfumed Garden" column in IT, John Peel wrote, "Sympathies and my love to all those humiliated during and following the recent raid on the Middle Earth. One girl told me that she was searched four times by an assortment of robust lady policemen. They found nothing, but didn't seem to mind. In view of all this, may I urge your renewed support for Release. You may be next…"

Release was the 24-hour free legal aid organization, similar to San Francisco's Switchboard, set up in 1967 specifically to help with drug busts

RIGHT: Ringo Starr and George Harrison appear unperturbed by the presence of the Blue Meanie behind them from the animated film Yellow Submarine. In Berkeley this term became a less offensive way of insulting the pigs.

Iron Butterfly

In-A-Gadda-Da-V

Album sleeve art attempted to reflect the band's state of mind.

"When you stop exploring with drugs, now that's a bad scene. I never want to stop exploring."

Stevie Winwood of Traffic, 1968

and other related hippie legal problems. In fact Release's cofounder, Caroline Coon, had just spent a night in jail herself for refusing to pay a ten guinea fine relating to the Free Brian Jones demonstration, but the Bernard Braden TV show paid it for her, gaining extra publicity for the organization.

IT sent three people over to cover the events of May in Paris, the aftermath of which was schisms and splits within the paper. After much debate, the original founders stayed to act as an advisory editorial board, and the paper itself

LEFT: British psychedelic band Tomorrow, featuring guitarist Steve Howe (later to form Yes) and drummer Twink, were a permanent fixture of the underground psychedelic scene in England. They would have one hit single, My White Bicycle, released this year.

became a worker's cooperative. Most of the original founders continued to write or work for it.

PERFORMANCE

1968 was the year of Performance, Nicholas Roeg and Donald Campbell's thriller featuring Mick Jagger and James Fox. Warner Brothers were so disturbed by the sex and violence in it that they shelved the movie for two years. It was finally released in a heavily cut version, so there was no more footage of Jagger's penis and the naked romps with Anita Pallenberg and Michele Breton were severely edited.

There was more stoned behavior in The Rolling Stones' Rock & Roll Circus by Michael Lindsay-Hogg, which remained unreleased for

more than 30 years because the Stones had played so badly. Today it is considered a record of an extraordinary moment in time, with the Who, John Lennon, Marianne Faithfull, Dr. John, Traffic, and full supporting cast.

It was also the year of the Beatles' animated feature Yellow Submarine, which, though they had very little to do with it, was surprisingly good and featured some wonderful psychedelic sequences. Ringo also starred as the gardener in Christian Marquand's forgettable Candy, based on Terry Southern's hilarious book. There was further peripheral Beatles involvement in Wonderwall, Joe Massot's film about voyeuristic sex, LSD sessions and hip photographers with a score by George Harrison. Apple released the soundtrack.

STREET FIGHTING MAN

There were a number of demonstrations in London in 1968. On March 17 Tariq Ali led his followers in The Vietnam Solidarity Campaign straight into the arms of the police, as he headed an anti-Vietnam War action against the American Embassy in Grosvenor Square. They were repelled by mounted police, who charged into the crowd, beating the protesters with batons. This happened again on April 15 in a demonstration against the German Springer Press outside the Daily Mirror building. Both times Ali was at the front of the column, but when the police made an appearance he slipped away. As he put it, "My comrades got me away from the fighting because they felt it couldn't do to have me arrested." There was a lot of criticism in the underground press of Ali, suggesting that if he was going to encourage bloodshed, he should at least train his followers in karate or self-defense. Mick Jagger had been on the first march to Grosvenor Square and found the inspiration to write "Street Fighting Man."

On March 2 Syd Barrett left the Pink Floyd; acid had made him so unstable that for some gigs he just strummed the same chord, or detuned the strings so they were slack. Eric Clapton, Jack Bruce and Ginger Baker's Cream were gaining in popularity on both sides of the Atlantic and their long guitar solos and big beat drum sound had begun to influence others. One such band had evolved from the ashes of the Yardbirds. Guitarist Jimmy Page and bassist John Paul Jones hired a 20-year-old high-pitched screamer from the Midlands named Robert Plant, who in turn recommended a 20-year-old session drummer named John Bonham. They called themselves Led Zeppelin and began to write songs that owed a lot to old bluesmen of America's Deep South. By the end of the year Led Zep had toured the US as support to Vanilla Fudge and the MC5 and been a huge success.

LEFT: The battle of Grosvenor Square. Tariq Ali's Vietnam Solidarity Campaign attempts to occupy the American Embassy.

ABOVE: The banned cover design for the 1968 Rolling Stones' LP Beggar's Banquet. The album contained "Street Fighting Man" and "Sympathy For The Devil." It was the last Stones album to feature Brian Jones.

"I'm rather pleased to hear they have banned 'Street Fighting Man' as long as it's still available in the shops. The last time they banned one of our records in America it sold a million."

Mick Jagger on hearing that "Street Fighting Man" had been banned in Chicago for fear that it might invoke civil unrest, September 1968

It was a year of extremes, of violence and madness as well as achievement and success. The Rolling Stones' experience encapsulated it all. Brian Jones became the first of many rock casualties when his drug taking made it impossible for him to function as a member of the group and he was thrown out. No one

6566676869707071

expected him to die, but he did shortly afterwards as the result of careless behavior at a party at his country house. At a concert swiftly dedicated to his memory in Hyde Park, London, the Stones performed for half a million people on a beautiful English summer afternoon. It was an idyllic day with no trouble. But when they tried to repeat it in San Francisco, at the Altamont Speedway six months later, they inadvertently presided over a murder as Hell's Angels ran amok and stabbed a man to death right in front of the stage. This was the year that hippies realized once and for all that the Hell's Angels never did believe in love and peace, and were not about to change.

In August, despite two downpours, the Woodstock festival had demonstrated how the communal spirit should work. Most people agree that the actual experience was horrible, but it was that shared experience that created the so-called Woodstock Generation. However, the happy communalism of a circulating joint and shared spiritual experiences on acid resulted in big-time drug dealing. And wherever there are millions of dollars to be made illegally, there are also beatings and murders as people carve out their territory.

POWER TO THE PEOPLE

"An angel who came and paved a road white chicks hadn't walked before."

Etta James on Janis Joplin

Jefferson Airplane were officially rich. Grace Slick surprised a car salesman by pulling out $18,000 cash to buy an Aston Martin. Yet they continued to support a pro-drug, anti-cop radicalism, making revolutionary political statements in interviews. For Grace Slick, the New Year opened in silence: she had an operation on her throat nodes and spent January 1969 without speaking. She also traded in Spencer Dryden for Paul Kantner. Dryden lasted another year before being replaced by Joey Covington. Meanwhile Jorma and Jack Casady, who loved to play, grew restless waiting for Grace to recover. They began jamming at the clubs around San Francisco. People seemed to like it so they decided to record and signed a $25,000 deal as a duo, calling themselves Hot Tuna (RCA wouldn't go for Hot Shit).

Janis Joplin was now a solo artist but she had assembled a band who were heavily into heroin, as she was herself. In March she played three nights at Winterland, her first post-Big Brother gig in San Francisco. She was nervous about the reception she was likely to get from her home-town audience, but fought it with heroin and the false bravura of a prima donna attitude. She kept the audience waiting for an hour, then performed so badly that people began to leave midway through and no one called for an encore. Hurt, humiliated and angry, she shot up backstage. There was one final blow waiting for her: someone had stolen her psychedelic painted

Porsche from the garage, claiming they were fetching it for her. The critics savaged her.

In April, though, she began a European tour and performed brilliantly, culminating at the Royal Albert Hall. She got the audience dancing at what many people regard as one of the best rock concerts of the 60s.

Unfortunately the celebration in the hotel room afterwards saw tragedy, as Sam Andrews, strung out on junk but unused to the purity of London heroin compared to American street smack, overdosed and had to be thrown naked into a bath of cold water to get him breathing again. Suzie Creamcheese, the famous groupie who had moved to London, did her bit to resuscitate him by jumping into the tub and sitting astride him, naked. When they got back to California, Janis asked him over to her room in the Landmark, where she lived with her girlfriend, Peggy Caserta. They both shot up, then she fired him. He was so out of it that he even stayed on until Janis could find a replacement.

Like Jefferson Airplane, Janis liked to whip up the crowd, getting them to leave their seats and dance, to defy the cops whom she insulted from the stage. On November 15, in Tampa, Florida, it didn't go over so well. Police dragged her from

PREVIOUS PAGE: At the barbed wire on campus at Berkeley.
RIGHT: Janis Joplin with her psychedelic Porsche.
OVER: The National Guard's barbed wire fence surrounding People's Park, Berkeley, is draped with the American flag.

"Power to the imagination, all power to the people."

The Berkeley Liberation Program statement, Summer 1969

the stage and put her in jail for "vulgar and indecent language." The chaos and shouting was now a substitute for a genuine blues performance. Thanks largely to heroin, Janis had lost her power. The screaming and sobbing on stage were now empty, inauthentic histrionics. A concert at Carnegie Hall was just about saved by some blues jamming by Paul Butterfield and Johnny Winter.

It was a bad year also for Tim Leary. Richard Nixon had been elected president and had personally vowed to "get" him. The story of Leary's legal difficulties is an enormously complicated one, with numerous charges in both local and federal court. He did win a significant victory when the Supreme Court threw out his original Laredo bust, by nullifying the Tax Stamp Act—it was illegal not to pay tax on marijuana imported into the country, but to declare it would, of course, have been self-incriminatory. Tim was so elated that he decided to run for Governor of California. He got together with John Lennon and Yoko Ono, who were holding a bed-in for peace in Montreal, and Lennon gave him a campaign song. It was the Laguna bust that was his undoing. On March 11 the judge gave Tim a six-month to ten-year sentence for the two roaches found in the car ashtray. Jackie got three months and Rosemary was put on probation. This time, there was no bail allowed. And after he'd served that, there was a ten-year sentence from the original Texas bust four years previously. The campaign to free Timothy Leary now began in earnest. What no one expected was that on September 12, 1970 Tim Leary, with the aid of the Weathermen, escaped from jail and, having successfully left the country, issued a declaration that showed that prison had changed him: "Warning. I am armed and should be considered dangerous to anyone who threatens my life or my freedom."

PEOPLE POWER

In Berkeley, the area to the south of the campus was Hippie high street. Telegraph Avenue was an

area of old wooden houses that were rented by students and hippies. The university did not like this and, using its right of eminent domain, they purchased three acres for $1.3 million and bulldozed the buildings, claiming they were going to build student dorms. But Ronald Reagan, governor of California, had cut off funds for dorms, so the land lay vacant. In April 1968 Mike Delacour had had the idea of using it as a public space for rock concerts, a meeting space and a playground for children. The Telegraph Avenue merchants raised a few hundred dollars and bought a truckload of plants and earth. Landscape architects at the university drew up a plan and within days hundreds of people were working on the site. On weekends as many as 3,000 people turned up to build swings, a slide, a wading pool and sandbox and to plant trees and flowerbeds. It was a beautiful thing.

Four weeks later Berkeley chancellor Roger Heyns acted. On May 15, before dawn, 300 police sealed off eight square blocks while city workers bulldozed the park and children's playground and erected an eight-foot cyclone fence around their property. At noon there was a rally of several thousand people on campus and student-body president elect Dan Siegel gave the word: "Let's go down there and take the park." It was only four blocks away.

Seeing a line of police in a side street, someone opened a fire hydrant to wet them if they charged. The police responded with tear gas, but Berkeley students had learned to always wear gloves so they could throw the hot gas canisters back. There was an exchange of fire, with the students also throwing rocks. A police car was set on fire and the Bank of America's window smashed and the building fired. A squad of Alameda County sheriff's deputies appeared in their blue jump suits—dubbed the "blue meanies" after the Beatles' Yellow Submarine— and the Berkeley police began issuing them with shotguns. There is a law in Berkeley that the police cannot use guns unless it's to save life or to protect their own, but it does not apply to out-of-town police.

The Sheriff's deputies began firing into the crowd. For several hours they fired buckshot and birdshot at students, people running away,

passers-by, lawyers and reporters. There were people watching the action from the roof of the Telegraph repertory Cinema and they shot them, too. An artist named Alan Blanchard was permanently blinded by buckshot, and James Rector, a visitor from San Jose who had nothing to do with the park, was murdered, his belly ripped apart by buckshot. One hundred people were hospitalized and many more had minor injuries.

Any reasonable administration would have negotiated with the park builders and permitted them to use the land until funds for student dorms were available. But not in Reagan's California. Two thousand National guardsmen were brought in, with bayonets fixed, and 700 cops patrolled the area. Public meetings were banned and a curfew was imposed, as helicopters buzzed around the town. Troops threw tear gas at Junior high schools, causing them to be evacuated and outraging normally acquiescent parents.

When a rally was called on the campus, a National Guard helicopter dropped CS gas on the crowd, blanketing the entire campus, including the hospital and nearby schools, with gas. The troops moved in and arrested 482 people, who were made to lay on the concrete for between four and seven hours as they were processed and taken to Santa Rita prison. Anyone who moved was hit. No wonder some students began enquiring as to what type of gun would bring down a helicopter. Troops built a machine gun emplacement in People's Park, installed chemical toilets and flew the American flag.

A People's Park Annex was built on public land across town, but police moved in and destroyed it. Small parks began popping up everywhere, only to be destroyed by cops and troops. On May 30, 25,000 people marched peacefully to the park, now guarded by police sharpshooters on the rooftops and ringed with Guardsmen with fixed bayonets. People put flowers in the barrels of their guns. Seventeen days later the guardsmen left, but the fence remained—proof of the power of the State.

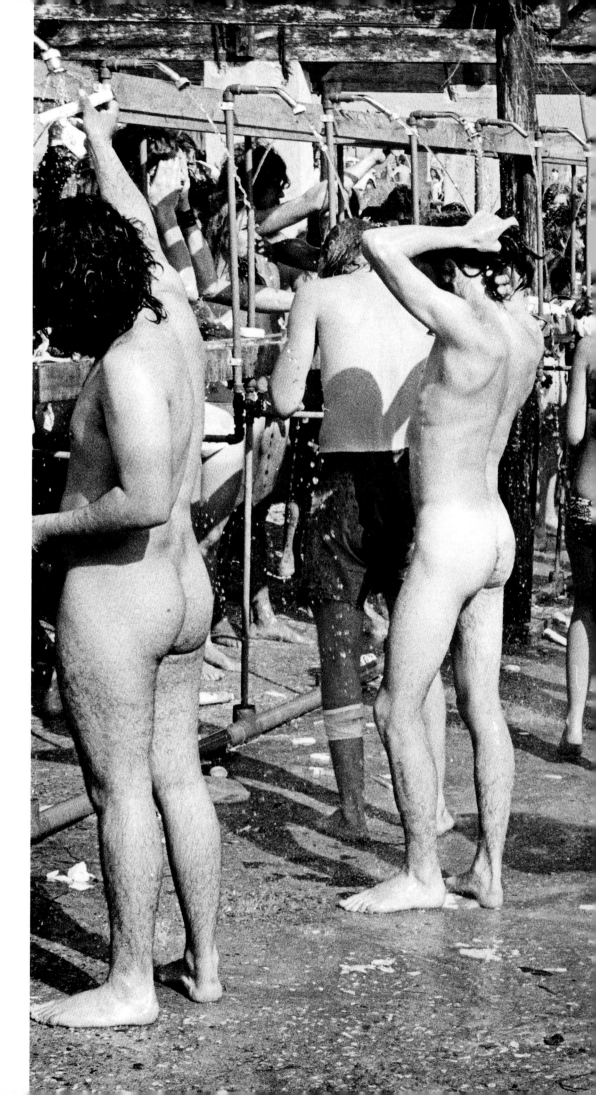

RIGHT: A big rock festival was like an instant small town—it needed communications, food, drink and toilet facilities, often for tens of thousands of people.

THE WEATHERMEN

Opposition to the war in Vietnam had radicalized many of the students and anti-war protesters. Nixon's government and the organized right harassed the Black Panthers and attempted to

National War Council in Flint, Michigan, where a huge cardboard machine gun hung from the ceiling and the speeches were about "organizing a city-wide anti-pig movement ..." Participants romanticized Manson's killing spree. Speaking of the LaBianca murders, Bernardine Dohrn, who became the organization's spokesperson, said, "Dig it. First they killed those pigs, then they ate dinner in the same room as them. Then they even

Induction Center, where every draft-eligible male in Manhattan reported for his army physical, was virtually levelled, although there were no injuries. The note sent to the press read: "Tonight we bombed the Whitehall Induction Center. This action was in support of the NLF, legalized marijuana, love, Cuba, legalized abortion, and all the American revolutionaries and GIs who are winning the war against the Pentagon. Nixon, surrender now!'

"You don't need a Weatherman to know which way the wind blows."

Bob Dylan

intimidate the underground press. The battle of Chicago had shown that normal free speech no longer existed in America and a faction of the SDS broke off to become the Weathermen. Their 16,000 word manifesto in the June 18, 1969 issue of New Left Notes was headed: "You Don't Need A Weatherman To Know Which Way The Wind Blows," a line from Bob Dylan's "Subterranean Homesick Blues." (They became the Weather Underground, in deference to the newly emergent women's lib movement). They held a

shoved a fork into a victim's stomach. Wild!" It was a standing joke that you couldn't be a Weatherman unless your father earned at least $30,000 a year; a majority of them were well-educated, upper middle-class kids who came from the same social stratum as the dead LaBiancas. After the conference, the Weathermen went underground. That summer there were bombings all across the country of federal and corporate offices, including Federal Plaza in New York. On October 8 the Whitehall

The Weathermen had been making a bomb in a Greenwich Village brownstone when it went off accidentally. Three Weathermen were killed: Terry Robbins, Ted Gold and Diana Oughton. Cathy Wilkerson, whose father owned the building, survived, as did Kathy Boudin, who was taking a shower when it happened. She ran into the street naked and was taken in by a neighbor. She borrowed clothes before slipping away to go underground for ten years.

The Weathermen claimed responsibility for dozens of explosions, and only disbanded when the war in Vietnam ended.

ABOVE: Three Weathermen died in an explosion in their bomb factory in a Greenwich Village brownstone, just off Fifth Avenue.
RIGHT: Weatherman Brian Flanigan is arrested in Chicago.

WOODSTOCK

"The New York State Freeway's closed, man. Far out!"

Arlo Guthrie

The Woodstock Aquarian Music and Art Fair was held on August 15, 16 and 17, 1969 at Max Yasgur's 660-acre dairy farm in White Lake, near Bethel, about 100 miles north of New York City.

The original plan was for "three days of peace and music" in Woodstock, the village in the Catskills where Dylan, his manager Al Grossman and the Band all lived in upstate New York. They expected about 50,000 people a day, and the toilets, plumbing, water supplies and catering were all for that many people. What they got was well over 400,000 people, the equivalent of the population of the third largest city in New York State, with all the problems that brings—in particular the need for trash collection, sanitation and food supplies. There were two births, three deaths and a few thousand injuries, though these were mostly cuts to bare feet. Amazingly, the facilities just about held up.

After months of work at Wallkill, a small industrial town near Woodstock, the city council changed their mind and, four weeks before the festival, a new site had to be found and all the equipment moved. Most of the Arts Fair had to be cancelled because of the move. Max received $50,000 for having his farm destroyed. The promoters of Woodstock were Michael Lang, a dealer who owned a head shop in Coral Gables, and Artie Kornfeld, a rock promoter of bubblegum bands. And on the money side there were Joel Rosenman, a lawyer, and John Roberts, whose father owned a multimillion dollar pharmaceutical firm.

LEFT: Woodstock became synonymous with the hippie lifestyle despite the fact that many groups played badly and most of the time the audience was sitting in a sea of mud.

The Hog Farm were asked to come and help out. Eighty of them were flown in two weeks early from New Mexico in a rented plane at a cost of $17,000 (the stewardesses locked themselves in the bathrooms). They helped build the site and provided food and security. Their way of stopping a fight involved a pie in the face and tense situations were diffused by lobbing balloons at people, who immediately began tossing them to each other.

Abbie Hoffman threatened Michael Lang with disruption right from the start if his various demands were not met, accusing the organizers of "ripping off the culture" (as if bands like the Who would have played for free). In the end they gave him money to set up booths and provide a free daily newspaper, but most of the money went toward his trial instead.

Four hours before the festival began, there was a fifteen-mile traffic jam all around the town of Bethel. People had been arriving for days before and the organizers rented additional space behind the stage for a tent and teepee city that soon needed its own roads and street signs.

A 35-acre field sloped down to form a natural amphitheater, though the stage was so far away that many people could barely see anything. At the time it was the largest performing stage ever constructed and it took a month to erect. It was originally equipped with a turntable so that one band could set up on the back half while another was performing, but this broke down early on, meaning there were unavoidable delays between acts as they changed equipment. The audience were able to hear the music though, from a huge speaker system mounted on 80-foot scaffolds on either side of the stage.

"There was no violence, but lots of marijuana and LSD."

www.hippy.com glossary

The music program changed quite a bit from the advertised line-up. The festival opened on the Friday evening with Richie Havens, who walked on stage at 5:07pm. Country Joe McDonald performed a solo set, including the infamous "Fixin-to-Die-Rag," and was followed by John Sebastian, also performing solo. Then it was Swami Satchadinanda, Bert Sommer and Sweetwater, who were originally scheduled to open the festivities.

Tim Hardin came on at 9pm. Many people were hoping that this appearance would revitalize his career, which had been badly damaged by heroin, but he stumbled onstage smacked out and performed badly. Then came Ravi Shankar, but he had to quit his set at 10:35 because the first of the rainstorms set in, breaking a long dry spell. After a fifteen-minute break, he was followed by sixteen-year-old Melanie, who claimed later to have had an out-of-body experience on stage, and Arlo Guthrie, whose "Coming Into Los Angeles" went down well with the dopers. Then Joan Baez played for an hour, ending the evening at 2am.

Saturday began at 12:15pm with Quill, who cut short their set. This was when the revolving stage broke down, and there was a 45-minute break before British rockers Keef Hartley came on. It was their American debut and they soon kicked some life into the crowd with an hour-long set. The energy level grew even higher with Santana, playing one of their first large concerts. The Incredible String Band were supposed to play the Friday night, but their set was postponed due to rain, so they had been waiting a long time. They did a credible 75 minutes that helped establish their quirky folk-rock in the States. The evening was designed to get heavier and heavier, first with Canned Heat, then Mountain, followed by Creedence Clearwater Revival. It was already 11:10pm when the Grateful Dead rambled on stage.

The organizers had expected to sell tickets at the gates but, by Thursday, the ticket booths and the hurricane fencing were not yet up, and so many thousands of people had already arrived

LEFT: Naked chick dances at a festival.
RIGHT: Jimi Hendrix's management insisted that he headline the festival. So he came on after dawn on a Monday morning and most people missed his set.

"Good morning. What I have in mind is breakfast in bed for 400,000."

Wavy Gravy gets cooking, Woodstock

that the organizers had little choice but to declare it a free festival. The organizers knew the film rights would bring in big money. The only people who in fact paid were those who bought tickets in advance. This meant there was no cash on the site and the bands were used to being paid in cash. The only two managers to make trouble over this were from the Grateful Dead and the Who, both of whom wanted certified checks, even though it was Saturday and the banks were not open. In the end Michael Lang said he would announce to the crowd that these bands were not playing because they wanted money up front and, at this, their managers backed down and settled for regular checks— which were in fact good.

The Grateful Dead, by their own admission, performed very poorly, even though they did a 90-minute set. After a 40-minute break, Janis Joplin came on and also performed badly. By the time Sly and the Family Stone came on, it was already 3am, but they played a brilliant set that was generally regarded as one of the best of the festival, and got the audience dancing.

The Who came on at 5am. Pete Townshend had brought his wife, Karen, and their baby daughter to Woodstock, but he had been spiked with acid, had waited 16 hours, then had to clear photographers off the stage before going on. He was not feeling the love and peace vibe. The last set of the night—or morning—was by Jefferson Airplane, who went onstage at 7am.

People had six hours to rest up before the Sunday concert began. Wavy Gravy and the Hog Farm kitchens swung into action. By the time everyone had eaten, done a little naked bathing in the lake and visited one of the portable toilets, it was 2pm and time for Joe Cocker to play air guitar. His 90-minute set was just ending when the second big storm broke. Rain tipped down for an hour and a half, soaking the audience, their sleeping bags, their clothes and food. By the end of it the site was a sea of mud and some people preferred to simply go naked, rather than walk around covered in mud.

When it was safe enough to use the equipment again, Max Yasgur, whose farm it was, said

a few words before Country Joe and the Fish came on and brightened everyone up with the Fish Cheer. As it was Sunday, Swami Satchidananda came on to deliver the sermon, followed at 8pm by Ten Years After. It was most people's first exposure to these British rockers and they did a solid two-hour set, followed by a tired, uninspired set from The Band. Throughout the festival, the acts that everyone thought would have captured the spirit of things were usually the ones who played badly. Many of the acts were tired and had taken too many drugs to perform at peak intensity. Blood, Sweat and Tears came on at midnight, followed by Texas bluesman Johnny Winter.

By the time Crosby, Stills, Nash and Young came on at 3am, the audience was beginning to drift away; many of them had jobs to go to that morning. Crosby, Stills and Nash played for 30 minutes before Neil Young joined them on stage for a further hour. The Paul Butterfield Blues Band played next, followed by doo-wop revivalists Sha-Na-Na. The final act of the festival was Jimi Hendrix. He wanted to close the show because the headliner always closes the show and he could not be persuaded otherwise. He was offered the optimum midnight slot but his manager, Mike Jeffries, insisted. Most people didn't see him. When Jimi walked on stage at 8:30am on the Monday morning, there were a mere 30 to 40,000 people left to see him perform the brilliant version of the "Star Spangled Banner," which has become a musical icon for the whole festival.

Joni Mitchell wrote a song about it; Abbie Hoffman wrote a quick book, Woodstock Nation; Charles Schultz introduced a character called Woodstock in his "Peanuts" cartoon strip. Woodstock entered popular culture as shorthand for a period, an attitude, a generation. Just as the survivors of May 1968 in Paris are known as the soixanthuitiemeards, so American youth of the later 60s are the Woodstock Generation.

RIGHT: Cleaning up after Woodstock. Max Yasgur's farm housed a temporary city of half a million people, which produced hundreds of tons of trash as evidence of its existence.

ALTAMONT

"Ain't nobody gonna kick my motorcycle. And if you have to go through 50 people to get at him, you're gonna git him."

Sonny Barger, chief Hell's Angel

The Rolling Stones performed a fifteen-city tour of the United States in November and, after being criticized for the high ticket prices, agreed to do a free concert in San Francisco.

This was originally scheduled for Golden Gate Park, a perfect location that was capable of taking a crowd as enormous as the one the Stones played to at the free concert in Hyde Park, London in July. But the city authorities changed their mind and a new location had to be found quickly. The Altamont Speedway was selected for a concert on December 6. It was going to be the West Coast Woodstock. For the Stones it was little more than just another gig. The Grateful Dead's manager, Rock Scully, advised them to use the Hell's Angels as security since the Angels would turn up and cause trouble anyway. Emmett Grogan agreed. A deal was made that the Angels would get $500 worth of beer to guard the stage.

Santana had to stop after three numbers to ask that the fighting halt. While the Jefferson Airplane were on, the Angels began beating up a black man in front of the stage. When Marty Balin intervened, he was knocked unconscious by an Angel. Inflamed by drugs and beer, the Angels periodically attacked the crowd, beating fans with billiard cues and driving their motorcycles straight at people, breaking one girl's ankle. Dozens of people were injured. One of the Angels' bikes, parked in front of the stage, was overturned when the Stones finally came on.

Sonny Barger explained their reaction: "Ain't nobody gonna kick my motorcycle. And they might think because they're in a crowd of 300,000 people that they can do it and get away with it, but when you're standing there, looking at something that's your life, and everything that you've got is invested in that thing, and you love that thing better than you love anything in this world, and you see a guy kick it, you know who he is. And if you have to go through 50 people to get at him, you're gonna git him." The Angels' outrage was not helped by Mick's sarcastic remark from the stage: "Oh dear, someone's motorbike's fell over."

The climax of the violence came when the Angels murdered an 18-year-old black man, Meredith Hunter, by stabbing him and beating him with their billiard cues. Film shows that Hunter was brandishing a gun.

Characteristically, the San Francisco hippie papers blamed the Stones for the violence, but they had been the ones to champion and romanticize the Angels. The Stones didn't know; they'd never set foot in Haight-Ashbury in their lives and wouldn't have wanted to. Two days later Mick, Keith and Charlie were back in Europe.

Keith Richards later said, "I thought the show would have been stopped, but hardly anybody seemed to want to take any notice. The violence in front of the stage was incredible. Looking back I don't think it was a good idea to have the Hell's Angels, but the Grateful Dead who've organized these shows before thought they would be the best. I believe the alternative would have been the Black Panthers. I wouldn't like to say whether they would have been more vicious.'

RIGHT: Mayhem reigned in the front stage area as drunken, pilled-up Hell's Angels fought with the crowd. The climax of the chaos came with the death of Meredith Hunter, stabbed by an Angel.

BORN TO BE WILD

By now the counterculture was well established in American society and, though still largely frowned upon, it was now a subject for Hollywood. This was the year of Arthur Penn's Alice's Restaurant, the film of the song, based on Arlo Guthrie's "The Alice's Restaurant Massacree," about a real person and place. According to Arlo Guthrie, "That was Arthur Penn's idea about communes in America, my song was about the draft and garbage.'

The most famous film of the whole period was Easy Rider. Directed by Dennis Hopper with a script by Terry Southern and starring Peter Fonda and Jack Nicolson, it caught perfectly the mood of the times: the friendly hippies versus the ugly rednecks. This same year saw Revolution, Jack O'Connell's documentary of Haight-Ashbury hippie life—the summer solstice, a nude ballet, the Avalon, the Hare Krishnas and a visit to a hippie commune in the woods.

The summer of 1969 is most remembered for the spate of killings that took place in Los Angeles. They began on July 31, when the body of Gary Hinman, a music teacher, was found stabbed to death at his home in Topanga Canyon, with the words "Political Piggy" daubed on the wall in his own blood. But this was nothing compared to the slaughter of the night of August 9 at 10050 Cielo Drive, a cul de sac off Benedict Canyon. Amongst the dead was the actress Sharon Tate (Sharon Polanski), who was stabbed sixteen times; five of these wounds were fatal. She was eight months pregnant. Also found were Jay Sebring, a wealthy high-society hairdresser, who was shot once and stabbed seven times; Abigail Folger, heiress to the Folger Coffee fortune, died from 28 stab wounds; Voytek Frykowski, Gibby Folger's boyfriend and one of Roman Polanski's Polish friends, died of two gunshot wounds after he was battered over the head with a blunt object thirteen times and stabbed 51 times; and Steve Parent, who had just visited the housekeep, was shot in his car as he was leaving. The word "Pig" was written on the wall in the victims' blood.

Two days later there were two more killings, this time in Los Feliz. Leno LaBianca died from twelve stab wounds after enduring a further fourteen wounds from a carving fork, which was left sticking in his stomach. His wife, Rosemary LaBianca, was stabbed 41 times. The words "Death To Pigs" was written on the wall in blood, as well as "Rise" and "Helter Skelter."

Charles Manson, the illiterate psychopathic leader of the Family commune at the Spahn Ranch, had convinced his followers to engage in a series of killings in order to ferment a war between blacks and whites. The tortuous logic of his philosophy was a composite of his interpretation of Scientology and the Process, combined with a unique reading of the songs on the Beatles' White Album, which he thought were

RIGHT: Steppenwolf. Left to right, Goldy McJohn, Gabriel Melder, Nick St. Nicholas, Jerry Edmonton, John Kay. Their "Born To Be Wild" was the theme tune to the cult movie Easy Rider.

secret messages for him. He called the killing sprees "Helter Skelter" after the McCartney song.

In his rambling statement at the conclusion of his murder trial on November 19, 1970, Manson told the judge and jury: "Like, Helter Skelter is a nightclub. Helter Skelter means confusion. Literally. It doesn't mean any war with anyone. It doesn't mean that those people are going to kill other people. It only means what it means. It's not my conspiracy. It is not my music. I hear what it relates. It says 'Rise!' It says 'Kill!' Why blame it on me? I didn't write the music. I am not the person who projected it into your social consciousness."

Charlie Manson was going to lead his family into the desert. There was a hole in Death Valley that only he knew about which led to the center of the Earth, where there was a civilization that would receive them and where they would live while the blacks and whites engaged in a battle to the death. Charlie had let it be known that he was an incarnation of Jesus Christ, and the girls believed him.

Before he was caught Manson had often boasted of 35 murders, but the prosecutors only had evidence for eight, although they knew he was also responsible for the murder of Donald "Shorty" Shea. This took place at the Spahn ranch, but his body was never found. The Tate murders were committed by Tex Watson, Susan Atkins, Linda Kasabian and Patricia Krenwinkel. The LaBianca murders were committed by Manson, who had tied them up before sending in Watson, Krenwinkel and Leslie Van Houten with instructions to kill them. Bobby Beausoleil killed Hinman, a friend of the Family who had inherited some money but refused to give it to Manson. Linda Atkins was a witness.

At first the underground press supported Manson, because it seemed that this was yet another case of victimization of a hippie just because he had long hair and ran an unorthodox commune. Ex-Fug Ed Sanders wrote many articles for the Los Angeles Free Press and East Village Other on the trial, but when the truth emerged, everyone was horrified. Vincent Bugliosi, Deputy District Attorney for Los Angeles, questioned Manson about his beliefs: "We both know you ordered those murders," he told him. "Bugliosi," Manson replied, "It's the Beatles, the music they're putting out. They're talking about war. These kids listen to this music and pick up the message. It's subliminal." Charlie was completely mad but no one had noticed.

RIGHT: Susan Atkins, one of the members of the Manson Family, is escorted into the courtroom. She was found guilty, with other Family members, of the murders in the Sharon Tate household.

SEXUAL REVOLUTION

"The key energy for our revolution is erotic. A free person is one whose erotic energy has been liberated and can be expressed in increasingly more beautiful, complex ways. The sexual revolution is not just part of the atmosphere of freedom that is generating within the kids. I think it is the center of it. The reason the psychedelic drugs, particularly marijuana, are so popular is because they turn on the body. I'll say flatly that the meaning and central issue of the psychedelic experience is the erotic exhilaration. The increased freedom in sexual expression in art and mass media is symptom number one of our victory."

Tim Leary, EVO, June 1969

The 60s was characterized by a series of obscenity law suits brought against William Burrough's Naked Lunch, Henry Miller's Tropics and Ralph Ginzburg's Eros magazine. By 1969 it was safe to publish explicit sex photographs and Al Goldstein immediately did so with Screw, a weekly newspaper looking for all the world like an underground paper, but containing a few un-retouched nudes and pictures of people having sex. He had troubles, of course: "When I started Screw, the government didn't like what I was doing. Fuck the government. If we're not allowed to own our dicks and our pussies … we're not in a free country." It was a successful formula and was still going 30 years later. Jim Buckley, managing editor of New York Free Press, joined

Goldstein as the copublisher of Screw, launched that November. Not to be outdone, EVO launched its own sex paper, called Kiss.

The New York Free Press was one of the straighter underground papers, closer to the Village Voice than to the East Village Other. However, one week the lead story fell through and editor Sam Edwards ran a piece on Yayoi Kusama, the performance artist whose work involved lots of naked people, usually including herself, and lots of objects and people painted with dots. With a Kusama orgy on the cover, sales of the issue sky-rocketed, then fell again the following week. Naturally, there were nudes on virtually all the subsequent issues. But even with nudes they couldn't compete with EVO, so

Edwards and the owner, Jack Banning, folded the Freep. Instead they started The New York Review of Sex. It was not quite as in-your-face as Goldstein's paper and contained more to read. Kusama saw what was going on and published one herself called Orgy, a magazine of "nudity, love, sex & beauty." Rat, ever filled with sexist "radical males," did a sex and porn issue that differed little from Screw. It was too much for the radical women staffers, who staged a coup and threw the men out.

RIGHT (BOTTOM): In the early days of Rolling Stone they offered a free roach clip if you subscribed.
FAR RIGHT: Kusama's Orgy magazine.

"He doesn't play anything like Brian. He's a blues player and wants to play rock 'n' roll, so that's ok."

Mick Jagger on Mick Taylor replacing Brian Jones in the Stones

The Rolling Stones' troubles continued. On May 28 Mick and Marianne were busted at Mick's house on Cheyne Walk, Chelsea. Mick told the press, "The police, about six or seven of them, arrived at about a quarter to eight, just after Marianne and I had our tea." When the case finally made the court on December 18, Mick was fined £200 and 50 guineas at Marlborough Street Magistrates' Court for being found guilty of possession of cannabis resin. Marianne was acquitted.

Drugs had made Brian Jones a liability to the group; he often didn't turn up at recording sessions and when he did his playing was erratic. Mick and Keith reluctantly decided to replace him and, on June 9, it was announced that he had quit for "musical differences." He was replaced on June 13 by 20-year-old Mick Taylor, lead guitarist with the John Mayall group.

Being thrown out of the group had a catastrophic effect on Brian Jones, whose behavior became more and more erratic. On July 3 Brian died in a swimming pool accident at his home, the 16th-century Cotchford Farm at Hartfield, Sussex, where A. A. Milne had written the Winnie the Pooh stories. The official story had Jones take a midnight swim and drown from an asthma attack, but a number of witnesses revealed that a party had been in progress and he drowned after someone held his head under the water. It may have been a joke that went wrong, or it may not. He had a lot of enemies.

The Stones were due to play a free concert in Hyde Park in London on July 5 and they decided to go ahead with it. Mick Jagger explained, "Brian would have wanted it to go on. We will now do the concert for him. I hope people will understand that it's because of our love for him that we are still doing it."

On stage Mick told the audience, "I really would like to say something for Brian, and I'd really dig it if you would be with us, with what I'm gonna say." He then read from Shelley's

LEFT: Brian Jones, the first 60s rock superstar to die.
RIGHT: John and Yoko take to their bed for peace, and invite the world's press to interview them.

"All we are saying is give peace a chance."

John Lennon and Yoko Ono marry and spend a week in bed in Amsterdam spreading their message via the media, 20 March 1969

"Adonais." It was a beautiful day and an estimated half million people filled the park to listen to the Stones.

The next day Mick and Marianne flew to Australia, where they were to film Ned Kelly, but Brian's death was too much of a strain on Marianne and on July 8 she was found in a coma from a drug overdose in her room at the Chevron Hotel. She did not regain consciousness for five days and actress Diane Craig was brought in to play her role in the movie.

AMSTERDAM

Many of the things hippies were working for in other countries came to fruition in Amsterdam. The Fantasio on Prins Hendrikade and the Paradiso on the Leidseplein were clubs actually sponsored by the local government for young people, places where pot could be smoked without fear of arrest—though it was still technically illegal—though only one, the Fantasio, actually advocated its use. The Fantasio had rooms set aside for reading, for smoking, for debate; they wanted a forum for cultural and political projects. The Fantasio was probably the first community center for the counterculture ever paid for by the government. There was a restaurant offering cheap, substantial vegetarian food and a tea house. The director of the Fantasio was a pro-pot activist and made a number of public statements advocating the legalization of hashish. However, over at the Paradiso, their position was that "hash is illegal, however we do not know if you are smoking hash or tobacco." Other hippie hangouts included the Café Olympia at 7 Saint Jansstraat behind the Dam and the Phono Bar on Rembrandtplein, where the dealers in hard drugs met and did their deals. All the appurtenances of hippie society were available. A Scots woman, Jeanette, and a Dutch woman, Ineke, ran The Head Shop at 9 Zwanenburgwalstraat, featuring clothes from Afghanistan, the near East and Africa; they had a policy of eliminating the middle-man to keep prices as low as possible and the shop was a favorite hangout. There was an English language bookshop on Danstraat and the wonderful

Atheneum bookshop on the Spui, which was run as a cooperative. Outside stood the statue of the Little Rascal, a gathering point for the early Provo happenings. There were three underground papers and various crash pads, including the Boomstraat—"a house where the dispossessed and weary can find rest, refreshment and revolution." The place was thoughtfully equipped with a pile of military helmets in case of a police confrontation.

SQUATTERS

On November 18, 1968, after watching the third screening of "Cathy Come Home," Jeremy Sandford's television drama about homelessness, the London Squatters Campaign was started by fifteen people meeting at Ron Bailey's house. Their aim was the "rehousing of families from hostels or slums by means of squatting." They also hoped that "squatting on a mass scale … would start an all-out attack on the housing authorities with ordinary people taking action for themselves." Their first action was symbolic, to show the injustice of allowing flats to stand empty while thousands were homeless. On December 1, they occupied "The Hollies," a part-empty block of luxury flats in Wanstead High Street, East London, some of which had been empty for the four years since they were built. On the roof Alf Williams, one of the activists, unfurled a banner proclaiming: "I lived in hostels for four years while these flats were empty." One week later, a different group of activists demonstrated how easy it was to render empty houses habitable. For one day they took over a house in Notting Hill that had been empty for eighteen months, cleaning and decorating it. The message was clear.

On January 18. 1969, with the aid of the Notting Hill activists, Mrs. Maggie O'Shannon and her two children moved into No 7 Camelford Road in Notting Hill. The council reacted with outrage, but she wasn't jumping the housing queue; the house was condemned and empty but still a lot better after they had done it up than her damp basement. The newspapers and television took up the story and, after six weeks, a rent

book was pushed through the letterbox, making Mrs. O'Shannon the first person since the 40s to obtain permanent housing through squatting.

Squatting spread rapidly. On March 17 the Edinburgh Squatters organized a token occupation of a flat in the historic Royal Mile. Three homeless families moved into houses in Winnersh, near Reading, and a family squatted a private house in Yorkshire that had been empty for six years. A month later they were awarded legal tenancy by the courts. Squatting groups began in Edinburgh, Birkenhead, Brighton and Manchester. In Leeds an empty office block was occupied and squats began all over London.

In England and Wales, squatting is not a crime. Providing you can get in without causing criminal damage and secure it, it's legally your home, as long as someone is not being prohibited from moving in because you're there. By the mid-70s, an estimated 50,000 people were squatting in Britain.

RIGHT: Early members of the squatting movement whose actions in occupying unoccupied property did much to relieve the suffering of homeless people in Britain.

330

"I would like to say thank you on behalf of the group and ourselves and I hope we passed the audition."

John Lennon rounds off the unannounced live performance on the roof of the Apple building in London, January

🍎 *I am at 3 Savile Row, most days*

THE ROLLING STONES
You can't always get what you want
Honky Tonk Women

45 rpm F12952 DECCA

LEFT: Unable to agree upon a venue for a live concert to film for their movie Let It Be, the Beatles went to the roof of their own office building in Savile Row to play. It was their last concert.

The year was dominated by widespread protests against the renewed American bombing of North Vietnam and the illegal invasion of Cambodia, which resulted in National Guardsmen killing four students at Kent State University. As if the Chicago police riot of 1968 had not convinced Americans that their

65 66 66 67 68 69 70 71

country was heading towards a police state, the Chicago Conspiracy Trial in December 1969 did a lot to reinforce that idea when Judge Hoffman ordered Black Panther Bobby Seale to be bound in chains, shackled and gagged as he sat in court, unable to take part in the travesty of justice that unfolded before him at his trial for conspiracy. The split up of the Beatles, the most influential rock 'n' roll band of all time, left an enormous hole in popular music that has never been filled. Without their leadership, popular music began to fragment into a collection of competing genres, and today a band with such wide appeal is almost inconceivable. It was a new decade and many things began to change. 1970 saw the birth of the modern gay and lesbian civil rights movement, Gay Pride, in a series of marches to commemorate the Stonewall Inn rebellion. It was also the year of the first national Earth Day in the US, heralding the ecology movement and drawing support from all sections of society, from industrialists to students, Republicans to Democrats and ecology anarchists. Because it was organized by politicians, it quickly resulted in legislation, setting in place a number of important safeguards against pollution.

SINGER-SONGWRITERS

"My style … was very self-centered, very autobiographical and you could call it narcissistic."

James Taylor

The freak scene had changed dramatically since the mid-60s. Vito and Szou left Los Angeles in December 1968, packing their bags and new child, Gruvi, into a beaten up Volkswagen bus and setting off for Haiti, where they hoped to dance and hear real drums in the street. Real gunfire was more like it, but they were not to be deterred. "I know about the poverty and tyranny but they don't hassle creative people." The original Byrds had broken up, as had Buffalo Springfield, and in the spring of 1970 the Mothers of Invention radically changed their line-up after arguments over Zappa's film projects, Uncle Meat and 200 Motels. Zappa explained, "We had a business meeting with the Mothers, just prior to that week of shooting, and there was a whole bunch of arguments and bullshit and hysteria. Four of the guys decided they wanted to have nothing whatsoever to do with any of the projects." He brought in Howard Kaylan and Mark Volman from the Turtles.

It was the time of the singer-songwriter, a phenomenon always associated with LA even though most of its proponents were not originally from there—even Bob Dylan moved to the Malibu colony in the end. The singer-songwriters first began to get noticed in the late 60s, first with Randy Newman and Joni Mitchell, then with Neil Young, but it became a distinct musical direction with the release of albums by James Taylor and

Carole King. Taylor was the first of these mellow individualists to reach the general public in a big way with his album Sweet Baby James, which stayed in the Top 40 for more than a year. Taylor has said of his music, "My style at that time was very intimate. But the upside of that was that it was very accessible, and I think people liked that. It was just guitar and voice with some embellishments." The songs were mostly written while Taylor was kicking junk at a residential institution in Massachusetts, but it was made in LA. He moved into Joni Mitchell's wooden bungalow in Laurel Canyon and they lived and performed together for a year. She wrote about the affair in her seminal album, Blue, released in 1971.

Playing piano on Sweet Baby James was Carole King, who had moved from New York in 1969 into a house on Appian Way, hidden in the Canyons near Blue Jay Way. The mellow lifestyle of the Hollywood Hills clearly agreed with her. Her solo recording career had a couple of false starts, including an album with The City and a solo called "Writer" that was victim of a label change by producer Lou Adler. But in January 1971 she went into A&M studios and, in five days of recording, she and a group of friends (including James Taylor) cut Tapestry. She was a consummate craftsman and the songs were perfectly made, combining the laid-back musical style of the Canyons with intimate, seemingly personal

lyrics that were played millions of times in bedsits and hippie-pads across the world. It sold 24 million copies worldwide and is one of the best-loved albums of the era.

The early 70s were filled with laid-back rock. In December Warner Brothers signed the Doobie Brothers, who epitomized the style first introduced by the Allman Brothers. 1970 also saw the first album from Little Feat. This was ex-Mother of Invention Lowell George's new band, which was to achieve cult status even though they never really had any substantial sales.

One of the most influential artists on the burgeoning country rock scene was Gram Parsons. His work with the Flying Burrito Brothers (and before that with The Byrds) paved the way for the Eagles, but his records were never a commercial success. His self-destructive ways and seemingly limitless trust fund money made him a near perfect buddy to the Rolling Stones, and Jagger is quoted as saying that Gram really helped him learn how to sing country music. Unfortunately being around Keith Richards meant that Gram developed a heroin habit. Keith Richards said, "I'm aware of those rumblings—Oh Gram would still be around if it wasn't for Keith Richards—I've

heard it put as boldly as that. And there is a possibility, to be totally honest, that yes, maybe hanging around the Rolling Stones didn't help him in his attitude toward drugs. But I would honestly say that his attitude toward those things reminded me of what was going on everywhere."

The talk that summer at Doug Weston's Troubadour club—the favored hangout for Linda Ronstadt, the LA studio mafia and many singer-songwriters of the scene—was about the Manson trial. Many people had met him and some, like the Beach Boys, had been quite involved. He had lived with Dennis Wilson for some time. Each fresh revelation shocked, horrified and thrilled the community as they realized there had been a maniac in their midst, who was quite capable of killing them on a whim.

DEATH OF JANIS

It didn't take a psychotic to kill Janis Joplin; plain old heroin did the job. Janis died after a very successful recording session at Sunset Sound working on the Pearl album, during which they recorded "Me and Bobby McGee" and laid down the instrumental track for the last song, "Buried Alive In the Blues."

Back in the studio after a Chinese meal, Janis and her musicians recorded a cassette to send to John Lennon on his birthday; she was in a good mood and launched into the old Roy Rogers and Dale Evans theme song, "Happy Trails." She had been expecting to see her boyfriend, Seth Morgan, whom she was about to marry, and her girlfriend, Peggy Caserta, that night because they had arranged to have a threesome. But Morgan stayed in San Francisco with another woman, and Peggy spent the evening with several other girlfriends having sex and shooting heroin in her room at the Chateau Marmont.

Janis returned to room 105 at the Landmark Motel, where she and some of her musicians were staying, at about 1am. Earlier that day her connection had delivered $50 worth of heroin to her. But the dealer himself was not an addict and whenever he received a new consignment, he usually had a "tester" check it for him to see how pure it was before stepping on it accordingly. But his tester was away. He sent it out anyway. The smack turned out to be between 50% and 80% pure—about eight times stronger than people were used to. Eight people would die from using that batch over the weekend; Janis was one of them. She took a shot, then went to the lobby to ask the night clerk George Sandoz for change for a five-dollar bill for cigarettes. He gave her four singles and four quarters, and she stayed chatting for a quarter of an hour before getting her Marlboros from the machine and returning to her room. That evening she had already drunk a quart of tequila and taken a couple of Valiums. She had begun to undress when the smack hit her.

Janis still had the $4.50 clenched in her hand when she was found, dead of an overdose, eighteen hours later.

LEFT: British magazine Oz celebrates the genius of Bob Dylan, 1970.
RIGHT: The original Fallen Angel, Gram Parsons, in his infamous Nudie suit that had a huge cannabis leaf embroidered on the back.

GAY PRIDE

"We may have lost the battle, sweets, but the war is far from over."

A Christopher Street bar "queen" to the New York Times after the Stonewall Riot, July 1969

In June 1969 Police and Alcoholic Beverage Control Board agents had entered the Stonewall Inn, a gay bar on Christopher Street, looking for violations of the alcohol control laws, and abused the customers one by one as they threw them out. On June 28, 1970, exactly a year after the Stonewall "riots," about 2,000 demonstrators assembled in Waverly Place near Sheridan Square in Greenwich Village, New York and marched up Sixth Avenue from the former Stonewall Inn to Central Park, where a "gay-in" was held. They were commemorating the first occasion when gays fought back against police harassment and intimidation.

Billed as the Christopher Street Liberation Day, it was the first lesbian and gay pride march in the US and the beginning of Gay Pride celebrations as they are now known. A simultaneous march of about 1,200 people took place in Los Angeles and there were demonstrations in several other cities across America. During the summer and autumn following the three days of gay demonstrations outside the Stonewall in 1969, Gay Liberation Fronts had started up in New York, Berkeley, Los Angeles, San Francisco and San Jose and, by the end of 1970, 300 Gay Liberation Fronts had been created. Gay activists started planning for the first anniversary march almost as soon as the fighting had died down, recognizing the rebellion as a significant rallying point—the first time gays had stood up for their civil rights.

In London the first march took place on November 27, 1970, organized by the Gay Liberation Front, when about 80 GLF activists gathered for a torchlight demonstration on Highbury Fields, Islington. It was a low-key affair. Participants all lit candles, then walked around the fields three or four times before going home, but it carried great significance. It was the first ever public gay protest in Britain, and came three years after homosexuality had been legalized for consenting males over 21 years of age.

BELOW: Parents of gays demonstrate in support in New York.
RIGHT: A Gay Pride event in London featuring actors and mime artists marches through Soho, the capital's sex center, in 1972.

OHIO KENT STATE UNIVERSITY RIOTS: FOUR STUDENTS KILLED BY THE NATIONAL GUARD

On April 30 President Nixon told the American public that American troops supported by B-52 bomber strikes had entered neutral Cambodia. This illegal act was by presidential decree and was executed without the approval of Congress, who alone had the right to declare war. Reaction on campuses was swift, with students turning out to demonstrate that very night. The next morning Nixon dismissed them, telling the press, "You see these bums, you know, blowing up the campuses." In fact the protests so far had been entirely non violent, but that weekend demonstrations flared across the land. Stanford University had the worst riot in its history and a National Guardsman armed with a shotgun shot a student at Ohio State.

At Kent State—also in Ohio—students burned the ROTC (Reserve Officers Training Corps) building to the ground. Within days, more than 80% of the nation's universities had announced some form of strike action in protest. At Kent State 69 students were arrested and one girl wounded by a bayonet, as National Guardsmen and police herded students into their dorms.

The next day, Monday May 4, students at Kent State organized a demonstration at noon to protest the presence of the National Guard on campus. The troops were equipped with tear gas canisters and M-1 rifles, capable of killing at two miles and ready to fire. The order was given for the National Guard troops to disperse the crowd. The troops retreated to the top of a slope, then opened fire on the unarmed crowd. Sixty-one shots were fired in thirteen seconds, killing four students and wounding nine. (The event was commemorated by Neil Young in his song "Ohio," which was rush-released by his record company.)

The national response was unprecedented. Violence flared with bombings, battles with police and hundreds of arrests. In the week following the killings, 30 ROTC buildings were destroyed by fire or bombs. More than 500 campuses were closed and over four million students and faculty were involved in some form of protest. The White House was surrounded by protesters, resulting in Presidential Advisor Henry Kissinger having to sleep in the president's bedroom in the bomb shelter because he couldn't get out. Then on May 14, in an action unrelated to the war, two students were killed by police at Jackson State, a black college in Mississippi.

The true face of America was now obvious to its young people and an increasingly large number of its adults. The President's Commission on Campus Unrest later reported, "In May 1970, students did not strike against their universities; they succeeded in making their universities strike against national policy ... nothing is more important than an end to the war in Indo-China. Disaffected students see the war as a symbol of moral crisis in the nation which ... deprives even law of its legitimacy." But the war dragged on.

RIGHT: A Kent State protester returns a tear gas canister to troops.

CHICAGO

The Chicago Conspiracy Trial began in December 1969. David Dellinger, Rennie Davis, Abbie Hoffman, Jerry Rubin, Tom Hayden, Lee Weiner, John Froines and Bobby Seale were all charged with conspiring to incite a riot at the 1968 Democratic Party Convention. The defendants decided to fight the case together, with William Kunstler and Leonard Weinglass as their defense lawyers, even though anti-war organizers had gone to Chicago with very different agendas than Bobby Seale or the two Youth International Party organizers, Rubin and Hoffman.

The trial was presided over by 74-year-old Judge Julius Hoffman. Bobby Seale's trial was quickly separated off, and he spent much of it bound, gagged, and shackled to his chair by chains, in full view of the jury, which not surprisingly found him guilty. It was a complete travesty of justice but fortunately he was acquitted of all charges on appeal. Among those appearing in their defense was Allen Ginsberg, who testified that he had been asked to go to Chicago in case his knowledge of chanting was needed to calm the crowd.

Leonard Weinglass, for the defense, asked Allen to describe his role in the February 1968 news conference when plans for the Yippie Festival of Life were announced. Ginsberg explained that their plan had been to hold a peaceful festival like the San Francisco Be-In, not a riot. He said that he had concluded his speech by chanting the "Hare Krishna Mantra" for the television cameras. Then, to demonstrate, he launched into the mantra: "Hare Krishna, Hare Krishna, Krishna Krishna, Hare Hare, Hare Rama, Hare Rama, Hare Hare, Rama Rama." Prosecutor

"I alibied for him. Now he says peace was a lie, we meant to start a war. Guilty 1968."

Allen Ginsberg on Jerry Rubin's admission that he was guilty of starting a riot during the Democratic convention in Chicago, 1968

Thomas Foran laughed, but William Kunstler objected, saying that the chanting had been a presentation of a religious concept.

"I don't understand it," said Judge Hoffman. "The language of the United States District Court is English."

"I know," said Kunstler, "but you don't laugh at all languages."

"I didn't laugh, I didn't laugh," protested the judge. "I didn't laugh at all. I wish I could tell you how I feel. Laugh—I didn't even smile."

Allen pointed out, helpfully, that the language was Sanskrit. "That's why I didn't understand it," Hoffman said, and told Kunstler, "You may use an interpreter for the remainder of this witness' testimony."

The case had a predictable outcome. The academics Lee Weiner and John Froines were acquitted of all charges; all the defendants were absolved of conspiracy; Hoffman, Rubin, Dellinger, Hayden and Davis were individually convicted of crossing state lines to incite a riot. Judge Hoffman then spent two days giving 175 contempt of court citations, totalling nineteen years in prison, to the eight defendants and their attorneys, Weinglass and Kunstler.

Bobby Seale and Kunstler both received more than four years for contempt. Two years later the US Court of Appeals overturned the verdict and most of the contempt citations, finding that, "The demeanor of the judge and the prosecutors would require reversal if other errors did not."

Once all the jail time had been voided and the citations reversed, Jerry Rubin revealed, "We wanted disruption. We planned it. We were not innocent victims. Guilty as hell! Guilty as charged!" Allen, who had accepted all along that the Youth International Party were planning a nonviolent festival of youth, was as annoyed as everyone else to find that the original good intentions had been undermined.

ABOVE LEFT: Attorney William Kunstler (left) with members of the Chicago Seven. Left to right, Abbie Hoffman, David Dellinger and Jerry Rubin celebrate acquittal outside court.

ALICE COOPER

"We were the group that drove a stake through the heart of the love generation."

Alice Cooper

A regular fixture at the Sunset Strip clubs in 1968 was Arizona's Nazz, a bad, if theatrical, act that supported the likes of the Doors and Yardbirds. Five school friends from Arizona, Nazz (named after a Yardbirds song) were fronted by a Detroit-born singer named Vince Furnier, who liked to act kind of mad on stage. In 1969 Nazz had to change their name when Todd Rundgren decided to use it for his band. As legend has it, they chose the name Alice Cooper after their manager's mother had consulted a ouija board.

Not long after, Frank Zappa signed the band to his Straight label because, as the singer explained, "We were the most hated band in Los Angeles," and that's what Zappa liked. The band also came under the guidance of a new manager, Shep Gordon, attracted to the band by their ability to drive 2,000 people away from the stage after only two numbers.

After two poorly received Straight-released albums (Pretties For You and Easy Action) and an appearance in the 1969 movie Diary Of A Mad Housewife (the only recorded proof of the madness of the Alice Cooper show at that time), the band left Hollywood for the frozen north and Cooper's place of birth. The move, along with a burgeoning reputation as the sick face of rock 'n' roll music after love and peace—enhanced by false claims of Alice having ripped a live chicken to shreds on stage in Toronto—proved to be the making of the band.

With the fledgling producer Bob Ezrin at the recording controls, Alice Cooper's Love It To Death album was the first to be released on the major Warners label (parent company to Straight) in 1971. The anthemic single "I'm Eighteen" that was taken from it made No. 21 on the US charts. To most of the people of the US who believed that the hippie movement would end badly, Alice Cooper provided proof. Here was a man who dressed in ripped women's clothing and claimed to have a woman's name. He sang sick ballads to a live snake on stage and was clearly depraved, if not clinically insane. There was no way that Alice Cooper wasn't going to be a huge star.

Major worldwide stardom came in 1972 with the release of the No. 1 single "School's Out" from the album of the same name. With it's strident apathetic message and aggressive sound, it's little wonder that various UK punks in 1976 claimed their first sighting of Alice Cooper on Top of The Pops provided the impetus to make music with attitude. In fact, US Creem magazine readers voted Alice Punk of The Year in 1973.

Alice Cooper not only rejected the love and peace message of the hippie movement, he reversed it to hate and war before the Clash had even begun to think of the idea. Cooper's stage antics—including the simulated rape and murder of sex dolls, chopping the heads off baby dolls with a sword, wielding a chainsaw and simulating his own death on stage (variously by electric chair, hanging and poisoning)—predated and inspired a number of pop acts, from the New York Dolls to Eminem and (clearly Alice's love child) Marilyn Manson. Watching Alice Cooper in action in the early 70s left one in no doubt that the halcyon days of hippie had passed.

LEFT (TOP): Alice in full nightmare eye make-up.
LEFT (BOTTOM): The original artwork of the band's breakthrough album School's Out (1972).
RIGHT: The band pose with Yvonne, Alice's pet python.

EARTH DAY

"Why not a great global holiday in support of our common desire for peace, justice and the care of earth?"

Earth Day organizer John McConnell

Though the ecology movement had its roots in the counterculture and hippie underground, widespread consciousness of the environmental movement came from Earth Day, organized—astonishingly—by a politician. In 1968 Senator Gaylord Nelson had proposed a nationwide "Environmental Teach-In," based on the earlier anti-war teach-ins, to be held on American college campuses the following spring. The organizing focus was to be Earth Day, an idea suggested and named by John McConnell, who saw it as "a global holiday for the whole planet." He persuaded the City of San Francisco to proclaim March 21, 1969 as Earth Day. Streets were closed, trees were planted in Central Park by local children, there were booths with environmental information and music and dancing. If it had been organized by the Diggers they would have been busted, but now it was the city itself organizing the festival.

John McConnell explained how it came together, "Our big Earth Day in New York was the next year. The 1970 Earth Day in New York had the backing of United Nations Secretary General U Thant. He felt Earth Day could become a vital global holiday that would benefit people and planet. My conversations with Margaret Mead and UN Ambassadors in 1970 resulted in participation worldwide. The International Earth Day Proclamation I had written after San Francisco was signed by U Thant and other world leaders. Issued as a United Nations Release it helped bring global attention." Up until this time, the ecology movement was fragmented, but Earth Day helped people see how it was all connected. It brought together such diverse issues as the population explosion, urban sprawl, misuse of pesticides, oil spills, the dangers of nuclear power, automobile pollution and so on. By showing the ecological links between these concerns, the organizers were able to argue that environmentally illiterate government and business leaders were leading the world towards catastrophe.

About twenty million people took part in the first national Earth Day in order to discuss practical action to clean up the environment, with events held in almost every city and town in the US. In New York, over l00,000 people attended an ecology fair in Central Park. Fifth Avenue was closed to cars and Mayor Lindsay drove down it in an electric bus. All three major TV networks covered the events of the day, and the Public Broadcast System devoted its entire daytime programming to Earth Day coverage.

It achieved an enormous amount. Later that year the Environmental Protection Agency was established. The tough 1970 Clean Air Act was passed with very few dissenting votes in both Houses of Congress. The military was made to stop using mutagenic defoliants in Southeast Asia. Plans for supersonic aircraft along the lines of Concorde were halted. The Federal Occupational Health and Safety Act aimed at stopping hazardous pollution in the workplace was passed, as were the Clean Water Act, the Endangered Species Act and the Resource Conservation and Recovery Act, all during the next three years. Remarkable legislation, but of course subsequent neo-conservative administrations have tried to erode its powers.

RIGHT: An Earth Day activist on the streets of Manhattan, 1970, wearing a gas mask and holding a white bicycle and wilting flower amid the city traffic.

Music From The Motion Picture Soundtrack
ZABRISKIE POINT
The GRATEFUL DEAD
The KALEIDOSCOPE
The PINK FLOYD
The YOUNGBLOODS
and

ZABRISKIE POINT AND BEYOND

This was the year that "hippie" went mainstream. Long after the Death of Hippie march in Haight-Ashbury, the long hair, the psychedelic patterns and hippie clothing, the beads and quite often the marijuana reached all parts of American culture. Businessmen grew their hair, TV Talk show hosts sported mustaches and the newspapers tried in vain to be "hip." In Britain there was the "switched on Daily Mirror"—presumably "turned on" would have been a little too close to a drug reference. Every town and city now had its head shop selling candles, ultraviolet light posters, rolling papers and roach clips.

Kids had a poster of Allen Ginsberg in an Uncle Sam hat pinned to their wall even though they had never read him. Twelve-year-olds wore "Turn On, Tune In, Drop Out" badges while Tim Leary himself plotted how to escape from jail. The revolution was being commodified.

Though many Hollywood stars had long been involved in the scene, only now did the Hollywood moguls begin to finance films about the counterculture. There was Zabriskie Point, Michelangelo Antonioni's odd film about student unrest in America with music from Jerry Garcia, the Grateful Dead and the Rolling Stones. It featured the biggest controlled explosion ever filmed at that point in cinematic history, when a desert mansion went up in slow motion to the sound of the Pink Floyd's "Careful With That Axe, Eugene." Hippies liked it for the Love-In orgy scene in the desert.

It was also the year of Woodstock, Michael Wadleigh's film of the event—an overly long but accurate portrayal of the sea of mud, the out-of-tune guitars and the amazing sense of community among the audience. With its sometimes split screen (taken from Warhol's Chelsea Girls) and other techniques previously unknown to Hollywood, it really did capture the moment.

LEFT: The soundtrack to Antonioni's Zabriskie Point was a bigger success than the movie. RIGHT: Jack Nicholson had become a star of the counterculture after his role in Easy Rider. He went on to contribute to a number of similarly themed movies as producer and actor.

Another important documentary/movie was released in 1970. Medium Cool, Haskell Wexler's film about the 1968 police riots in Chicago, mixed actual news footage with a fictional story and featured Zappa and Wild Man Fischer on the soundtrack.

The exploitation movie Groupie Girl and the documentary Groupies also came out this year, as did Jack Nicholson's underrated Drive, He Said. Talking of his film, Nicholson said, "I was trying to convey not the shift in campus mood but the universal fact that most people do not respond to extremist behavior. Some critics think that I oversimplified by reducing everything to sex, but if you look at the real facts of your life you'll find if you're not releasing your sexual energy you're in trouble. It's a pure Wilhelm Reich theme and illustrative of Reichian politics."

SCHOOL KIDS RULE, OK?

JAIL BAIT of the MONTH

David Nutter

The underground scene in London had changed a lot since the mid-60s. Indica bookshop and the Indica gallery were both closed, and the only bookshop still catering to hippies was Compendium on Camden High Street, near the Roundhouse. The Roundhouse itself was now host to the weekly Implosion, run by Jeff Dexter, and provided a weekly income for Release. Rents were still cheap around there and head shops and hippie boutiques began opening up.

International Times (IT) was still being published, as were Friends and Oz. It was in 1970, however, that Oz published the fateful "School Kids" issue, which led to the longest obscenity trial in British history. Editors Richard Neville, Jim Anderson and Felix Dennis turned Oz magazine over to a group of 16-year-old school kids and let them run whatever they liked. The result landed them in court.

The offending material was a cartoon strip. One panel was taken from a Rupert cartoon in which the much loved Daily Express newspaper-owned bear, who is, as usual, running, was given a large penis, collaged on from a Robert Crumb cartoon. This clearly struck at the very heart of British decency and they were prosecuted under the Obscene Publications Act.

ABOVE: The "pin-up" poster of a schoolgirl from the offending School Kids issue of Oz. The irony of the issue was lost on the police and in particular the Vice Squad who were more used to raiding the premises of genuine sex shops and pornography magazines.
RIGHT: The front cover and excerpts from the same issue, with editor Richard Neville in schoolboy garb (inset).

BREAK-UP OF THE BEATLES

others he was leaving back in December 1969, but Allen Klein, their business manager, asked him to keep it quiet until contract negotiations with Capitol Records were completed.

John and Yoko had already released Live Peace In Toronto in December 1969 and Ringo was making Sentimental Journey. Paul had been working on McCartney since the end of 1969. In completing a press questionnaire to promote his solo album in April, Paul revealed that the Beatles effectively no longer existed. The press went wild, as he must have known they would. The final Beatles album to be released was Let It Be, which Paul hated because producer Phil Spector had added lush strings to his ballads without consultation.

The Beatles never re-formed, though they continue to be one of the highest earning groups in the world. Apple Records continued, but the ex-Beatles rarely went there and McCartney moved to Scotland for a while to get over the break-up. Who broke them up? The marriage was over between them, they found real wives and grew up. If anyone was to blame it was John Lennon for insisting that Yoko join the group.

LEFT: Lennon and Yoko, the unappreciated "fifth Beatle," peer into their future as a double act.
BELOW: The cover of Paul McCartney's debut album. Daughter Stella peers out from the leather jacket.
RIGHT: A final publicity shoot to promote Let It Be.

More than anything else, what marked the end of an era and the decade was the break-up of the Beatles. The fab four had single-handedly revitalized the whole rock 'n' roll industry, influencing countless groups, including virtually all the psychedelic bands. Uniquely, they had taken their fans with them as they evolved from the Four Mop Tops to the Lords of Psychedelia, with their strange electronic seagull-call solos, backwards tapes and Sgt. Pepper suits. The Beatles lasted from 1960 until 1970, spanning a decade that they have now come to represent.

Having achieved iconic status, their break-up was the cause of much weeping—some of it by record company executives—and the excuse for thousands of column inches of gossip and speculation. Most of all, the press and public wanted to find out who did it. Who broke up the Beatles? The finger appeared to point at Yoko Ono.

The 60s had been more or less heroin free, but hard drugs appeared to dominate the following decade. Among those who survived the drug were Eric Clapton (who was completely

strung out when he recorded his Layla and Other Assorted Love Songs as Derek and the Dominos in August 1970) and John Lennon. John had been fooling around with smack ever since he left Cynthia for Yoko. Lennon had become very disillusioned at being in the Beatles. At one point he almost became an acid casualty and actually convened a Beatles board meeting at Apple in order to tell the other three that he was Jesus Christ. "Right you are, John," they said. "Any other business?"

At recording sessions, John insisted that Yoko sit next to him on a piano stool and even accompany him to the bathroom, all of which caused the creative bubble in which the Beatles worked to be broken. Ringo felt intimidated and no one but John welcomed Yoko's suggestions about arrangements and material.

Relations between the members of the group were strained almost to breaking point. Three of them were working on solo projects and the group had, in effect, already broken up, but had not yet announced it to the world. John told the

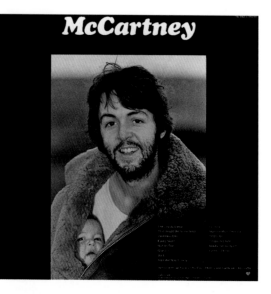

McCartney

TAKING A BATH

"A half an hour to set up—then the members of THE definitive heavy band strode on stage—Robert Plant, looking more like a Norse warrior than ever, Jimmy Page looking like mad Dan Eccles in an ankle-length overcoat and a yokel's hat over his ears."

The Melody Maker review Led Zeppelin at Bath Festival

By the end of the 60s music festivals had gained in popularity both in Europe as well as in the US. The idea of enjoying live music all day in the sunshine and open air, sleeping in tents or simply under blankets and developing a temporary community made up of like-minded people eager to share this new experience worked perfectly in California. In England things were not quite so sunny, but the festivals became equally successful. Although the first Bath Festival in 1969 attracted only 12,000 people (headline act Led Zeppelin were yet to achieve huge fame), it did manage to be financially viable for its promoter, Freddie Bannister.

A year later the Bath Festival was truly successful, however. This time around 150,000 people were attracted to the Shepton Mallet site over the weekend of 27, 28 and 29 June. Saturday's headline act were Steppenwolf, who had rounded off a day that featured Donovan, Fairport Convention and It's A Beautiful Day. From midnight through to Sunday morning,

albino blues guitarist Johnny Winter ignored the almost persistent rain to keep everyone awake.

Beginning at 3am and debuting the yet to be released Atom Heart Mother album, the Pink Floyd played for the best part of 90 minutes. They were followed by John Mayall and Canned Heat before a lengthy break. Donovan once again got things going in the afternoon, before Frank Zappa and Santana set the stage for Led Zeppelin to play an astounding two-and-a-half-hour set, which helped establish them among both their US counterparts and the British audience as a truly great live act. As they left the stage, apparently half the audience left the site.

Monday was America day. Country Joe, the Jefferson Airplane, the Byrds and Dr. John all performed. The festival was meant to end at midnight, but it carried on until 7am. Emcee throughout the weekend was DJ John Peel.

Despite the rain and inevitable traffic queues, the spartan facilities and the presence of UK Hell's Angels as "security," most Festival-goers

announced that it was the European Woodstock. Caroline Coon of Release said on-site, "Everything's fantastic, it's a beautiful atmosphere." Even the locals were happy it seems. Friends magazine reported one as commenting on the preponderance of marijuana smoke, "Don't know what they want that there pot for—not when they could have cider."

The fact that Bannister also made money from the enterprise encouraged other promoters to organize festivals in the UK—the biggest and longest-running of which, of course, is Glastonbury. The first took place in 1970, but was not a success. Things were changed for the 1971 event, which was so successful that it set the pattern for those that followed.

LEFT: Led Zeppelin singer Robert Plant with magician's white dove, cigarette and bottle of Newcastle Brown Ale on stage in front of thousands. For the next ten years, Led Zeppelin would be the biggest grossing live act in the world. Their Bath Festival appearance in 1970 is considered one of their best ever.

"They don't have summers like this in New York."

After a groundbreaking tour of the US in 1968, where they supported Vanilla Fudge, the next year had seen Led Zeppelin touring as a headline act and selling three million copies of their second Atlantic Records release, Led Zeppelin II.

In 1970 the band found themselves playing to audiences in excess of 15,000 people at a time. They were beginning to create what would become known as the Stadium circuit, with each tour employing ever larger venues to suit demand for tickets. Under the guidance of manager Peter Grant, Led Zeppelin were destined to become a legendary rock 'n' roll band. As far removed from the Chet Helms school of management and promotion as was possible, Grant was a big, tough Londoner who was used to bullying his way around. He reveled in a reputation (much of it of his own making) that credited him with various outrageous acts. One such saw him facing down an irate concert promoter with a gun in Memphis in April 1970. Apparently annoyed at the overrunning of the band's set, the promoter thrust a pistol in Grant's face and told him that he'd shoot him unless he pulled the band offstage. Grant laughed and took the gun from him. He argued that he couldn't shoot him since, at that moment, the Memphis city mayor was onstage giving the band the keys to the city (he was). It was the first time since the late 50s that the city had celebrated a rock act in that way and was symbolic of Led Zeppelin's appeal.

By mixing uncomplicated, blues-based riffs with pyrotechnic showmanship, Led Zeppelin took the music business in a new direction. They legitimized organized touring on such a grand scale for bands. They owned their own jet, refused to release singles—not wanting to be regarded as a mere flash-in-the-pan pop act— and, despite wearing a Freak look, had no message to impart to their fans, except "have a good time, all the time." Without Led Zeppelin, there would have been no Spinal Tap.

DEATH OF JIMI

Rock stars continued to die. Following in the steps of Brian Jones and Janis Joplin, it was now Jimi Hendrix who died from stupid, drug-related causes. Jimi and his girlfriend Monika Danneman spent Thursday September 17 shopping. After a meal of fish fingers and chips washed down with a bottle of red wine, Monika dropped him off for a party at a flat in Great Cumberland Street at about 1:45am on September 18. Monika returned to the Hotel Samarkand, 22 Lansdowne Crescent, where she and Jimi were living, and went to pick him up at about 3am. They talked until about 7:15 in the morning, then Jimi took some of Monika's sleeping pills because he said he really needed a good night's sleep. The reason he was up so late talking, the post-mortem showed, was that he had taken a load of speed sometime that evening. Speed, sleeping pills and wine are a fatal mixture. When she counted the pills the next day, Monika found he had taken nine—a handful.

Monika woke up about three hours later, got ready and made herself breakfast. She went to the Portobello Road to buy some cigarettes and, when she returned at about 11am, she noticed that Jimi had been sick. She couldn't wake him. An ambulance arrived at 11:27 but he had died some time before. Monika Danneman maintained that he was breathing when she left the flat. The ambulance men reported that some of the vomit was already dry, but there was a great deal of it, mostly red wine. His airway was completely blocked and his tongue had fallen back. Jimi had drowned in his own gastric contents.

LEFT and ABOVE: When the sun shone, festival crowds got closer to nature.

HOT LOVE

> ## "My people were fair and had sky in their hair, now they're content to wear stars on their brow."

Marc Bolan prophetically titles a Tyrannosaurus Rex album

Just as Led Zeppelin were busy building an audience from non–single buying "Freaks" across America, in the UK two former arch hippies were re-creating themselves in a Glam fashion.

David Bowie had been a Mod (Davey Jones) and an acoustic-guitar-strumming, long-haired hippie when he scored a UK Top 10 pop hit with Space Oddity in 1969. Subsequent releases failed to match its success however. So in 1970 Bowie changed his manager (taking on Tony de Fries) and his sound, using guitarist Mick Ronson and synthesizer player Ralph Mace to create The Man Who Sold The World. The album's dramatic vocals were matched by its provocative cover, which featured Bowie wearing a Mr. Fish designed dress—the same dress that the singer wore later that year in Houston, Texas and was arrested for. The sexual revolution begun by hippies in the 60s wasn't complete yet and a man who dressed like a woman and wore make-up was still regarded in great swathes of America and Europe as being as big a threat as a commie with a nuclear bomb.

Gender-bending and ambiguous sexuality proved to be a winning concept for Bowie. As the decade progressed he became more outrageous and created the sexually ambivalent Ziggy Stardust persona that won him enormous success around the world. In opposition to the "natural" appeal of singer-songwriters, Bowie became ever more theatrical.

In America the New York Dolls took Bowie's cross-dressing to trashy heights and copied guitarist Mick Ronson's raw and basic sound, but with little commercial success. However, Kiss took the art of dressing up a step further and became enormous stars, despite the fact that their fans wouldn't recognize them without their bizarre make-up.

Like Bowie, Marc Feld had been a Mod dandy—he was featured as a smartly dressed London boy at the age of fifteen for a London Sunday Times magazine article. By the heyday of hippie in 1968, however, Feld had become Bolan and was performing in an acoustic two-piece folk band named Tyrannosaurus Rex with Steve Peregrine Took. Even when they went electric, their Tolkien-esque mystic ramblings failed to yield sales success.

With the dawning of a new decade, Bolan shortened the name of his band to T. Rex, replaced Took with Mickey Finn and, in October 1970, T. Rex released "Ride A White Swan," which went to No. 2 in the singles chart. During their first Top Of The Pops TV performance Bolan wore glitter make-up under his eyes. Within weeks teenage girls and boys were to be seen on Britain's streets wearing the same sparkling make-up. The Glam era had been started by a former proto-hippie.

A year later saw "Hot Love" becoming T. Rex's first No. 1 single. Newspapers were claiming that Bolanmania was a match for Bealtlemania at its peak, but despite that Bolan never became a star in America.

He died in a car crash in 1977.

RIGHT (TOP): David Bowie in 1970 before inventing Ziggy Stardust and becoming a theatrical Glam star.

RIGHT (BOTTOM): Marc Bolan and Steve Peregrine Took when they were Tyrannosaurus Rex. At the end of 1970 Took was replaced by Mickey Finn and Bolan put glitter under his eyes, shortened the band name to T.Rex and became a Glam star.

In 1971 Jim Morrison joined Brian Jones, Janis Joplin and Jimi Hendrix in the roll-call of rock 'n' roll superhero deaths. Frank Zappa almost joined the list when a crazed fan threw him from the stage ten feet into the orchestra pit, knocking him unconscious. Zappa described his injuries: "I had a hole put in the back of my skull, twisted my neck, broke my wrist and leg. I was in a wheel chair for nine months and off the road for over a year." His voice dropped an octave as a result. The two main venues to showcase underground rock——Bill Graham's Fillmore East and Fillmore West——closed their doors this year, and "rock" as it was now called became increasingly a business rather than a calling. On 30 March, the Rolling Stones gave a huge party in London before moving to the French Riviera as tax exiles, once and for all removed from the everyday cares of life. On a more positive note, 50,000 people gathered in New York's Central Park for the 1971 Earth Day and the ringing of the United Nations Peace Bell to announce Spring received worldwide attention. And the hippies? The few hardcore ones left were mostly living in country communes. Many of their ideas had spread into the general community: vegetarianism, organic food, home-made bread. The consumer side of the movement caught on fast in America as people saw the value in the return to healthy living. Similarly, by the early 70s, most towns now had a yoga center, and possibly even a meditation center of some sort. By 1971 even politicians were wearing their hair down to the collar.

THIS IS THE END

"The sad death of Jim Morrison leaves a few unanswered questions. What were the full circumstances surrounding his death and why have they not been revealed?"

International Times reports the death of the Doors singer, issue 105

On March 5, 1971 Jim Morrison left Los Angeles to join his long time girlfriend Pamela Courson in Paris. She had gone on ahead a few weeks before and was already well established at the Hotel George V. When Jim arrived, he was overweight and heavily bearded; he brought with him cartons of books and papers, intending to devote his time to writing. At first all went well—he cut down on his drinking, lost weight and shaved his beard. They drove down through France and Spain to Morocco, they went to the opera and all the art galleries and museums, but most of the time Jim just explored Paris. A month later, they flew to Corsica for ten days. By then they were living at 17 rue Beautreillis, an apartment they sublet on April 10.

Then, at the end of June, Morrison developed a terrible depression. His drinking had increased once more but no one had seen him so low before. On Friday July 2 Pamela and a friend, Alan Ronay, managed to persuade him to go out for a meal, but he remained virtually silent throughout.

Afterwards he took Pamela home and went alone to a movie. He went to a club, the Rock & Roll Circus on the rue de Seine, where he was a regular. After almost three decades of silence, the manager finally revealed that Morrison had been there that night. There was a lot of heroin in Paris at that time and many of the dealers and users congregated at the Rock & Roll Circus. Jim liked cocaine, and it is possible that he snorted a line in the toilets thinking that it was coke. Pamela was taking heroin and had some in the flat, but witnesses place Jim in the club that night. He collapsed on the spot. The story has it there was a group on stage playing a number called "The Death of Rock 'n' Roll" as they carried him across the back of the stage and out through the kitchen, which connected with the back of a more respectable club called the Alcazar on the rue Mazarine. From here he was bundled—dead, dazed or in a coma—into a car and taken home to the rue Beautreillis where they appear to have tried to resuscitate him in a cold bath.

We do not know if Pamela was home when they arrived. Her official story was that they watched Doors footage at home that night after he got in from dining alone. She died of an overdose in 1974, having told many different versions of the story. We know that Pamela called the pompiers at 9:21am and they arrived a few minutes later. They found Morrison in the bath, dead, apparently from natural causes. As there was no suspicion of suicide or murder, no autopsy was performed. He was buried at Père Lachaise on 7 July. Because no one from the Doors office ever saw the body, rumors have been rife ever since that Morrison is alive and well and the coffin was empty, but Pamela's subsequent descent into a self-destructive life of hard drugs is the best proof possible that carelessness had taken a life.

PREVIOUS PAGE: No longer burning the flag, but wearing it.
ABOVE: How International Times reported Morrison's death.
RIGHT: A bust of Jim Morrison at his graveside in Paris in the 1990.

IT'S ONLY ROCK 'n' ROLL

The 1972 Rolling Stones US tour made Bill Graham big business

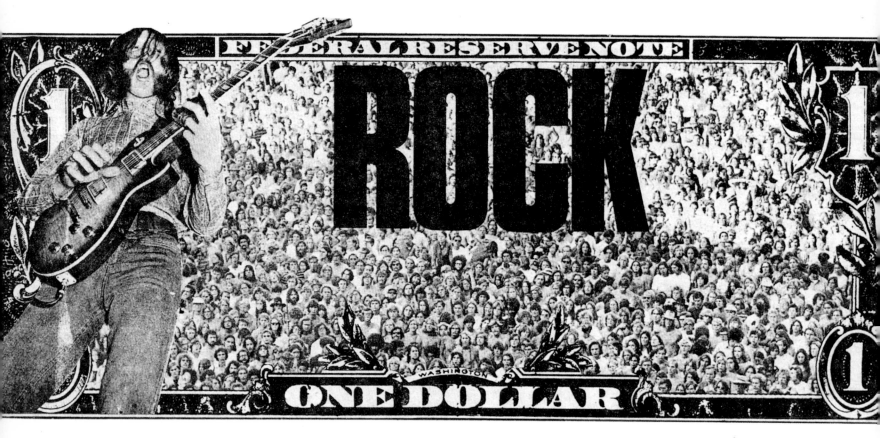

New York was going through a very bad period and as many people as were able had left town. At the Fillmore East, there were unpleasant scenes outside the theatre. The security team now consisted of really huge bouncers, but, even so, people were mugged, beaten up and thrown through plate glass windows. The atmosphere inside was not very pleasant either—the kids were puking in the toilets, passing out and pissing on seats. They would applaud anything, even Crosby, Stills, Nash and Young when they played out of tune and sang flat all evening. Being in the presence of the group had become more important than the experience of the music.

Also the groups had become greedy and this was what closed the Fillmore. The final incident came when Bill Graham wanted to put on the Band for a week at the Metropolitan Opera House. He called their manager, John Taplin, and explained that, because it was a unionized house and the overheads were very high, the Band would make $50,000 for eight shows. Taplin said, "Bill. Do you expect my boys to work for a lousy 50 grand a week?" Graham put down the phone and exploded. He announced that that was it, he had had enough. He was closing the Fillmores. Everyone was shocked because they were making more money than ever, but he was adamant. In April 1971 the Fillmore East closed its doors and, to make sure that he didn't have any second thoughts, he sold the building. Graham then flew back to San Francisco and closed the Fillmore West as well. He later explained, "We were making a fortune by the end. Between the tickets and the concessions. We could have gone on for another five years …

So money was nothing to do with my decision. Money never was a factor." From now on he put on events at Winterland if and when he wanted to: "I didn't have to fill a room where I was paying rent. At the Berkeley Community Theater, I only had to pay for the use of the hall when I actually used it. I was free to book any act I wanted." He put on shows at the Berkeley Community Theater and at Winterland. Soon he was doing more shows than ever, only this time he was just promoting. Then he took on the 1972 Rolling Stones American tour, and suddenly Bill Graham was in business big time.

ABOVE: The underground press satirize the sell-out of music.
RIGHT: Mick Jagger on the highest-grossing tour of the United States at that time, 1972. The promoter was Bill Graham.

"The Underground is turning sex back into play. Pure play has no rules. On your mark; get set. . ."

Richard Neville in Playpower, 1970

HOLLYWOOD LOVES ITS CRAZIES

After the success of Easy Rider and the Woodstock movie, the underground and Hollywood quickly cozied up together. Virtually every rock 'n' roll band had a film made about them, usually using concert footage, some of which were very good. In 1972 Ringo Starr made a surrealistic documentary about Glam teenybopper Mark Bolan, which also featured Elton John. Robert Frank accompanied the Rolling Stones on their 1972 American tour, but the resulting documentary was too close to the truth for the Stones to handle. They felt the naked groupies and the drugs would get them banned from the US so the film was never released. Frank could, however, screen it in person at film festivals and special showings. Chuck Wein's Rainbow Bridge had a loose story line, but was really concert footage of Jimi Hendrix playing with Mitch Mitchell and Buddy Cox at Hawaii's Haleakala Volcano.

The musicians soon took to being actors—a trend that started back in the 60s, most significantly with Mick Jagger's role in Performance. Claude Whatham's That'll Be The Day—a teddyboy movie set in a 1958 English holiday camp—featured David Essex and Ringo Starr in his best role ever. In 1976 David Bowie starred in his best ever role as the alien Thomas Jerome Newton in The Man Who Fell To Earth, a film by Performance director Nicolas Roeg. Kris Kristofferson, Rita Coolidge and Bob Dylan acted in Sam Peckinpah's 1973 Pat Garrett And Billy The Kid, but the results were disappointing due to MGM's post-production interference. Dylan played an inarticulate drifter called Alias and wrote the soundtrack, which gave him a Top 20 hit with "Knocking On Heaven's Door." James Taylor and Dennis Wilson starred in Two Lane Blacktop, a road movie directed by Monte Hellman in 1971 that has since achieved cult status. Time Out described it as "Self-enclosed, self-absorbed, self-destructive (as the last shot of the film catching in the projector and burning suggests), it's absolutely riveting." The other great road movie from this period was Richard Sarafian's Vanishing Point, which used Delaney, Bonnie and Friends, including Rita Coolidge, as J. Hovah's Singers. Underground ideas, if not exactly hippie ideas, certainly informed Stanley Kubrick's 1971 masterpiece A Clockwork Orange, just as they had his 1968 film, 2001: A Space Odyssey.

1971 saw the release of Shaft, directed by Gordon Parks and featuring Richard Roundtree essentially as a black James Bond. Isaac Hayes' extraordinary score and the endless tracking shot that opens the movie helped make this the first big Superspade film. It was followed by two sequels—Shaft's Big Score and Shaft in Africa—as well as a TV series. It established the genre that soon included Slaughter's Big Rip-Off (1973) with a score by James Brown, Cleopatra Jones (1973) and Foxy Brown (1974). Better than most was Superfly, which was made in 1972 by Gordon Parks Jr., the son of the director of Shaft. Curtis Mayfield's score gave him two US Top 20 hits with "Freddie's Dead" and "Superfly."

RIGHT: Film director Stanley Kubrick, whose 2001 A Space Odyssey in 1968 and A Clockwork Orange in 1971 represented the critical highpoints of "alternative" mainstream movies.

THE DAWNING OF THE NEW AGE

"The 60s interest in all things occult, spiritual and mystical had spread far and wide."

Miles

LIFE The Love and Terror Cult

Richard Nixon, cult leader

Many of the New Age spiritual groups, therapies and growth centers existed long before the 60s, but that was a time of rediscovery, as well as a time of invention. As part of the general increase in interest in spiritual matters there were naturally numerous Christian groups, amongst them David Berg's Children of God, which began in 1968 in California and adopted a strict communal lifestyle, as well as the Lonesome Stone group, founded in 1971 in a commune in Milwaukee. There were literally hundreds of others.

Hippies were more interested in Oriental religion and philosophy, so dozens of swamis, roshis and gurus migrated to the US and Britain to set up centers. Most of them were Hindu. One of the first to achieve a huge following, thanks to the Beatles and the Beach Boys, was the Maharishi Mahesh Yogi, whose Transcendental Meditation Centers—TM—are in every major city. The followers of A. C. Bhaktivedanta's Krishna Consciousness are also hard to miss, as they chant the Hare Krishna mantra down the high streets of the world. The Guru Maharaj Ji's Divine Light Mission also achieved a high profile in the early 70s, particularly when the 13-year-old guru arrived in London in 1971. Hippies were also attracted to Sri Chinmoy, popularized by Santana and guitarist John McLaughin. They also liked Bagwan Shree Rajneesh and, as popularized by Pete Townshend of the Who, Meher Baba, who remained silent from 1925 until his death in 1969. Subud attracted the attention of Roger McGuinn of the Byrds. The Hindu practice of yoga developed into literally thousands of centers, many of them with no religious connection at all.

The Beat Generation had shown a great interest in Zen Buddhism, but not until the 60s did it become popular. Then a number of Tibetan lamas arrived in the west and this very different form of Buddhism attracted thousands of fol-lowers, possibly because of the mystical nature of the chants, the visualizations, the hints of tantric sex and the possibility of instant enlightenment. The biggest group was formed by Chogyam Trungpa, whose original Tale of the Tiger group mushroomed into the Naropa Institute, which now has centers all across the US and Canada.

But most of the hippie-oriented groups were started by self-appointed gurus. These included Russell Paul Schofeld's Actualism, Master Morihei Uyeshiba's Aikido, Frederick Alexander's Alexander Technique (described by William Burroughs as "learning how to wear your head"), Ida Rolf's Structural Integration, Oscar Ichazo's Arica, Werner Erhard's Erhard Seminars Training, Nathaniel Branden's Biocentric Psychology, Jose Silva's Silva Mind Control, Eric Berne's Trans-actional Analysis and George Ohsawa's Macrobiotics.

Fritz Perls started Gestalt Therapy. Perls had practiced for five years, from 1964 at the Esalin Institute in Big Sur, before setting up his Gestalt centers across the US and UK. Arthur Janov's Primal Therapy got off to a good start when John Lennon and Yoko Ono enrolled for scream therapy. Wilhelm Reich spawned so many groups that he has followers in the areas of psychotherapy, Vegeotherapy (later Orgone Therapy) and even rain making. Also popular were Carlos Castaneda and his teacher Don Juan, a Yaqui Indian shaman, as well as Edgar Cayce, the "sleeping prophet." There were, and still are, many more.

Casting the I-Ching, reading tarot cards and calculating astrological signs are now practiced by millions of people, very few of whom first read about them in the San Francisco Oracle.

LEFT (TOP): Wilhelm Reich in 1946.
LEFT (BOTTOM): Oz magazine spoofs the cult of Cults.
RIGHT: The Children of God commune give thanks.

THE TRIAL OF OZ

OZ Obscenity Trial Old Bailey London 1971

Trial begins 22 June
Any information contact Friends of Oz,
39a Pottery Lane, London W11. 01-229 5887

On Wednesday June 23, 1971, at Court number 2 at the Central Criminal Courts of the Old Bailey in the City of London, Britain's longest obscenity trial got under way. The three defendants—Jim Anderson, Richard Neville and Felix Dennis—were charged with having "conspired with certain other young persons to produce a magazine" that would "corrupt the morals of young children and other young persons" and had "intended to arouse and implant in the minds of these young people lustful and perverted desires." There were four other charges to do with publishing "an obscene article," possessing copies of the magazine, sending it through the postal system and so on. The trial was a farce—the contents of the magazine were so tame that the Soho sex shops would not have stocked it. In reality it was an attempt by the authorities to curb the growth of the underground press and to stop the spread of pernicious ideas about sexual freedom, the rights of school children and other hippie notions.

Oz had previously published a Homosexual Oz, edited by homosexuals but aimed at the usual Oz readership. The Women's Liberation Oz was edited by feminist author Germaine Greer but distributed to Oz magazine's usual underground readership. There had even been a Flying Saucer Oz, edited by people who believe in such things. The School Kids Oz was edited by school kids, but aimed at Oz's usual readership. The court, of course, thought they were aiming the magazine at children, which was the main reason given for the case. Richard Neville represented himself. He told the jury, "One of the reasons we invited adolescents to edit this special issue of Oz was to combat the tendency for everyone to try and shut them up. We were interested in what they had to say. But we didn't want to be like the headmasters who censor everything they don't happen to agree with … Oz 28 is the result of this experiment. 'School Kids Issue' it says on the cover—which means of course, the issue edited by school children, not aimed by others at them.'

They advertised for school children between the ages of 14 to 18 to come and edit Oz, offering them freedom from editorial interference. Mostly they wrote about the iniquities of the school system: arbitrary punishments, vindictive teachers, sexually predatory teachers and grading systems. Being school kids, there was a lot of smut, including a collage of Rupert Bear with a huge phallus that had been taken from a Robert Crumb cartoon and stuck on him.

The trial result could be easily predicted. Judge Argyle made life as difficult and worrying as possible for the defendants, from not allowing an adjournment when their barrister dropped out, to remanding them in custody for social, medical and mental reports before he would pronounce sentence. The defendants' long hair was forcibly shorn in prison. They were given 15 months each, and Neville was to be deported back to Australia, his birthplace. Once more the law was shown up and, once more, an appeal was needed to overturn the sentences and set the Oz Three free.

TOP (LEFT): The staff of Oz who produced the Schoolkids issue.
RIGHT: The three Oz defendants, left to right, Richard Neville, Jim Anderson, Felix Dennis.

THE HIPPIE LEGACY

"What have we got?"
"No beer, no pot!"
"What have we got?"
"No beer, no pot!"

Cypress Hill and the crowd at Woodstock 94 bemoan the no alcohol and no drugs policy of the show's organizers

What actually remains from the counterculture of the 60s? The closest we have to a memorial is the Woodstock Festival, which has so far been celebrated by a 10th, a 25th and a 30th anniversary reunion. The 1979 reunion was divisive, with several competing events. These included a scrappy affair in upstate New York with Johnny Winter as the biggest name, and a concert at Madison Square Garden featuring Rick Danko with Paul Butterfield, Richie Havens, Canned Heat, Country Joe and The Fish, Kenny Rankin and others.

The 1994 festival was a much more commercial affair with big name bands, sponsorship by Pepsi and the entertainment conglomerate Polygram, and a ban on beer and tent poles—no wild camping in the woods, or anywhere else, allowed. It took place on the Winston Farm, 16,000 acres in the Saugerties from 12 to 15 August. Among the 30 bands were Aerosmith, the Allman Brothers, Aphex Twin, Arrested Development, Joe Cocker, the Cranberries, Crosby, Stills and Nash, Sheryl Crow, Metallica, Del Amitri, Bob Dylan, Melissa Etheridge, Peter Gabriel and Green Day. The Band, a pickup group consisting of Bruce Hornsby, Roger McGuinn, Bob Weir, Jorma Kaukonen, Jack Casady, John Sebastian and Country Joe McDonald, performed a lot of 60s numbers that appeared to be familiar to the largely young audience. Ed Sanders of the

Fugs had been living in Woodstock for twenty years, and organized his own alternative festival: The Real Woodstock Festival, featuring the Fugs, Allen Ginsberg and Country Joe (who also played yet another alternative festival held at the Woodstock Festival's original site in Bethel, NY). Sanders wrote, "The pandemic grovelling for money, the hypocrisy, the banning of tent poles and beer, with nods of joy." Their poster advertised that the first ten people to arrive with tent poles would get in free. They also suggested that beer and wine would be available and that no one would be searched unless they requested it. In fact a good time was had at both festivals. The Pepsi one was the biggest event most of the kids had ever been to and had the hallmarks of the original Woodstock—thunderstorms turned the site into a sea of mud, the 4,000 portable toilets did not work very well, the fences were torn down, there were drugs everywhere and a low police presence.

All of this, of course, made Woodstock 1999, held in Rome, NY, an even more commercial event. Bush, The Chemical Brothers, George Clinton, Collective Soul, Counting Crows, Creed, Sheryl Crow, DMX, Everlast, Fatboy Slim, Guster, Ice Cube, Jewel, Korn, Limp Bizkit, Live, Los Lobos, Dave Matthews Band, Metallica, Moe, Alanis Morissette, Willie Nelson, Rage Against

The Machine, Sugar Ray, Red Hot Chili Peppers, Rusted Root, Brian Setzer Orchestra, Offspring, the Tragically Hip, Jamiroquai, Our Lady Peace, Kid Rock, Mickey Hart Planet Drum, Mike Ness, Godsmack, Everclear, Lit, Insane, Clown Posse, Moby, Oleander, Umbilical Brothers, Buckcherry and Megadeth. A surprise ending was promised, but the organizers were not expecting the actual finale when much of the stage, a row of trucks and vendors stalls burned down.

The speed metal line-up guaranteed that most of the audience would consist of 18- to 25-year-olds. Ogden Entertainment, the parent company of the promoters, held the food concessions and gouged the kids throughout the weekend with grossly overpriced water, beer and food, charging $10 for a burrito, $4 for a soda, $12 for a mini- pizza and $30 for a T-shirt. Unlike the original Woodstock, there was no Hog Farm to feed the 250,000 kids who attended. The audience relished the opportunity to cut loose and soon the festival became a virtual nudist camp, with body painting booths and naked people running everywhere out of their minds on drugs. Organization was poor: with water mains broken the drinking

RIGHT (TOP): A bunch of happy Woodstock 1994 campers get set to leave the site. RIGHT (BOTTOM): It rained at Woodstock 1994, which meant that there was mud. Lots of mud.

"History books will probably remember Woodstock 99 as a festival that went down in flames, but many concertgoers might not remember it at all. For three days in Rome, NY, drug use was as much a part of the festivities as the mud, moshing, nudity and music. Marijuana was the most predominant among an assortment of illicit substances that included LSD, Ecstasy, Special K, nitrous oxide, PCP and heroin. In fact, the air was even more polluted with the smell of pot than it was with the stink coming off of the 250,000 unwashed campers.

"But pot smoking was child's play compared to the heavy-duty drugs that turned many in the festival's audience into tripped-out zombies. During Fatboy Slim's set at one of Woodstock's nightly raves, partyers openly snorted Special K, ate mushrooms and sucked on balloons filled with nitrous oxide. 'You can get your hands on just about anything,' said one stoned audience member."

Jenny Eliscu reports for Rolling Stone magazine on the Woodstock 1999 festival

water got contaminated by overflowing sewage. A huge pool of impure water turned into a giant mud hole as people wallowed in it. Saturday night ended with Limp Bizkit, R.A.T.M. and Metallica working the kids into a fine frenzy. Kids began torching the huge piles of trash, dancing around the bonfires naked. One fire got out of control, and a row of twelve parked trucks containing propane gas cylinders exploded in huge fireballs when a burning tent fell on one of them. Excited by the flames, kids took their revenge on the greedy organizers by tearing down parts of the stage and scaffolding and starting more fires. Vendors stalls were destroyed, cars were overturned and portable toilets were pushed over. Order was only restored when riot police moved in and secured the area. Twelve riot police later appeared in court for neglecting their duty by posing for photographs with naked girls while tents and stalls burned in the background.

But even though Woodstock 1999 was an organizational disaster, most of the kids had the time of their lives, dancing naked and high, away from the constraints of school and parents.

If nothing else, Woodstock, Earth Day and Gay Pride represent some of the major changes wrought by the 60s counterculture. Rock 'n' roll has divided hydra-like into different strains, many of which can legitimately be regarded as art, and despite its commercialization rock 'n' roll is no longer just an American phenomenon—even Iceland has its superstars. The women's move- ment had its beginnings in the underground scene, as did most of the resistance movements since the 60s: the tribes, the anti-motorway protesters, the travellers, the squatters, the free festivals and mass raves, the animal rights protesters and eco-revolutionaries, Greenpeace and Friends of the Earth.

The hippie experience gave people a heightened awareness. Young people are no longer as acquiescent as they were, they know they have the power to change things and with luck they will save the planet.

RIGHT: The event ended in flames as concession stalls were set on fire. Peace, man. . .

INDEX

PICTURES

All images thanks to Miles except the following:
Gene Anthony: page 31, 97, 107, 110, 111, 112, 113, 115, 128, 207, 269

Corbis: page 12 Hulton-Deutsch Collection, 14/15 Ted Streshinsky, 19 Henry Diltz, 24/25 Bettmann/Corbis, 34, 38 Alan Ginsberg, 36, 37 Ted Streshinsky, 41 Bettmann/Corbis, 42/43 Hulton-Deutsch Collection, 47 Jonathan Blair, 49 Bettmann/Corbis, 53 Jonathan Blair, 57 Flip Schulke, 63 Hulton-Deutsch Collection, 67, 75 Bettmann/Corbis,, 98 102, 103, 105, 106, 108, 109, 118/119, 121, 124/125 Ted Streshinsky, 120 Henry Diltz, 129 Bettmann/Corbis, 133 Henry Diltz, 138 Malcolm Lubliner, 140, 142 Bettmann/Corbis, 144 Henry Diltz, 148, 153, 156/157 Bettmann/Corbis, 158 Flip Schulke, 185, 196, 198/199, 201, 205, 213, 214/215 Ted Streshinsky, 187, 189, Henry Diltz, 191, 193, 202, 208/209, 211 Bettmann/Corbis, 204 Robert Holmes, 218, 220, 221, 224 Henry Diltz, 227, 229, 230 Bettmann/Corbis, 252 Shepard Sherbell, 259 Douglas Kirkland, 261, 264/265, 267, 272 Ted Streshinsky, 263 Bettmann/Corbis, 271 Henry Diltz, 273, 279, 280, 283, 284 Bettmann/Corbis, 277 Wally McNamee, 303, 306/307, 308 Ted Streshinsky, 312, 313 Bettmann/Corbis, 317 Corbis, 319, 322 Henry Diltz, 321, 325 Bettmann/Corbis, 335, 337 Henry Diltz, 340, 343, 347, 348 Bettmann/Corbis, 346 Lynn Goldsmith, 351 Condé Nast Archive, 355 Underwood & Underwood, 356 Neal Preston, 363 Wally McNamee, 365 Corbis, 367 Shepard Sherbell, 370, 372 Bettmann/Corbis, 373 Hulton-Deutsch Collection, 377 Kraft Books/Corbis Sygma (bottom), Henry Diltz (top) 379 Mitchell Gerber, 380/381 Lichtenstein Andrew/Corbis Sygma

John "Hoppy" Hopkins: page 77, 78, 79, 81, 84, 86, 87, 88/89, 163, 165, 171

Hulton Archive: page 58/59, 146/147, 159, 178, 180 (bottom), 181, 236, 242, 286, 287, 291, 298, 331, 332, 341, 344/245

Pictorial Press: page 8, 10, 11, 13, 17, 21, 83, 85, 92/93, 116/117, 130/121, 141, 147, 150/151, 164, 167, 179, 180 (top), 182, 232/233, 235, 241, 244, 248, 250, 254, 255, 274, 293, 296, 314, 328, 329, 361 (both)

Redferns: page 137, 275, 305 plus 29 Herb Greene, 64, 99, 122/123 Michael Ochs Archives, 69, 95, 168/169 Adam Ritchie, 101 Glenn A Baker, 134/135 Chuck Boyd, 339 Jim McCrary

Topfoto.co.uk: 238